Thomas Frost

The Life of Thomas Lord Lyttelton

Thomas Frost

The Life of Thomas Lord Lyttelton

ISBN/EAN: 9783743337350

Manufactured in Europe, USA, Canada, Australia, Japa

Cover: Foto ©ninafisch / pixelio.de

Manufactured and distributed by brebook publishing software (www.brebook.com)

Thomas Frost

The Life of Thomas Lord Lyttelton

CONTENTS.

CHAPTER I.

Birth and Parentage—Education—Early Promise of future Fame—Journey through Scotland with his Father—His Proficiency in Drawing and Painting—Encomiums of Mrs. Montagu—His Admiration of Milton's Poetry—Development of the Family Foible—Flattering Opinions of his Abilities formed by his Father and Earl Temple—Dr. Barnard compares him with Charles James Fox 1

CHAPTER II.

Thomas Lyttelton's Engagement with Miss Warburton—His Tour through France and Italy—John Damer—Thomas Lyttelton's Duels at Bologna—Rupture of the Matrimonial Treaty—Prolongation of the Tour—Return to England—Masque at Stowe—Returned to Parliament for Bewdley 10

CHAPTER III.

Politics of the Period—Men of the Commons—The Damers—George Durant—Petition against Lyttelton's Return—His Maiden Speech—Complimented by Wellbore Ellis—Reconciliation with his Family—Unseated—"Junius"—Hypothesis that Lyttelton was the Author of the Famous Letters—Second Continental Tour—Quarrel with George Ayscough—Return to England 36

CHAPTER IV.

Overtures for Domestic Reconciliation—Lord Chatham congratulates Lord Lyttelton on his Son's Return—Lord Lyttelton's Reply—Thomas Lyttelton's Letters to his Friends—The

Miseries of having nothing to do—Regret at the Loss of his Seat in Parliament—"Dialogues of the Dead"—His own Version of the Causes of his Disgrace—Claude Anet—Story of the Quaker and his Dog—Bishop Lyttelton and the French Hornblowers—Comparison with Mirabeau	61

CHAPTER V.

Morals of the Eighteenth Century—Gambling and Gallantry—Mania for Card-playing and Betting—Singular Wagers—Lyttelton's Wager with Blake—Elopement of Sally Harris with Lyttelton — Letter about George Ayscough — John Courtney—Mrs. Dawson—Letter on the Passions—Mrs. Peach—Lyttelton's Account of his Courtship and Marriage—Letters to his Father on the Subject—Anecdote of Lord Lyttelton—Letter from Lord Chatham to Lord Lyttelton—Lord Lyttelton's Reply—A Contrast	88

CHAPTER VI.

Separation—Journey to Paris—Death of Lord Lyttelton—Letter on the Event—Return to England—Letter of Condolence from the Earl of Chatham—Correspondence with Earl Temple—Letters on his New Position—Hopes of Moral Amendment—Dissatisfaction with Hagley—Letter to Sir Richard Lyttelton—Political Views—The American Troubles—His Estimate of Public Men—Hopes and Aims for the Future	116

CHAPTER VII.

Parliamentary Session of 1774—Appeal to the Lords in Beckett *v.* Donaldson—Speech on Literary Property—Letter to Earl Temple—Speech on the Booksellers' Copyright Bill—Dedication of his Father's Works to him by George Ayscough—Letter on the Subject—Thoughts about Maids of Honour—Speech on the Government of Quebec Bill—Meeting of the New Parliament—Debate on the Address—Speech on the American Question—Secrecy of the Lords' Debates—Motion on the Subject—Rejection of the Motion—Successful Second Attempt—Project of Selling or Leasing Hagley	137

CHAPTER VIII.

Lord Lyttelton's Speech on the Earl of Chatham's Proposal to withdraw the Troops from Boston—Speech on the Provisional Bill for the Settlement of the American Difficulty—Strictures on Lord Camden—Complaints of the Duke of Richmond and the Duke of Manchester—Lord Lyttelton's Exculpation—Speech on the Administration of the Poor Law—Debate on the Licensing of the Manchester Theatre—Speech on the Quebec Act—Strictures of Horace Walpole—Visit to Bristol—Parson Adams—Story of a Lost Sermon—The Lyttelton Pudding and the Parson's Cradle—Scheme for relieving Hagley of the Jointures of Lady Lyttelton and the Dowager 157

CHAPTER IX.

Opening of the Parliamentary Session of 1775-76—Debate on the Address—Speech of Lord Lyttelton—Speech on the Introduction of Foreign Troops without the Consent of Parliament—Change of Relations with the Ministry—Appointment as Chief Justice in Eyre, north of the Trent, and a Privy Councillor—Letter on his Appointment—Opposition to the Duke of Grafton's Motion for Return of Troops in America—Defence of the Prohibitory Bill—Vindication of his Conduct against the Duke of Richmond—Calumnies of Horace Walpole—Trial of the Duchess of Kingston 201

CHAPTER X.

Speech on the Proposal of the Duke of Richmond to Countermand the March of the German Troops—Debate on the Duke of Grafton's Motion for Conciliatory Measures—Lord Lyttelton's Speech—Letter on the American Question—Visit to the "Justitia" hulk—Anecdote of David Hume—Letter on his Political Position—Lord Lyttelton's Double Life—His Opinion of Literary Ladies—Mrs. Montagu and Miss Carter—Gambling Debts of the Damers and the Foleys—Suicide of John Damer—Letters of Horace Walpole, the Earl of Carlisle, and Lord Lyttelton on the Subject 231

CHAPTER XI.

Lord Lyttelton's Moral Amendment—Testimony of his Friends—His Thoughts on Scepticism and Revealed Religion—Satirical Reflections on Credulity and Incredulity—Stormy Debate on the Earl of Chatham's Motion against the War—Lord Lyttelton's Profession of Whig Principles—Letter to Lord Westcote—Opposition to raising Troops without Consent of Parliament—Speech on the State of the Country—Defence of the Conciliatory Bills—Speech on the Duke of Richmond's Proposal to withdraw the Troops from America—Strictures on the Earl of Sandwich—Death of the Earl of Chatham—Letter on the Subject—Speech on the Annuity Bill 266

CHAPTER XII.

Lord Lyttelton's Occupations at Hagley—Views on the Game Laws—Speech on the American War—The Earl of Bristol's Motion against the Earl of Sandwich—Lord Lyttelton's Speech—His Political Status in 1779—Relations with the Earl of Shelburne—Pitt Place—Reasons for preferring it to Hagley—Discussion on the Locality of the Soul, and the End of the World—Death of George Ayscough—Letter on the State of Public Affairs—Visit to Ireland—The Irish Volunteers—Agitation in Ireland for Free Trade 294

CHAPTER XIII.

Lord Lyttelton's Secession from the Ministerial Ranks—Great Speech on the Irish Question—Opinions of the Whig and Tory Journals—Lord Sandwich and Miss Ray—Understanding between Lord Lyttelton and the Earl of Shelburne—More Calumnies of Horace Walpole—Lord Lyttelton's Famous Dream—Various Versions of the Story—New Light on it from the Family Archives at Hagley Hall—The Dowager Lady Lyttelton's Picture—True Circumstances of Lord Lyttelton's Sudden Death—His Will—Conclusion 328

THE LIFE

OF

THOMAS LORD LYTTELTON.

CHAPTER I.

Birth and Parentage—Education—Early Promise of future Fame—Journey through Scotland with his Father—His proficiency in Drawing and Painting—Encomiums of Mrs. Montagu—His Admiration of Milton's Poetry—Development of the Family Foible—Flattering Opinions of his Abilities formed by his Father and Earl Temple—Dr. Barnard compares him with Charles James Fox.

THOMAS LYTTELTON, the second Baron of that name, was born on the 30th of January, 1744. His father was the son of Sir Thomas Lyttelton, of Hagley, in Worcestershire; and his mother, whom Sir George Lyttelton married in 1741, was Lucy Fortescue, a Devonshire lady, whose untimely death, five years after marriage, deprived the hope of the family of maternal care during the years when he most needed it, and afforded her husband a theme for the poetical effusion by which he is best known to the present generation of readers.

Young Lyttelton gave promise, at a very

early age, of the intellectual ability displayed by so many of his family, and was in due time sent to Eton, where his conduct seems to have been as free from blame as his progress in his studies was remarkable. His father wrote in 1758, when Thomas was fourteen years of age, of "the promise afforded by his opening talents;" and in the following year, when the lad accompanied his father in a tour through Scotland, as far as Inverary, Lord Lyttelton—he had been raised to the peerage during the Pelham Administration for his opposition to Sir Robert Walpole—wrote to his brother William: "Much the greatest pleasure I had in my tour was from the company of my son, and from the approbation (I might say admiration) which his figure, behaviour, and parts drew from all sorts of people wherever he went. Indeed, his mother* has given him her *don de plaire*, and he joins to an excellent understanding the best of hearts, and more discretion and judgment than ever I observed in any young man except you."

During this Scottish tour young Lyttelton produced some views of the beautiful scenery through which he passed, which, though it is probable that some allowance must be made for partiality

---

* Lord Lyttelton had married, in 1749, Elizabeth, daughter of Sir Robert Rich. The union was unfortunate, and resulted in separation.

on the part of his critics, must have been above the average excellence of amateur productions, to have evoked such praise as was awarded them by Mrs. Montagu, in a letter to his father. "Mr. Lyttelton," says the lady, "is a charming painter. His views of Scotland appear as the scenes of Salvator Rosa would do, were they copied by Claude, whose sweet and lovely imagination would throw fine colours over the darkest parts, and give grace to the rudest objects. I design at some time to visit Scotland, but I do not expect more pleasure from Nature's pencil than I have had from his pen. I can trust with equal confidence and delight to all you say of him. Pray God preserve you to guide him, and preserve him to make you happy."

It is not surprising to find, combined with the admiration of Nature which is essential to the landscape artist, a love of the grandest conceptions of the poet; but it must surprise those who regard Thomas Lyttelton as a mere scapegrace, remarkable only for his profligacy and the strange circumstances that attended his death, to learn that his favourite poet was Milton. "Of all the poets that have graced ancient times, or delighted the latter ages," he says, in a letter to a friend, "Milton is my favourite. I think him superior to every other, and the writer of all others the best calculated to elevate the mind, to form a nobleness of taste, and to teach a bold, commanding, energetic language. I read him with delight as soon as I could read at all; and I remember, in my father's words, I gave the first token of premature abilities in the perusal of the 'Paradise Lost.' I was quite a boy when, in reading that poem, I was so forcibly struck with a passage, that I laid down the book with some violence on the table, and took a hasty turn to the other end of the room. Upon explaining the cause of this emotion to my father, he clasped me in his arms, smothered me with embraces, and immediately wrote letters to all his family and friends, to inform them of the wonderful foreboding I had given of future genius. Your curiosity may naturally expect to be gratified with the passage in question; I quote it, therefore, for your reflection and amusement:

> "'He spoke; and, to confirm his words, out flew
> Millions of flaming swords, drawn from the thighs
> Of mighty Cherubim: the sudden blaze
> Far round illumin'd Hell!'"

Too much reason is afforded by the letters of his father, of Mrs. Montagu, and others, for the belief that the praises which his budding talents called forth were too lavishly and indiscriminately awarded to be good for the mental and moral health of their recipient. In after-life he saw the mistake that had been made, and complained of it with the bitterness that pervades many of the letters of the period when he roused himself for a time from the influence of the Circean draughts of which he had so deeply drank. "I have been," he said, "the victim of vanity, and the sacrifice of me was begun before I could form a judgment of the passion." The friend to whom this remark was made wishing for its explanation, he wrote a letter, which will be further quoted in another chapter, and from which only as much need be given here as relates to the defects of his early training.

"You will," he says, "I believe, agree with me that vanity is the foible of my family. Every individual has a share of it for himself, and for the rest. They are all equally vain of themselves and of one another. It is not, however, an unamiable vanity: it makes them happy, though it may sometimes render them ridiculous; and it never did an injury to anyone but to me. I have every reason to load it with execration, and to curse the hour when this passion was concentrated to myself. Being the only boy, and hope of the family, and having such an hereditary and collateral right to genius, talents, and virtue (for this was the language held by certain persons at that time), my earliest prattle was the subject of continual admiration. As I increased in years, I was encouraged in boldness, which partial fancy called manly confidence; while sallies of impertinence, for which I should have been scourged, were fondly considered as marks of an astonishing prematurity of abilities. As it happened, Nature had not been a niggard to me. It is true she has given me talents, but accompanied them with dispositions which demanded no common repressure and restraint, instead of liberty and encouragement. But this vanity had blinded the eyes, not only of my relations, but also of their intimate connections; and, I suppose, such an hot-bed of flattery was never before used to spoil a mind, and to choke it with bad qualities, as was applied to mine. The late Lord Bath, Mrs. Montagu, and many others, have been guilty of administering fuel to the flame, and joined in the family incense to such an idol as myself. Thus was I nursed into a very early state of audacity; and being able, almost at all times, to get the laugh against a father, or an uncle, I was not backward in giving such impertinent specimens of my ability. This is the history of that impudence which has been my bane, gave to my excesses such peculiar accompaniments, and caused those who would not have hesitated to commit the offence loudly to condemn the mode of its commission in me."

One specimen of the praise that Lord Lyttelton lavished upon his son has been given. That he wrote of him to Mrs. Montagu in terms equally eulogistic may be gathered from a letter from that lady to his lordship, written in August, 1759, in which she says: "Your lordship's commendations of Mr. Lyttelton not only make me happy, but make me vain. He is every day going on to complete all I have wished and predicted on this subject." Earl Temple joined in the chorus of praise, as we learn from a letter addressed in after years to its object, in which he says: "I have in very early days acknowledged and done justice to your talents."* Dr. Barnard, the headmaster at Eton, often compared Thomas Lyttelton with Charles James Fox, to the advantage of the former; and though it must be remembered that young Lyttelton was five years the senior of the future Prime Minister of England, it is probable that Dr. Barnard was not unmindful of the difference of age, and had in his mind, when making the comparison long after both men had left Eton, the intellectual powers which they had respectively displayed at the same age. The master's estimate

---

* Correspondence of the Earl of Chatham, vol. iv., p. 222.

has been thought partial. But it is impossible to compare the oratorical efforts and few literary productions of both men without feeling that the intellectual superiority assigned to Lyttelton was a reality, and that he might, had he attained the same years as Fox, have achieved greater distinctions both in literature and in politics. At Eton, and at the same age, there was no reason to anticipate for Fox a degree of fame and distinction higher than might be won by Lyttelton.

But for the injudicious training that developed the foibles that should have been counteracted, and the undiscriminating flattery that was lavished upon him by all with whom he came in contact, the youth of Thomas Lyttelton would have been passed under favourable auspices. His father was honoured with the friendship of the Prince of Wales and the leading men of the day; he was a Privy Councillor, a Lord of the Treasury, and, later, Chancellor of the Exchequer. The future peer enjoyed the advantage of social intercourse with most of those who had achieved political or literary distinction, his father blending both characters, and being a patron of literary men, as well as himself a contributor to the literature of the period. It was Lord Lyttelton who obtained for Thomson his pension, and for Fielding his appointment as a magistrate; he was the first to encourage the poetical efforts of Mickle, who came to London when Thomas Lyttelton was twenty years of age, and he was a fellow-labourer with Horace Walpole, Soame Jenyns, the Earl of Chesterfield, and other remarkable men, in the columns of the *World*.

"Coventry dined yesterday at Claremont," says George James Williams—commonly called Gilly Williams—in a letter to George Selwyn, written in the summer of 1763, when Thomas Lyttelton was in his twentieth year. "The dinner consisted of Lord Spencer, the Rockinghams, little Villiers, Lord Lyttelton and his son, General Mostyn, and his lordship." Claremont was at that time the seat of the first Duke of Newcastle. This is the earliest mention of Thomas Lyttelton in the letters and memoirs of the period, subsequent to the date of the eulogies of Mrs. Montagu. He was the youngest of the party at Claremont, and may be excused if he felt a sense of rising importance in the world upon which he was preparing to enter, with all the *éclat* derivable from his father's social and political position and associations. As yet he viewed life through the "golden exhalations of the dawn," and everything was to his youthful vision beautiful and bright. A brilliant future was anticipated for him by all his friends; and the blight and chill of the future were as yet in the thoughts of none.

CHAPTER II.

Thomas Lyttelton's Engagement with Miss Warburton — His Tour through France and Italy — John Damer — Thomas Lyttelton's Duels at Bologna — Rupture of the Matrimonial Treaty — Prolongation of the Tour — Return to England — Masque at Stowe — Returned to Parliament for Bewdley.

ABOUT the time of the dinner at Claremont, a matrimonial project was planned by the Lyttelton family for its hope, the young heir of Hagley, and acceded to by him with a readiness which the beauty and amiability of the young lady of their choice sufficiently explains.

Miss Warburton, the only daughter of General Warburton, belonged to a good family, and possessed both great personal attractions and an excellent disposition, as well as a considerable fortune; and young Lyttelton, enraptured with her beauty, and viewing life through the rose-coloured glasses of youth, anticipated with eagerness the felicity which seemed to be in store for him. Letters are extant in which he speaks of Miss Warburton in the highest terms, and looks forward to their union with the most passionate devotion; and it is not improbable that, if this dream of his youth had been realised, he would have lived in the memory of posterity, not as "the wicked Lord Lyttelton," but as one of the greatest statesmen of the eighteenth century.

But, as he was at this time only nineteen years of age, and no marriage-settlement could be made until he had attained his majority, it was suggested by Sir Richard Lyttelton, one of his uncles, that he should pass the intervening time in travelling on the Continent. It does not seem the course best calculated to give steadiness to the character of a young man, who, from hints which he has given in letters written in after life, seems already to have shown symptoms of moral aberration, or to ensure the future happiness of the young persons whom it was thought desirable to unite in marriage, that they should not see each other during the period between betrothment and union, and that the interval should be passed by him in rambling with companions of his own age and dispositions from one foreign capital to another, and joining in the pleasures and dissipations of all. The admonition of Lord Burghley was thrown away upon Lord Lyttelton, and fashion and conventionality held their sway as potently as with inferior minds.

Thomas Lyttelton saw, later in life, the grievous

mistake that was committed by his elders, and has placed on record his view of the matter in the letter quoted in the preceding chapter, and to which I now return. "When I drew towards manhood," he says, "it will be sufficient to say that I began to have some glimmering of the family weakness. However, I was still young, dependence was a considerable restraint, and I had not acquired that subsequent knowledge of the world which changed my notions of paternal authority. I was, therefore, without much difficulty brought to consent to the design of giving solidity to my character, and preserving me from public contagion by marriage. A rich and amiable young lady was chosen to the happy and honourable task of securing so much virtue as mine, to correct the natural exuberance of youthful inexperience, and to shape me into that perfection of character which was to verify the dreams of my visionary relations.

"I must own that the lady was both amiable and handsome, but cold as an anchorite; and, though formed to be the best wife in the world to a good husband, was by no means calculated to reclaim a bad one. But, to complete the sensible and well-digested plan, in which so many wise heads were concerned, it was determined for me to make the tour of Europe previous to my marriage, in order to perfectionate my matrimonial qualifications; and the lovely idea of the fair maid I left behind was presented to me as possessing a talismanic power to preserve me from seduction. But this was not all. For the better enabling me to make a proper and becoming appearance, or, in other words, to give me every means of gratification, the family purse was lavishly held forth; I was left almost without control in point of expense, and every method pursued to make me return the very reverse of what expectation had painted me."

The expenses of the Continental tour were borne by Sir Richard Lyttelton, a circumstance which explains the allusion to "the family purse." It may be remarked here that this circumstance was not likely to be known beyond the family circle, and its mention goes far to prove the genuineness of the letters which the Lytteltons strove to persuade the world were the spurious concoctions of William Combe, the author of "Dr. Syntax." How should this circumstance have been known to Combe? The fact itself does not rest solely on the authority of the letter that has been quoted; it is mentioned in a letter from Lord Lyttelton to his brother Richard.*

---

* *Quarterly Review*, December, 1851.

Thomas Lyttelton set out on his travels in the summer of 1763, and was either accompanied by John Damer, the eldest son of Lord Milton, and probably by that gentleman's brother George, or met them on the Continent. They had been at Eton together, and continued through life on terms of the closest intimacy. John Damer was the same age as Lyttelton, whom he resembled in temperament and aspirations.

It seems to have been contemplated at the outset that Lyttelton should have the advantage of paternal companionship and guidance during the greater part of the Continental tour; for his father wrote, towards the close of September, "He is just setting out from France to go to Italy, and I hope next summer to come to him at Florence, and make with him the tour of the Milanese, part of Germany, and all Switzerland by the end of October."* But this intention was not realised; and if the cause is to be found in the parental displeasure which Thomas Lyttelton soon evoked by the follies and dissipation in which he indulged during this tour, both he and his friends must have often regretted that an endeavour was not made to preserve him from the temptations with which a youth of rank and

---

* "Memoirs and Correspondence of George Lord Lyttelton." 1845.

fortune could not fail to be beset while travelling through France and Italy with young men of his own age and of similar temperaments.

The first of the letters which the courtesy and kindness of the present Lord Lyttelton enables me to place before my readers was written from Turin, on the 19th of November, and is addressed to Sir Richard Lyttelton. Though he had been absent from England about five months, he had not then received a single letter, a circumstance which seems to have caused him some uneasiness, and which the letter-writing habits of the age among the higher classes renders the more remarkable :—

"My dear Sir Richard,

"I am at length got over those impending precipices, covered with frozen snow, (that certainly Hannibal alone had the secret of melting with vinegar,) and repose myself now in the delicious plains of Italy. My eye has seen only what the French call the *affreuses beautés* of nature from Lyons quite to the Alps. I need not describe to you their horrible grandeur. But from the foot of Mount Cenis to Turin the lovely vale of Piedmont opens to you a thousand beauties, and all the *dolce* and *amabile* is laid before you.

"But I will not enter into minute descriptions

of a country you have so lately seen, and will only in general tell you that I am much delighted with all I have seen, and liberally feast my imagination on the thoughts of what I am to see. I found every house open to me at Lyons, and everywhere the most polite and friendly reception. But I do not place this to my account, and I am pleased to tell my dear uncle the respect was shown to me as *to his nephew*; and there is nothing they would not do to oblige anybody you recommended.

"I have not yet received any letters from England. The silence of my friends I can attribute to a thousand accidental causes, from some of which they certainly proceed; *but Love will not be satisfied by Reason*, and ever suspects the worst. When you see my sweet girl, do, my dear uncle, tell her all my fears. I know the value of her too well not to be afraid of losing her. She is a treasure that multitudes long to possess. In my absence, every device will be conceived, and every means made use of, to deprive me of her. New lovers will be fired by her beauty, and importunities she will be forced to submit, though I hope, and rest assured, never to yield to. All that can make the ties of affection binding certainly has been used to make our love so, but time and absence may efface the tender impressions that early love has made upon her heart. Objections, too, may possibly arise, and *her parents*, and even my father, may possibly be inclined rather to divide than unite us. This, indeed, is to me a cruel consideration. 'Dark as I am, unconscious of their will,' I cannot prevent whatever may be done in my prejudice. I therefore stand much in need of one who loves me by inclination. I know of none who have given such proofs of love as you. To you, therefore, I apply, and entreat you to guard this fairer than Hesperian fruit. She will in everything be directed by you, and make you the confidant of her most secret thoughts. My lord she respects and loves, but she looks upon him as a father, and to him she fears to throw off all reserve.

"I am interrupted by a pacquet of letters from England—one from you, one from my father, and one from Miss Warburton. It always diminishes the pleasure I should have in hearing from you to see upon the superscriptions of your letters the doctor's hand. You say, my dear uncle, you have been ill ever since I left you. I hope only *ill with the gout*. Indeed, there is more vivacity in your letters than men generally have when they are oppressed with sickness. I trust, therefore, the pains in your hands and feet, though bad, are the worst you feel. I will leave you to think how sincerely I wish those pains were removed.

"Miss W.'s letter has removed all jealous suspicions of her constancy. She professes herself, in the language of desiring love, to be *mine, and only mine*. She has promised to send me her picture, and I will bid her deliver it to you as soon as it is painted. You will be so good as to order it to be enclosed in such a frame as will make it fit to be hung to my watch, and then will send it immediately to me. I believe I can not have it before I get to Venice.

"I reflect with pleasure, my dear uncle, upon the conversations that passed between us at Richmond; and it is a great happiness to me that your inclinations and mine should be the same in points of so great importance to my future welfare.

"Ambitious, to you I confess myself to be, but I am also diffident of myself. I have something of the presumption, but all the heat, of youth about me. To your advice and direction I give up myself. Tempered and influenced by your judgment, my ambition may not be fruitless.

"I have wrote a long letter, and not said a word about Turin. The town, you know, is a fine one, and the society I am got into is very agreeable. The women, too, are most incitingly handsome. I am *cecisbeo*,* *en passant*, to her who I think is much the prettiest in the place. I shall set out to Milan in three days, or perhaps I may prolong it to a week. I told you in my last that Pernon was to supply me with all my clothes. I have found some at Turin much handsomer (and I think cheaper) than any he has got. I therefore intend to have only one *habit de galas* of him, and the other made here. Adieu.—I am ever your most dutiful nephew,

"T. L."

He proceeded from Turin to Venice, as indicated in the preceding letter; for in a subsequent letter he alludes to a gambling transaction in the latter city, which seems to have been the first incident of his tour which drew down upon him the reproaches of his father and uncle. It must not be forgotten, in justice to young Lyttelton, that the institutions and habits of Italian society at this period were not favourable to morality. Gambling and gallantry (as unbridled libertinism was then called, in the delicate phraseology of fashionable life) were the vices of the age; and in none of the European capitals were they more prevalent than in Turin and Florence. "Gambling,"

---

* *Chaperon* had been written here, but scored out with the pen.

says Lady Morgan, " was the prevailing vice, from the king to the least of his courtiers. Pharobanks were publicly kept ; jewels and trinkets were staked when all else was gone ; and the enormous sums won from young English travellers at the court of Turin by the native nobility could not save them from ruin, brought on by play and by a total neglect of their affairs. The bond of marriage was one of mere accommodation. The necessity (originating in fashion) which every man was under of neglecting his own wife, and entering into the service of his neighbour's, while it undermined morality, deprived taste of its preference, and passion of its excitement ; and general gallantry was so blunted by authorised libertinism that lovers became as stupidly loyal as husbands were confessedly faithless."*

There is no doubt that it was in Italy that the germs of the twin passions that dominated the life of Thomas Lyttelton were implanted. Between the letter from Turin and the next which I have before me—thick, gilt-edged post quarto, yellow with age, and the ink faded to a yellowish-brown hue—there is an interval of six months. In that period occurred the gambling loss at Venice, two duels at Bologna, and several

---

* " Italy," vol. i., p. 90.

affairs of gallantry with Italian women, which we shall find alluded to in a subsequent letter, but concerning which no details appear ever to have been known in England.

While at Bologna, or shortly after leaving that city, he wrote to Sir Richard Lyttelton an account of the circumstances connected with a duel in which he had there been engaged with an Italian gentleman; but it seems that his uncle thought that something had been withheld from him, and Thomas Lyttelton, in a letter written from Naples, on the 11th of May, 1764, while assuring him that he had withheld no circumstance connected with that affair, acknowledged that there had been another, at the same place, concerning which he had been silent, " because it happened with an Englishman who is too much my friend for me to let it be known that my honour obliged me to purchase a just satisfaction at his expense."

It appears from the statement which he wrote from Naples, that the Englishman, whose name was Pigott, had been at Eton with him, and that the quarrel out of which the duel arose occurred at a little dinner-party, given by himself, the other guests being two English artists, named Brumpton and Wilson. The conversation took a literary turn, and some difference of opinion arose between

Lyttelton and Pigott, which, owing probably to both being heated with wine, culminated in hasty and offensive words, followed by a challenge and a hostile encounter. Each of the parties regarded the other as the aggressor, and it is evident from Lyttelton's explanation that there was wrong on both sides, though the cause was so trivial that it might well have been adjusted by an exchange of apologies.

The gambling losses at Venice were, however, regarded as the most serious of young Lyttelton's follies, both by himself and the family. Sir Richard's purse-strings had again to be untied, and his nephew expressed the deepest gratitude for the relief. "Is it possible," he wrote, "for me to express by words the acknowledgments I owe you for your most noble and disinterested generosity to me? Henceforward, in every action of my life, I will endeavour to show the deep gratitude your unwonted kindness has raised in my heart. Guided and directed by you, to your opinion I submit everything that concerns me, and should hold myself unworthy to live if I disobliged you in any one instance, who have added to the strong ties of relationship the infinitely more strong ones of unbounded love. It is indeed the debt immense of endless gratitude still owing, still to pay.

"Nothing I can ever do can balance the account, but no future ill-conduct of mine shall, at least designedly, lower me in your opinion and affections. In respect to the cursed transaction that raised your just anger against me at Venice, I do give you the most solemn and sacred assurances that you have nothing to fear upon that account. Gaming I hold in detestation, and if again I ever relapse in that most absurd vice, I will forfeit my life, my estate, or what is as dear to me as either, the good opinion of men, and will allow myself patiently to be treated with universal contempt. Moderate play, too, when it is absolutely for amusement, I hold in great aversion, for, as I always either lose or am cheated out of my money, it is no amusement to me. Last night I lost thirty ounces at a game I thought it impossible to lose ten at; and at sober whist, at seven ounces the rubber, I lost seven rubbers together. So I have now determined never again (at least while I am abroad) to play, even for trifles. Of this you, *upon my honour*, may be as well assured as of my determination about gaming."

The next of the unpublished letters is undated, but was written from Toulon, probably in the latter part of 1764. The time was approaching for his return to England, and his union with Miss Warburton, for which he was as anxious as he had been before his departure. Though there is nothing in the published letters of his father to indicate the nature and extent of the causes of the displeasure with which he was regarded on his return to England, the rupture of the matrimonial treaty has generally been regarded as due to his misconduct while in Italy; but the following letter, addressed to Sir Richard Lyttelton, throws a new light on the subject, and, if it does not fully explain the cause of the rupture, exonerates the writer from the suspicion of having been the cause of it:—

"I have the pleasure to inform you that I have left Italy, though allowed by a charming woman to give some time more to the most delicious pleasures I have ever yet enjoyed. It is, indeed, a land of softness and delight. The women, like Armidas, have the power of fascinating their lovers, and of instilling into the most ambitious minds the love of ignoble ease and voluptuous refinement. But when the love of honour predominates they charm in vain. For myself, I can answer that I would as lief spend my days among the savages of wild America as in the arms of the most charming of the fair Italian ladies.

"I embarked last week with Lord Ossory from Genoa, and we purposed to continue our voyage, without stopping, towards Antibes. We were carried on by a very favourable wind to Hospitaletto, a little village about twenty miles from Monaco, when the wind suddenly changed, and we were forced to quit our feluccas, and continue our route upon mules to Monaco. We stayed there two days, and then, as the wind was fair, we again embarked. The sea, which had been agitated by violent storms, was much more swelled than we supposed, and the waves ran so high that we more than once expected to be overset. By good luck, however, we got to Villafranca, where we remained until the sea was quite calm, and from thence sailed most agreeably to Antibes.

"I write you this letter from Toulon. As the weather has been bad, I have not yet been able to see the port, which is the finest the French have in the Mediterranean, and where there are at this time twenty ships of the line.

"In the last letter I wrote to you, I desired *your directions* in respect to the future course of my travels. You well know the situation of my affairs in England. I am *betrothed* to a woman whom I would give the world to enjoy, and whom I cannot marry until those preliminaries are settled which *cannot be settled* until the General has sold his estate. *The estate is not sold*, as I know of, and my marriage is no farther advanced than it was a year and a half ago. To what purpose, then, should I return in so nice a conjuncture? The sight of my mistress will raise to an ungovernable height that desire of possessing her which the enjoyment of the finest Italian ladies has never been able to diminish.

"I love you, my dear uncle—I love you in my heart. I wish to live with you. I prefer Miss Warburton's love to that of any other woman; but, *in this crisis*, I had rather be *a banished man, condemned abroad to roam*. Time, that great artificer of men's fortunes, may work some lucky change. Her father is very old; he is turned of seventy. When the old man dies, she will have at once, and in her own power, a fortune of fifty thousand pounds. It is also probable he may sell the estate. He must some time or other find a purchaser. Was anything, in short, to happen that might facilitate this wished-for alliance, I would instantly direct my course to England; but till some preparatory step be taken, *I think I am better where I am*, improving myself by foreign observation and experience. I mean only for some months to come. Before the summer ends, I would, I think, at all events be in England; and by prolonging thus much my stay abroad, I gain many considerable advantages, and finish more completely this most useful part of my education. I propose these doubts *to you only*, and I beg, my dear uncle, you will not betray to anybody the unlimited confidence I have in your goodness and friendship. Write me soon an answer.—T. LYTTELTON.

"I beg you would excuse my ending so abruptly my letter, but I was led on unawares to the end of my paper. Accept my most grateful thanks for the thousand favours I have received from you, and believe me for ever attached to you. Direct *aux soins* of John Birkbeck, Esq., à Marseilles."

The projected marriage with Miss Warburton must have been broken off shortly afterwards, for on the 1st of January, 1765, his father wrote as follows: "My son is in France, where, I believe, he will stay till about the beginning of April. His match is off. If you will ask the reason, I can give it you in no better words than those of Rochefoucault, who says that *une femme est un bénéfice qui oblige à la résidence*." He adds, in another letter: "By his letters it appears that there is a great energy and force in his understanding; and as his faults are only those of most of our young travellers, I hope his return to England, and cool reflection on the mischief of his past follies, will enable his reason to get the better of any recent ill habits contracted by him already, and that his natural goodness of heart will give a right turn to the vivacity of his passions."* There is nothing in this extract to show that the tinge given to young Lyttelton's character by Italian manners and institutions was deeper than was usually contracted by young men on their travels; but it can scarcely be doubted that it was deeper than was then feared.

His resolution to avoid gambling was not abiding. The disappointment of the hopes he had so long indulged with regard to Miss Warburton may have led him to seek the excitement of play as a means of diverting his mind from it; but he informed Sir Richard Lyttelton, in a letter from Dijon, dated the 15th of February, that it was an Italian, not an English lady, who had been the innocent cause of his moral aberration. He at first won largely, and then had a run of ill-luck, which obliged him to draw for £500 to satisfy his debts of honour, and for £250 for his expenses at Marseilles and Aix.

"I will not presume," he wrote, "by any excuse to endeavour to regain your favours and affection. I am sensibly enough convinced that I have the *very great misfortune* to have lost them *irrecoverably*. I shall always remember with most heartfelt gratitude the tenderness and confidence reposed in me by the most generous of parents.

---

* "Memoirs and Correspondence of George Lord Lyttelton." 1845.

The debt I owe you is too immense ever to be repaid. In regard to the money I have spent, I will confess myself legally your debtor for all or any part of the sum. In times to come I may be able to discharge it."

His Continental tour had already been prolonged beyond the period originally fixed for it; and he did not return until the summer, when the first thing that we hear of him is the part he took in a masque at Stowe, for which he composed some tolerable verses, which were spoken by a little girl in the character of Queen Mab, and embodied a very graceful compliment to the character and abilities of the host, Earl Temple. With the exception of this pleasing little incident, the three years succeeding his return to England are a blank; but his letters show that, during at least a portion of this time, he was under the cloud of paternal displeasure and social proscription, the causes of which can only be inferred from the manner in which his candour invariably led him to speak of his own faults. The chronological arrangement of his letters can be determined only by internal evidence, which is often very slight or wholly deficient; but it appears from the eleventh of the series* that he was in the position de-

---

* "Letters of the late Lord Lyttelton." 1806.

scribed in the spring of 1768, and it was probably some time before that period that he wrote the following letter to a friend who had accused him of neglect, and reproached him with his failings:—

"My dear Friend,

"You do me great injustice. I receive your letters with the greatest pleasure; and I gave your last the usual welcome, though every line was big with reproaches to me. I feel myself greatly mortified that you should have a suspicion of any neglect on my part. When I cease to answer your addresses you will be justified in supposing me careless about them: till then, you will, I hope, do me the justice, as far at least as relates to yourself, to think well of me. I very sensibly feel the advantage of your good opinion, and the loss of it would greatly affect me. You may be assured that my insensibility to reputation is not such as some part of my conduct may have given you reason to believe; for, after all his blustering and looking big, the heart of the worst man cannot be at ease, when he forces a look of contempt towards the ill opinion of mankind. In spite of all his bravadoes, he is a hypocrite twelve hours out of the four-and-twenty; and hypocrisy, as it is well said, is the homage which Vice pays to Virtue: unwillingly, I confess; but still she is forced to pay it.

"I will most frankly acknowledge to you that I have been as well disposed to turn my back upon the good opinion of the world as any one in it; and that I have sometimes accomplished this important business without confusion of face, but never without confusion of heart. On a late very mortifying occasion, it was not in my power to possess myself either with one or the other. At a public and very numerous meeting in the county where my father lives, where great part of his property lies, where his influence is considerable, and his name respectable, I was not only deserted, but avoided; and the women could not have discovered more horror on my approaching them if I had been Tarquin himself. I found myself alone in the crowd, and, which is as bad, alone out of the crowd. I passed the evening without company; and two or three such evenings would either have driven me to despair or have reformed me. I was then convinced, as I always am when I write to you, that there is some particle of good still remaining in me: but I flew from that solitary scene which gave such a conviction, to renew that dissolute intemperance which would destroy it.

"It is a great misfortune that vice, be it what

it may, will find some one or other to flatter it; and that there should be assemblies of people, where, when public and honourable society has hissed you from the stage, you may find, not only reception, but applause—little earthly pandemoniums, where you meet with every means to hush the pains of reflection, and to guard against the intrusions of conscience. It requires a most gigantic resolution to suffer pain when passion quickens every sense, and every enticing object beckons to enjoyment. I was not born a Stoic, nor am I to be made a martyr. So much do I hate and detest pain, that I think all good must be dear that is to be purchased with it. Penitence is a rack where offences have been grievous. To sit alone and court reflection, which will come, perhaps, every moment, with a swinging sin at her back, and to be humble and patient beneath the stripes of such a scourge, by heavens, it is not in human nature to bear it! I am sure, at least, it is not in mine. If I could go to confession, like a good papist, and have the score wiped off at once, *à la bonne heure!* But to repent like a sobbing paralytic Presbyterian will not do for me; I am not fat enough to repent that way. George Bodens may be qualified for such a system of contrition, but my skinny shape will not bear mortification; and if I were to attempt the subdual of my carnal lust by fasting and prayer, I should be soon fasted and prayed into the family vault, and disappoint the worms of their meals.

"I have had, as you well know, some serious conversations with my father upon the subject; and one evening he concluded a Christian lecture of a most unchristian length by recommending me to address Heaven to have mercy upon me, and to join my prayers to his constant and paternal ones for my reformation. These expressions, with his preceding counsels, and his affecting delivery of them, had such an effect upon me, that, like the king in Hamlet, I had bent the stubborn sinews of my knees, when it occurred to me that my devotions might be seen through the key-hole. This drew me from my pious attitude, and, having secured this aperture, so unfriendly to secret deeds, I thought it would not be an useless precaution to let down the window-curtains also; and, during the performance of that ceremony, some lively music, which struck up in the street, caught my attention, and gave a sudden flirt to all my devout ideas; so I girded on my sword, and went to the Little Theatre in the Haymarket, where Mrs. Cole and the Reverend Dr. Squintum soon put me out of humour with praying, and into humour with myself.

"I really began this letter in very sober

seriousness; and, though I have strayed from my grave airs into something that wears a ludicrous appearance, I beg of you not to give up all hopes of my amendment. If there were but half-a-dozen people in the world who would afford me the kind encouragement I receive from you, it would, I verily believe, work a reformation in the prodigal; but the world has marked me down for so much dissoluteness as to doubt, at all times, of the sincerity of my repentance. ——— has already told me, more than once, that I am got so deep into the mud as to make it highly improbable that I should ever get out; that I am too bad ever to be good; and that my future lot is either to be an open villain or an undeceiving hypocrite. Pretty encouragement, truly! Lady Huntingdon would tell me another story; but, however that may be, I shall never give myself up for lost while I retain a sense of your merit and a value for your friendship."

George Bodens, whose name appears more than once in the letters which must be frequently quoted in these memoirs, has not left his name on the records of the age; but that he was one of the associates, whose influence upon the character and career of Thomas Lyttelton was feared by the friends of the latter may be inferred from a letter written at a subsequent period by Earl Temple, and which will be given in its proper place.

There were probably alternate storms and calms in the relations between Lord Lyttelton and his scapegrace son, and the scene related in the foregoing letter must have taken place during one of the intervals of peace. Earl Temple seems always to have used his influence in his young relative's true interests; and his counsels had probably their due weight in the decision that was arrived at in 1767, that the family influence should be used to give the energies and abilities of Thomas Lyttelton an useful and honourable field for their exercise by obtaining him a seat in Parliament. At the ensuing general election he became a candidate for the representation of Bewdley, a little borough in which his family possessed considerable interest, and which had been represented by a Lyttelton on several previous occasions. Great exertions were made to secure his return, but he headed the poll by only a small majority over Sir Edward Winnington. He seems to have attached much importance to the attainment of this position, which would give him occupation, and open a career for him; but both himself and friends were again doomed to be disappointed.

CHAPTER III.

Politics of the Period—Men of the Commons—The Damers—George Durant—Petition against Lyttelton's Return—His Maiden Speech—Complimented by Wellbore Ellis—Reconciliation with his Family—Unseated—"Junius"—Hypothesis that Lyttelton was the Author of the Famous Letters—Second Continental Tour—Quarrel with George Ayscough—Return to England.

FOR nearly half a century, from the change of dynasty which took place on the death of Queen Anne until the accession of George III., the government of this country had been almost constantly in the hands of the Whigs. Sir Robert Walpole, Pelham, the Duke of Newcastle, and the Earl of Chatham had all been taken from this party, which, as long as the national liberties seemed to be threatened by the pretensions of the Stuarts, had the support of the landed interest, as well as the sympathies of the trading and industrial classes. The cessation of this fear wrought a change in the policy of the Crown and the aristocracy. George III., who had the most exalted notions of the royal prerogative, showed, from the beginning of his reign, a strong desire to extend the power of the Crown and to keep that of the people within the strictest limits that the Constitution rendered possible ; and hence the storm with which the Crown and its advisers were assailed from the first year of the Administration of the Earl of Bute down to the dawn of the era of Parliamentary reform. Grenville, who succeeded Bute in 1763, left the Wilkes prosecution and outlawry and the American Stamp Act as legacies to his successors, under whom they bore bitter fruit. The Stamp Act was repealed under the Whig Ministry formed by the Marquis of Rockingham, but the right to tax the colonies, which was the matter in dispute between them and the mother country, was reserved.

The Rockingham Administration did not long continue in power, being supplanted by the second Ministry of the Earl of Chatham, which was, however, less popular than the first. Indeed, all the Cabinets of this period suffered from the popular suspicion that they were composed of mere puppets, moved at the will of the Crown, and the strings of which were pulled by the Earl of Bute. The Earl of Chatham was, unfortunately, prevented by ill-health from taking an active part in the business of the State, and, on the death of Charles Townshend, who was, after the Premier, the most able member of the Cabinet, he resigned. Early in 1768, a new administration was formed by the Duke of Grafton, and a general election took place. Such was the state of affairs when Thomas Lyttelton entered Parliament as the representative of Bewdley.

John and George Damer sat in the same Parliament, the former for the now extinct borough of Gatton, and the latter for Cricklade. Another of his fellow-members was George Durant, who sat for Evesham, and of whose history and connection with the Lyttelton family we have the following account in a letter from Thomas Lyttelton to a friend :—

"Your usual accuracy has failed you in your suggestions concerning the rise and rapid progress of Mr. [Durant's] fortune. The history of that gentleman's advancement to his present affluence, if my immediate recollection does not fail me, is as follows : That he was appointed to his first employment in the service of Government by my father's interest is true; and it may, perhaps, have been procured for him from the motives which current opinion has assigned; but of this I do not pretend to be better informed than the rest of the world. Thus placed in a situation of little or no leisure, he was left, I believe, by our family patronage, to look for any future promotion from his own industry, the chance of succession, or the casual boon of fortune. The latter was disposed to smile upon him, or, it may be said with more propriety, to reward the prudent modesty with which he retreated from her first advances to secure her greater favours. In the usual course of promotion he had an acknowledged claim to succeed to a vacant place of no inconsiderable profit. On this occasion Lord Holland, for some particular reason which I have forgotten, or perhaps never heard, wished to make an irregular appointment in favour of some other person; and, to comply with his lordship's wishes, Mr. [Durant] wisely waived his right of succession. That nobleman, who never suffered a good office to be long unreturned, soon after procured him to be named commissary-general to the expedition then preparing to attack the French West India islands. The success which attended it, together with the regular profits of his appointment, placed him in a situation, with respect to fortune, with which, it may be imagined, he was more than satisfied; and I have been told that he then looked no farther.

"But Lord Holland never thought he did enough for any one that had obliged him; and I am greatly mistaken if his influence did not name Mr. [Durant] to the same employment in the formidable armament which was sent against the Havannah, and succeeded. The fortunes acquired by that capture are well known, and Mr. [Durant's] was among the largest of them. On his return to England he soon began to display a love of ostentation, which he displayed, however, as I understand, without injuring his fortune; for, though George has no small share of vanity, it has seldom operated so far as to make him inattentive to the *summum bonum* of life. He built a fine house in Portman Square, and purchased the very capital estate of Tong Castle, in Shropshire, of the Duke of Kingston. He immediately renewed, or rather improved, the ancient form of the decayed edifice, adorned with the venerable decorations of Gothic architecture, beautified its surrounding lawns, and conducted through them a long extent of fine water, which flows on three sides of the stately edifice. The castle is a very large building, contains many very capacious apartments, and is furnished with a profusion of pictures and splendid upholstery. Though it is not situated in a fine part of the country, yet, taken in all its circumstances, it may lay no small claim to the character of magnificence. The owner of it might have built a new and more commodious house for much less money than has been expended in the reparations of the old one; but the word *castle* is a sounding word. It was in unison with Mr. [Durant's] notions of grandeur; and, apprehensive that this favourite title might, by degrees, be forgotten with the lofty turrets and stately battlements, he resolved to clothe them in more than pristine grandeur, and thus secure their ancient, honourable name, till time or chance should destroy them for ever. Some of my old neighbours positively assert that they remember to have heard George [Durant] declare, when he was a youth, that he hoped, one day or other, to be possessed of a larger house than Hagley; and they insist upon it that he gives such great extent to the limits of Tong Castle merely to fulfil his own prediction.

"But this by the way. The world in general, who were not acquainted with the ambition of his early days, have thought that by this creation of splendour he hoped to allure some lady of noble birth and great connections to become the mistress of it. The bait offered by so handsome a man as he certainly is would, in all probability, have been soon taken, but, in this particular, expectation has been very much disappointed, for he has actually made a kind of half-runaway match with a little Quaker of eighteen years of age, and educated in all the rigour of her sect. She has no pretension to beauty (I write merely from information), but possesses a very agreeable person, with a most amiable simplicity, and loves her husband to idolatry. I have heard your friend, Councillor Day, speak in high terms of her father, as a man of excellent understanding, polite manners, and generous disposition. Since this marriage, the superb service of plate very seldom makes its appearance; and the master of the noble castle, as I am told, now lives in a corner of it, with a small party of his relations, and seems to be growing into a disregard of the intrigues and fashions of public life. His brother* is the parson of my parish, and is called Doctor John; but the divine and the squire do not hold a very friendly intercourse.

"I rather think that this little piece of biography is pretty well founded: if, however, it should possess any errors, I beg leave to assure you that they are not of my invention. As to Mr. [Durant's] unpopularity with the Lyttelton family, it does not arise, perhaps, from what you and the world may, with some reason, suppose; but from a subsequent circumstance, of which you and the world are, in general, ignorant. When my [uncle] was governor of [Jamaica], he received positive orders to raise and discipline a regiment of negroes for the service of the

---

* Rev. John Durant, D.D., Vicar of Hagley.

Havannah expedition. As this supply did not join the grand armament at the time appointed, Mr. [Durant] was despatched to Jamaica by the commander-in-chief, to chide the tardy levies; and, as report says, he found a very surprising languor in obeying these very important orders of Government. On such an occasion he was, perhaps, instructed to threaten an accusation of delinquency against the governor to the powers at home; and it is equally probable that he did not forget his instructions. Whether this neglect was repaired by subsequent exertions, or whether it was forgotten in the successes which followed, I do not know; but I very well remember that at the time my father was very uneasy about it, and complained, in angry terms, to the clergyman of Hagley of his brother's forwardness to disgrace a branch of that family by which his own had been so warmly protected. Here the matter rested; but that George [Durant] should have been elevated to a situation wherein he could repeat what was called an insolent menace to one of the Lyttelton family will never be remembered without much mortification, and therefore can never be forgiven. Adieu."

This letter, with its revelations of irregular appointments and fortunes made by commissaries-general under a corrupt system of Government, constitutes an appropriate commentary on the results of that condition of the representative institutions of the country of which we have illustrations in the existence of such constituencies as Gatton and Old Sarum, and the return of such men as the Damers by means which were no secret. The return of Thomas Lyttelton was petitioned against, on the ground of fraud, it being alleged that recourse had been had to the system of manufacturing "occasional burgesses," in order to secure his election. But it is probable that he was quite as much the choice of the electors of Bewdley as the majority of the members of the Commons' House of Parliament at that day were of the constituencies of which they were the ostensible representatives.

Parliament assembled on the 10th of May, and on the 18th Thomas Lyttelton delivered his maiden speech, the occasion being one of the many stormy debates that arose out of the case of John Wilkes, of *North Briton* and *Essay on Woman* notoriety. Not a line of this first oratorical effort is to be found in "Hansard," but we learn from the meagre sketch of it in the "Cavendish Debates," that the line of argument adopted by the speaker was, that it was unwise to bestow so much time upon such an insignificant subject, when the American colonies were so disturbed on account of the fiscal measures of the late Administration, and a strong Government was so obviously and imperatively required. The speech made a favourable impression upon the House, and elicited a compliment from Wellbore Ellis, who observed that the honourable member for Bewdley had spoken with hereditary ability.

The compliment was sweet incense to the family foible; and its occasion brought about a temporary reconciliation between young Lyttelton and his offended relatives. The truce was as brief, however, as the future orator's possession of his seat. The Committee to which the petition against his return was referred reported unfavourably to him; and, on the 28th January, 1769, he was declared not to have been duly elected, and the seat was transferred to Sir Edward Winnington.

It was at this time that the celebrated letters of "Junius" began to attract that large share of public attention which they received during several years, and which has, from time to time, been directed to them from that period to the present day, through the efforts which have been made to fix the identity of their author. Three-quarters of a century afterwards, an attempt* was made to assign the authorship of these famous letters to Thomas Lyttelton, on the ground of certain

---

* *Quarterly Review*, December, 1851.

expressions and turns of thought which are found both in the letters of "Junius" and in those of Lyttelton, and others which, in the opinion of the writer, favour the hypothesis that Woodfall's mysterious correspondent was "a dissolute young man." Wade had just taken equal pains to prove that "Junius" could have been neither a peer nor a member of the House of Commons; but, without entering into the often-discussed question as to who "Junius" really was, it will be sufficient here to show that there are very small grounds for identifying him with Thomas Lyttelton.

The similarities of thought and expression which are found in the letters of "Junius" and in those of Lyttelton are not remarkable enough to warrant the inference that the two sets of correspondence emanated from the same mind and hand. Most of them are coincidences which are almost certain to occur to any two writers of the same period, regarding the same topics from the same point of view, or from similar points; and though, unfortunately for his memory, it cannot be contended that Thomas Lyttelton was not a dissolute young man, there were so many young men of the same character, in and out of Parliament, who were contemporary with "Junius," that dissolute habits can scarcely be regarded as a characteristic by which the authorship of the letters in the *Advertiser* can be assigned to him. He was only twenty-four years of age when the letters signed "Junius" began to appear, and, though he had given considerable attention to the political questions of the day during the short period that he sat in the House of Commons, and, in the words of the author of the theory under consideration, "those who knew him intimately discerned very early the superiority of his genius, and gave him credit, while yet plunged in profligacy, for qualities which would conduct him to eminence, should he ever resolve on doing justice to himself," he can scarcely have possessed the experience and knowledge of public affairs evinced by "Junius."

In order to account for "the profound knowledge and matured political opinion he displayed on his first appearance" in the House of Lords, and to explain the "confidence in his powers that distinguished his speeches, and surprised even more than his eloquence," the writer in the *Quarterly Review* states that, "for seven years previous to his father's death he studiously shrouded his motions, frequently concealing his residence from his friends," and infers "that that time—despite profligate habits—must have been spent in intellectual exercises." That much of the time referred to was thus creditably and profitably employed, there is abundant evidence in his letters and speeches to prove; but the fact does not help us very far to the conclusion that he was "Junius."

Seven years previous to the death of his father carries us back to the summer of 1766, one year after his return from his Continental tour, and when he was in his twenty-second year. In 1768 he was in Parliament, and he seems, during the short time that he held his seat, to have given an exemplary attention to his legislative duties. There is not much data as to the manner in which the next three years were spent, but he was at Ghent in 1769, and in Italy during the following year; and it seems probable that he left England for a second Continental tour soon after he lost his seat in Parliament, and remained abroad until the end of 1771, or the beginning of 1772.

The misty veil that conceals his movements during the interval is explicable without recourse to the supposition that he withdrew from the world for the purpose of forging in retirement the weapons of future political controversy. His public career had received a check that had disappointed himself equally with his friends, and he was, besides, under the ban of paternal and family displeasure. No one was concerned as to where he was or what he was doing. Hence it is that there is not a line about him—not the merest mention of his name—either in the letters of his father or in those of his noble relative, the Earl of Chatham. What his relations with his family were at this time can be seen from two letters written shortly before his return to England, and the first of which is as follows :—

" So [George Ayscough] turns up his eyes and significantly shrugs his shoulders when my name is mentioned, and, to continue the farce, pretends to lament me as a disgrace to his family! I am almost ashamed to acknowledge it, but this idle history has given me a more stinging mortification than I almost ever felt. How insignificant must he become who is openly despised by insignificance! and how loud must the hiss of the world be when such a puny whipster insults me! If honourable men were to speak of me with contempt, I should have submitted without resentment, for I have deserved it. If they should bestow their pity upon me, I should thank them for giving me more than I deserve. If mankind despise, I have only to resist, or fly from the contempt; but to be an object of supercilious airs from one who, two years ago, would have wiped the dust from off my shoes, and who, perhaps, two years hence will be proud of the same office— a puny prattler, who does not possess a sufficient degree of talent or importance to give dignity either to virtue or crime—I say to be the butt of such a one severely mortifies me. Were I on the other side of the water, his back-biting looks and shrugs should be changed in a moment to well-made bows and suppliant postures. If I live, the scurvy knave shall do me homage! It really frets me that I cannot in four-and-twenty hours meet him face to face, and make his subservient attentions give the lie to his humbling compassion in the presence of those before whom he has traduced me. The day of my revenge will come, when he shall open his mouth for me to spit in it, as he was wont to do, and perform every dirty trick for which parasites were formed. His genius is to fetch and carry—a very spaniel, made to fawn and eat your leavings, whose whole courage rises no higher than to ape a snarl. If I live to outlive this sniffling pedagogue, I shall see him make a foolish end of it. Mark my words, I am a very Shylock, I will have Revenge!

"The last word I have written puts me in mind of telling you that —— has been with me for some time. The rascal, who is a priest into the bargain, carried *aqua fortis* in a syringe for three months together, to squirt the fiery liquor into the eyes of a fortunate rival. In this diabolical design he succeeded, and the object of his malice was for ever deprived of half his sight. I have conversed with him on the horrors of this transaction, but the Italian finds a consolation in his own infernal feelings, and a justification in the dying commands of his father, whose last words composed this emphatic sentence: 'Remember, my son, that revenge is sweet!'

"This man is capable of any villainy, if money is to be got by it; and I doubt not but he might be bribed to undertake, without hesitation, robbery, seduction, rape, and murder. However, my superior virtue for once overawed his villainy; for he most certainly had it in his power to have robbed me of a large sum of money without the possibility of a discovery, and, if he thought it necessary, he might have despatched me with as little danger. I have since asked him what strange fit of virtue or fear of the devil came across him when he had such an opportunity to make his fortune? The impudent rascal replied at once that he had very powerful suggestions to send me to the other world, and that if, fortunately for him, I had possessed one single virtue, he should, without ceremony, have despatched me to my reward. This event will, I think, make a complete Mandevillian of me. You see, for your encouragement, that a bad life is good for something; and for the good example which the world will receive from me in times to come, it will be indebted to the very bad one I have already given it. After this signal and providential preservation, I cannot but think that Heaven has something particularly great in store for me.

"As I tell it you, this history has the air of a *badinage*, but you may be assured that it is a real fact, and I am sorry that the circumstances of it are too long and various to be inserted in a letter. I believe you know something of the man, but if you repeat what I have written to any one who is acquainted with him, you will soon find that I have had a very narrow escape. I have bribed him to leave me, and he is gone for England. The story of Lewis the Fourteenth and his barber is well known, and you may, if you please, apply it to your affectionate," &c.

George Edward Ayscough was the son of the Rev. Dr. Francis Ayscough, who had been tutor to Lyttelton's father at Oxford, and afterwards married Anne Lyttelton, the peer's sister, and became Dean of Bristol. George was, therefore, Thomas Lyttelton's cousin, and held a lieutenant's commission in the First Regiment of Foot Guards. That in the foregoing letter, and in the one that follows, he has not been misrepresented, is shown by the manner in which he is treated by Nichols. "It is painful," says that author, "to reflect on the miscarriages of families, or the profligacy of individuals; yet truth obliges me to observe, that the honour of the respectable house of Lyttelton derives little advantage from the conduct of this unhappy member of it. Though a military man, he submitted to be insulted by a gentleman* who repeatedly treated him as a poltroon; and, though in no affluent circumstances, he gave up his commission, to avoid doing his duty when called upon by his Sovereign to fight in America."† What Nichols says of his vicious and debauched conduct, may for the present be omitted. That it was to him the following letter was addressed, there can be no doubt :—

"You have certainly given yourself very unjustifiable airs upon my subject: neither your talents, knowledge, figure, courage, nor virtue, afford you the shadow of that superiority over me which, I understand, you affect to maintain. However imprudent or bad my conduct may have been, whatever vices I may unfortunately possess, be assured I do not envy you your snivelling virtues, which are worse than the worst vices, and give an example of meanness and hypocrisy in the

---

* Swift, author of a poem entitled "The Gamblers."
† "Literary Anecdotes of the Eighteenth Century."

extreme. Your letter is a *farrago* of them both; and since the receipt of it I despise you more than ever.

"What, sir? Has my father got a cough, or does he look thinner than usual, and read his Bible? There must be some certain symptoms of his decay and dissolution that could induce you to address yourself kindly to one who, to use your own expression, is, as he ought to be, abandoned by his family. You have dreamed of an hatchment upon Hagley House, and seen a visionary coronet suspended over my brow. You are a simpleton and a parasite to let such weak reasons guide you to wag your tail and play the spaniel, and renew your offers to fetch and carry. Be assured, for your comfort, that, if ever you and I have any future intercourse together, it will be upon such terms, or worse.

"I have heard it said, and I believe it to be true, that you pretend to lament your poor uncle's fate, and, with a more than rueful visage, prognosticate the breaking of his heart from the wicked life of his graceless son. Now, I will tell you a secret, that, supposing such a canting prophecy should take place to-morrow, you would be the first to flatter the *parricide*. I consider you with a mixture of scorn and pity, when I see you so continually pampered in difficulties from your regard to the present and future Lord: though you order your matters tolerably well, for there is not one of our family to whom your hypocritical canting will not answer in some degree, but to myself. I know you, and I declare you to be incapable of love or affection to any one, even to a mother or a sister. You know what I mean; but to quit an idea abhorrent to human nature, let me entreat you, if it is in your power, to act with candour, and, if you must speak of me, tell your sentiments openly, and not with those covert looks and affected shrugs, which convey so much more than meets the ear: and be so good, I pray you, as to raise your merit upon your own mighty stock of virtues, and not upon my vices. The world will one day judge between us, and I must desire you to be content with the acknowledged superiority you will receive from the arbitration in your favour.

"'Oh, *stultum nimis est, cum tu pravissima* tentes,
Alterius censor ut vitiosa notes!'

"I have not yet sung a requiem to my own honour; and, though you and some others of my good friends may have chaunted a dirge over the grave you have yourselves dug for it, it does not rest, however, without the hopes of a joyful and speedy resurrection. To have done with you for the present, I have only to desire you to be an open enemy to me, or a real friend, if you are capable of either; the halting between two opinions on the matter is both disgraceful and contemptible. Be assured that I give you these counsels more for your own sake than for that of your humble servant,

"[THOMAS LYTTELTON.]"

It is probable that Lyttelton, leaving England in disgrace with his family, and almost an outcast from reputable society, left debtors unsatisfied; and that to this circumstance must be ascribed the attempt to conceal his movements on his return, which elicited the friendly remonstrance to which the following letter is a reply, and which seems to constitute the slender foundation upon which the writer in the *Quarterly Review* built up the theory that he secluded himself from the world to study politics and write letters to the *Advertiser*:—

"You accuse me of neglect in not informing you that I was in London. Believe me, I had every disposition in the world to do it, but was opposed by circumstances, which, among other mortifications, prevented me from seeing you. I came to England in so private a manner that I imagined no one would, or, indeed, could know of my arrival; but, by a combination of unlucky circumstances, the secret was discovered, and by those who were the most likely to make a very unpleasant use of their knowledge. I was, therefore, obliged to shift my plan, and to beg H—— to give me an asylum in his house, where he very kindly received and entertained me. My abode was not suspected by any one; and I remained there till certain people were persuaded that I had never left the Continent, or was again returned to it; and till the hell-hounds which were in pursuit of me had relaxed their search.

"You must certainly have heard me mention something of my host and hostess; they are the most original couple that ever were paired together, and their singularity effected what, I believe, no other amusement could have attained—it made me forget the disagreeableness of my situation. He possesses a strange, wild, rhapsodic genius, which, however, is not uncultivated; and, amid a thousand odd, whimsical ideas, he produces original bursts of poetry and understanding that are charming. She is a foreigner, assumes the title of countess, and, without knowing how to write or read, possesses, in the circumstances of dress, behaviour, &c., all her husband's dispositions. She is fantastic, grotesque, *outré*, and wild; nevertheless, at times, there are very pleasing gleams of propriety in her manners and appearance.

"I cannot describe so well as you may conceive the striking and odd contrast of these two characters, and what strange sparks are produced by the collision of them. When she imagines that Cytherea acknowledges her divinity, and he grasps in his hand the lyre of Apollo; when the goddess unfolds herself to view with imaginary millions at her feet, and when the god chides the chairs and tables for not being awakened into a cotillion by his strains; in short, when the sublime fit of madness is on, it is an august scene; but if the divinities should rival each other, heaven changes instantly to hell, Venus becomes a trull, and Phœbus a blind fiddler. It is impossible to describe the riot; not only reflections, but things of a more solid nature are thrown at each other. Homer's genius is absolutely necessary to paint celestial combats. But it ends not here: this superb opera, which was acted at least, during my stay, three times a week, and rehearsed generally every day, for the most part has an happy conclusion. The contest requires the support of nectar, which softens the edge of resentment, puts the parties in good humour, and they are soon disposed to acknowledge each other's merit and station, with a zeal and fondness superior, if possible, to their late rage and opposition. A number of collateral circumstances serve as interludes to the grand piece, and though less sublime, are not less entertaining.

"You will now, probably, be no longer displeased with me for making my hiding-place a secret. One hour's attendance upon our orgies would have done for you; on the contrary, they suited me. I wanted something to hurry my spirits, to dissipate my thoughts, and amuse my mind; and I found it in this retreat. You know enough of the parties to enter into my description. I hope it will make you laugh; but, if my pen should fail, I will promise to make your sides ache when we meet again, a pleasure which I look to with a most sensible impatience."

He had not, it may be safely assumed, passed the period of his second Continental sojourn in scenes or with companions conducive to moral amendment. For ever making resolutions for the future, which he had not firmness enough to keep, he returned to England in a state of mind which forcibly illustrates the Zoroastrian creed, the powers of good and evil contending for mastery over the heart of man, and each in turn gaining the advantage over the other. Weary of his wandering life, surfeited with sensual pleasures, disgusted with the degradation of his surroundings, feeling with all the bitterness of his passionful nature his exclusion from the family circle, and from the society of his best friends, he came back to England with contrition on his lips; and who shall say that it was not in his heart? But at the bottom of that mysterious well-spring of human passions were pride and vanity, and an inordinate love of pleasure—the pride of intellect, the love of power, the thirst for applause, the worship of the flesh; all these, cast down for the moment, were ready to spring up and renew the struggle with every better feeling of the heart, every higher aspiration of the soul.

CHAPTER IV.

Overtures for Domestic Reconciliation—Lord Chatham congratulates Lord Lyttelton on his Son's Return—Lord Lyttelton's Reply—Thomas Lyttelton's Letters to his Friends—The Miseries of having nothing to do—Regret at the Loss of his Seat in Parliament—Dialogues of the Dead—His own Version of the Causes of his Disgrace—Claude Anet—Story of the Quaker and his Dog—Bishop Lyttelton and the French Horn-blowers—Comparison with Mirabeau.

THERE can be no doubt that Thomas Lyttelton returned to England with a sincere desire for restoration to the family relations, which, by various circumstances, had been ruptured. He wrote to the principal members of his family, expressing regret for his past misconduct, assuring them of his contrition, and asking for their intercession with others on his behalf. Only one of these letters has been preserved.* It was probably addressed to Earl Temple, and is as follows:—

"It is so long since I received your letter that I am almost ashamed to answer it; and be assured that, in writing my apology, and asking your

---

* "Letters of the late Lord Lyttelton." 1806.

pardon, I act with a degree of resolution that I have seldom experienced. I hardly expect that you will receive the one, or grant the other. I do not deserve either, or indeed any kindness from you of any sort, for I have been very ungrateful. I am myself very sensible of it, and very much apprehend that you will be of the same opinion. I was never more conscious of my follies than at this moment; and if you should have withdrawn yourself from the very few friends which are left me, I shall not dare to complain; for I deserve the loss, and can only lament that another and a deeper shade will be added to my life. The very idea of such a misfortune is most grievous; and nothing can be more painful than the reflection of suffering it from a fatal, ill-starred, and abortive infatuation, which will prove my bane. I have written letters, since I received yours, to many who have never done me any kindness, to some who have betrayed me, and to others whose correspondence administered no one comfort to my heart, or honour to my character; and for them, at least engaged with them, I have neglected you, to whose disinterested friendship I am so much indebted, and which is now become the only point whereon to fix my anchor of hope.

"But this is not all; if it were, I have something within me which would whisper your forgiveness; for you know of what frail materials I am made; and have ventured, in the face of the world's malice, to prognosticate favourably of my riper life. But I fear that you will think meanness added to ingratitude when I tell you that I am called back to acknowledge your past goodness to me, and to ask a repetition of it, not from any renewed sentiment of honour or gratitude, but by immediate and wringing distress. In such a situation your idea presented itself to me—an idea which was not encouraged in seasons of enjoyment: it never wished to share my pleasure, but, like the first-born of friendship, it hastened to partake my pain. Though it came in so lovely a form, I dared not bid it welcome; and I started, as at the sight of one whom I had severely injured, whose neglect, contempt, and revenge I might justly dread, while I did not possess the least means of resistance, nor had a covert left where I might fly for refuge.

"This is a very painful confession, and will, I hope, plead my cause in your bosom, and win you to grant my request. I have written to —— for some time past, and have never been favoured with one line of reply. Indeed, it has been hinted that he refuses to read my letters. However that may be, he most certainly does not

answer them. In order, therefore, that I may
know my fate and be certain of my doom, I most
earnestly and submissively entreat you to deliver
the enclosed letter into his hands. If I should be
deserted by you both, the consequences may be of
such a nature as, in the most angry paroxysm, you
would neither of you wish to your most obliged," &c.

It is doubtful whether the person mentioned
in this letter as not answering his appeal was his
father or Sir Richard Lyttelton, and the blanks
in the next epistle throw no light upon the point.
The latter was evidently addressed to a friend
who was entirely in his confidence, the previous
commission referred to in the first sentence relating to inquiries which he had asked his correspondent, while in Paris, to make concerning
a lady whom he had met there. He respected
the lady as much as he admired her, but he says
that, of ten calls he had made upon her, he had
been admitted only thrice, "when there was a
great deal of company. This," he continues, "is
a very superior woman; for, while she conducts
herself in such a manner towards me as to tell me
plainly, that the respect she has for my family is
the only inducement to give me the reception she
does, there is not a single look suffered to escape
her from which any person might form the most

distant suspicion of her sentiments concerning me." He had been unable, from indisposition, to bid her farewell in person, and had consoled himself "by writing her a letter, which was half serious, more than half gallant, and almost sincere." He wished to know whether, and in what manner, the lady had spoken of him; but his friend had been unable to learn, and Lyttelton thought it probable that his epistle had been consigned to the fire-grate.

"I have another commission for you, in which I flatter myself you will be more successful than in your last. You must know, then, that I am in a bad plight, and there is no good ground of expectation that matters will go better with me: on the contrary, the prospect is a dark one, and the gloom increases every step I take. To extricate myself, if possible, I wrote to ——, who has not answered my letters, and, I am disposed to think, never opens them. I was, therefore, under the necessity of addressing a very pitiful, penitential epistle to ——. I have used him scurvily, and made such an ill return to all his zeal to serve me, that I have too much reason to apprehend his resentment. He passed through —— about six weeks ago, without inquiring after me. However, without appearing to know anything of that circumstance, I ventured to tell a miserable tale to him, and to beseech his kindness would once more interest itself in my behalf, by delivering a letter into ——'s own hands. It would be an easy matter, I should imagine, to discover if he has complied with my request. T—— will inform you if he has been lately, and when, in —— Street. Perhaps he may have scented out something more; and whatever you can discover I should be glad to know with all possible despatch. They will probably be slow in their operations, whatever they may be; and your information will direct my hopes, or confirm my fears,—will either give a sunshine to the present shade, or prepare me for the worst."

He seems to have been some time in London before his return was known to the family, for Lord Chatham, in a letter to his father,* speaks of his return and the reconciliation as events more nearly connected in point of time than they appear to have been. The letter is dated February 16, 1772, and is as follows:—

"MY DEAR LORD,—The sincere satisfaction I feel on what I hear of Mr. Lyttelton's return, with all the dispositions you could wish, will not allow

---

* "Correspondence of the Earl of Chatham." 1838.

me to be silent on so interesting an event. Accept, my dear Lord, my felicitations upon these happy beginnings, together with every wish that this opening of light may ripen into the perfect day. I know what it is (thank God!) to be happy hitherto in my children; and I grieve for those who meet with essential disappointment in that vital part of domestic happiness. May you never again know anguish from such a wound to your comfort, but the remainder of your days derive as much felicity from the return as you suffered pain from the deviation."

Lord Lyttelton replied to these felicitations and good wishes as follows: "I give you a thousand thanks for your very kind felicitations on the return of my son, who appears to be returned, not only to me, but to a rational way of thinking, and a dutiful conduct, in which if he perseveres, it will gild with joy the evening of my life."

There are letters which appear to have been written by Thomas Lyttelton about this time, which afford further insight into his strangely compounded character, and throw light upon the causes of his long estrangement from his family. "There is nothing," he says in one of them, "so miserable, and, I may add, so unfortunate, as to have nothing to do. The peripatetic principle, that Nature abhors a vacuum, may be applied, with great propriety, to the human intellect, which will embrace anything, however criminal, rather than be without an object. It is a matter of indubitable certainty with me that, if I had kept my seat in Parliament, most of the unpleasant predicaments in which I have been involved since that time would have been avoided. I was disposed to application in the political line, and was possessed of that ready faculty of speech which would have enabled me to make some little figure in the senate. I should have had employment; my passions would have been influenced by a proper animating object, and my vanity would have been sufficiently satisfied. During the short time I sat in Parliament, I found myself in the situation I have described: I was pleased with the character; I availed myself of its privileges while I possessed them; I mingled in public debate, and received the most flattering testimonies of applause. If this scene had continued, it would have been very fortunate for myself, and have saved my friends great anxiety and many alarms: you, among the rest, would have been spared the pain of much unavailing counsel and disregarded admonitions.

"You know me well enough to be certain that I must have a particular and not a common object to employ my attention; it must be an object which inspires desire, calls forth activity, keeps hope upon the stretch, and has some sort of high colouring about it. Power and popular reputation are of this kind, and would greatly have engrossed my thoughts and wishes; they would have kept under the baser passions; I should have governed them at least; and my slavery, if I was destined to be a slave, would have been more honourable. But, losing a situation so suitable to me, I fell back, a prey to that influence which had already proved so fatal, and yielded myself a victim to an habitual dissoluteness which formed my only pleasure.

"I do not mean to write a disrespectful thought of my father; I would not offend you by doing it; but, surely, his ignorance of mankind is beyond all conception. It is hardly credible that a man of his understanding and knowledge, whose life has been ever in the world, and the most polished societies of it, who writes well and ably on its manners, should be so childish in its concerns as to deserve the coral that amused, and the go-cart that sustained him sixty years ago. I write in confidence, and you know what I assert to be true. Indeed, I might go further, and trace the errors of my own life from the want of that kind of paternal discernment which sees into the character of his child, watches over its growing dispositions, gently moulds them to his will, and completes the whole by placing him in a situation suitable to him.

"I have been the victim of vanity, and the sacrifice of me was begun before I could form a judgment of the passion. You will, probably, understand me; but if there should be the least gloom in my allusions, I will, with your leave, explain the matter more clearly in some future letter. There is a great deal of difference between a good man and a good father. I have known bad men who excelled my father as much in parental care as he was superior to them in real virtue. But more of this hereafter."

He continued the subject in the letter from which extracts are given in the first and second chapters of these memoirs, and which concludes as follows :—

"You know as well as myself what happened during my travels, as well as after my return; and I trust that you will impute my misconduct, in part at least, to its primary cause.

"In this short sketch of the matter, which consists rather of hints than descriptions, you will see the drift of my reasoning, and know how to apply it to a thousand circumstances in your remembrance. You were present at my being received into the arms of my family with a degree of warmth, delight, and triumph, which the brightest virtue could alone have deserved; and you recollect the cause of all this rapturous forgiveness, which, I believe, penitence itself would not, at that time, have effected; it was my having made a speech in Parliament, flowery, indeed, and bold, but very little to the purpose, and at a time when, as I was certain that I should lose my seat, it would have been prudent in me to have remained silent. However, Mr. Ellis thought proper to compliment me upon the occasion, and to observe that I spoke with hereditary abilities; and this circumstance instantly occasioned the short-lived family truce that succeeded.

"That my relations may have cause to complain of me, I do not deny; but this confession is accompanied with an opinion, in which I doubt not of your acquiescence, that I, on my side also, have no small cause of complaint; and, however black the colour of my future life may be, I shall ever consider that the dusky scenes of it are occasioned by the vanity of my family, and not by any obdurate or inflexible dispositions inherent in my own character."

He had written at this time two "Dialogues of the Dead," one between Jesus and Socrates, the other between David and Cæsar Borgia, from hints given him at Turin by a free-thinking Frenchman. They are said to have been extremely irreverent and profane; but the suspicion that they were intended to ridicule the similar compositions of his father is declared by him to be without foundation. "Bad as they may be," he observes, "they were not writ for so bad a purpose; and, if I had considered the possibility of such an idea becoming prevalent, they would never have been exposed to inspection. I wrote them originally in French, and never, to my recollection, gave them an English dress, but when I read them to some one who did not understand the former language. I was flattered into the suffering of some copies to be taken by the declaration of a respectable literary company that they were superior to Voltaire's tragedy of *Saul*; and these copies must have been greatly multiplied to have made it possible that one of them should have reached you. I am very sorry for it; for you have already more than sufficient reason to fill your letters to me with reproaches, and I to curse the chance that has thrown another motive in your way to continue a train so disagreeable to us both.

"It is true that my father is a Christian, and has given an ample testimony of his faith to the world by his writings; but it was long after he attained to my age that he became a convert to that system which he has defended. It is painful to me, and hardly fair in you, to occasion our being brought together in the same period; it takes from me the means of justification where I could use them, and of palliation where a complete defence might not be practicable. As to my right reverend uncle, I shall consider him with less ceremony. He also may be a good Christian; but I recollect to have heard him make a better discourse upon the *outside* ornaments of an old Gothic pulpit—I think it was at Wolverhampton—than he ever delivered *in* one throughout the whole course of his evangelical labours. He seems much more at home in a little harangue on some doubtful remnant of a Saxon tombstone than in urging the performance of Christian duties, or guarding, with his lay brother, the Christian fortress against infidel invasion. I well remember, also, to have heard his right reverence declare that he would willingly give one of his fingers (that was his expression) to have a good natural history of Worcestershire. What holy ardour he may possess as an antiquarian, I cannot tell; but, in my conscience, I think he would make a sorry figure as a Christian martyr, and that a zeal for our holy religion would not inflame him to risk the losing of a nail from his finger.

"I repeat to you, upon my honour, that I did not wish these *jeux d'esprit* should have gone beyond the limits I had prescribed for them. The very few persons to whom I gave them were bound, by a very solemn promise, not to circulate their contents or to name their author. If they have forfeited their word, I am sorry for it; but the failure of their engagement cannot be imputed to me, and the severest judge would not think me guilty of more than chance-medley on the occasion. In your breast, I hope there is a complete and full acquittal for your most sincere and obliged," &c.

This letter, and others, show that he had read many of the deistical works of the period, and that he was suspected of having imbibed the sceptical views of revealed religion which were then beginning to pervade all classes of society in every civilised country. He is credited, however, in a passage of one of Pennington's works, which has been quoted by almost every subsequent writer by whom he has been mentioned,*

---

* "With great abilities, generally very ill applied—with a strong sense of religion, which he never suffered to influence his conduct—his days were mostly passed in splendid misery, and in the painful change of the most extravagant gaiety and the deepest with "a strong sense of religion;" and such a sentiment is not incompatible, as some of the most celebrated divines of the present day have shown, with views of the divine inspiration and literal interpretation of the Scriptures which, a century ago, were considered inconsistent with the belief of a Christian. Thomas Lyttelton, whatever else he was, was not a hypocrite; and his letters and speeches must be accepted, therefore, as evidence that he never ceased to be a Christian, though he may have had reasonable doubts upon some matters which it was then held to be impious to doubt. He lived in an age of active thought, when the minds of all who were capable of thinking were, at some period of their lives, more or less disturbed, as even his father's had once been, as he acknowledged on his death-bed to Dr. Johnstone.*

The revolt of the intellect against old forms of religious belief was accompanied by a corresponding movement against the restraints of custom

---

despair. The delight, when he pleased, of the first and most select society, he chose to pass his time, for the most part, with the most profligate and abandoned of both sexes. Solitude was to him the most insupportable of all torments, and to banish reflection he flew to company whom he despised and ridiculed. His conduct was a source of bitter regret both to his father and to all his friends."—*Memoirs of Elizabeth Carter*.

* "Memoirs and Letters of George Lord Lyttelton." 1845.

and convention, and society was threatened with the loss of its cohesion. It was heaving already with the coming throes of revolution. Young men like Thomas Lyttelton, endowed with active intellects and ardent temperaments, breaking the chains which had bound the minds of past generations, were dazzled by the illumination into which they rushed, and groped about as blindly as those who remained in the dark. They found the fences and landmarks of the moral world thrown down, and they wandered about in it, without guides, scoffing at warnings of their danger, and absorbed in the triumphs of the intellect and the pleasures of the senses.

It is impossible to understand the character of Thomas Lyttelton, and to do justice to it, without understanding the character of the age in which he lived. It was not a religious age; still less was it a moral age. The evidence afforded by contemporary memoirs, letters, and journals is conclusive upon this point. Religion was dead, morality at the lowest ebb; and the creeds, customs, and conventionalities which are their mere husk, and which alone remained, and passed current for them, were everywhere struggling to maintain themselves against the rising tide of new ideas. There was necessarily a large amount of hypocrisy in the world; for an outward reverence for religion and regard for morality was enforced by the example of the Court, and self-interest was a potent agent in prompting men who cared nothing about either to be loud in their professions of attachment to the Church, and unquestioning belief in the Articles of Religion.

Thomas Lyttelton was at least no hypocrite; whatever his other faults may have been, he was one of the most candid of mankind. "Open and ingenuous in his disposition," says one who knew him well,* "he soon became disgusted at the hypocrisy of mankind. . . . . Less cautious in his amours than a more prudent, though not less guilty, man would be, it is not at all extraordinary that his lordship should have met with obloquy and reproaches, since there is no situation in life which will admit of an avowed contempt of vulgar prejudices." In several of his letters he attributes his bad reputation to these features of his character; and no one who has studied it, and the times in which he lived, can doubt that many worse men have enjoyed a better repute,

---

* The author of the character of Thomas Lyttelton, prefixed to the volume of poems attributed to him, and published after his death. This brief essay is anonymous, but Roberts, who edited the volume, and wrote the preface, states that it was written by a gentleman who had been intimate with him.

simply because they took more care to seem better than they were, and put on the semblance of a piety and a virtue which they did not really possess.

"The world at large," says he, in a letter to a friend, "is so disposed to generalise, that it is seldom right when it descends into the detail of opinion. It has so many eyes and objects that, in the act of particularising the sources of its favour or disapprobation, the rectitude or error of its conclusions are both the effect of hazard. I, as you too well know, have been the subject of its severest censure; but, with all my faults, I have much reason to complain of its precipitate injustice.

"Among other instances of its premature indisposition towards me, the circumstance to which you have alluded with so much humour is in proof of my assertion; and, to heighten my mortification at that time, my own family joined the popular cry, so that, in pronouncing all possibility of amendment,* the devoted prodigal was driven to a situation which absolutely precluded him from it.

---

* There seems a slip of the pen here, unless we suppose a typographical blunder to have been made; the writer must have intended to say, "all amendment impossible."

"My father, in a long detail of my unworthiness, which, with his usual tenderness, he dealt forth to Harry de Salis, as a climax to the amiable history, concluded the list of my enormities with declaring that I actually intrigued with three different women of fashion at one and the same time! Without making any comment on the very creditable account given of me, and the favourable picture which his pious lordship displayed of our first-rate females, permit me to assure you that neither my prowess with the ladies, nor any foolish, unworthy deed of mine, occasioned the paternal displeasure of that moment. The subject of an occasional morning's reading was the true, but unacknowledged, cause of my disgrace. I shall do myself the justice of relating the fact to you in all its circumstances.

"You must have heard of the celebrated sceptical writer, Claude Anet. His works, and the prosecution which they brought upon him, have conspired to give his name no small share of public notoriety. It will be also necessary to inform you that, after the sacred writings, Lord Lyttelton has directed his partial estimation to two popular theological productions. The one details, explains, and observes upon the resurrection of Christ; and the other defends the character and conduct of the Apostle Paul. The former was written by his dearly beloved friend, Mr. West; the latter by *himself*. The infidel, Claude Anet, among other matters, thought proper to give these two publications a particular and separate consideration. He had the abominable impudence to declare, that they were not only deficient in their principles, but that they were logically defective in the means they took to support them; nay, he undertakes to give them arguments superior to any they have used, and then to confute them.

"On this ground he opens his battery, and makes his attack; nor is he without his partisans among men of learning and talents, as I have been informed, who do not hesitate to assign him the victory. Of this I do not pretend to determine; I have, in truth, no genius for that line of criticism. The mode of proceeding, however, must be acknowledged to have been accompanied with an air of insolence and contempt which might have been the cause of mortification to men of a less sensible fibre than one, at least, of those against whom it was directed. It had this effect in the extreme: for the pity of the Christian gave way to the pride of the author, and the damnable sceptic, instead of being the object of fervent prayer that he might be converted from the error of his way, was wafted, in a moment, by his pious antagonist, to the howling portion of the devil and his angels.

"In an unlucky hour it was discovered that this offensive volume was in my possession, and the subject of my occasional meditation; and from hence arose that unexpected burst of displeasure that fell with so much weight upon me, and which had instant recourse to my graceless life as the pretended reason for its justification. I do not know a quality of the human mind that is of such an absorbent nature as vanity; in one disappointed moment it will suck up the virtue of years. If Claude Anet had levelled his shafts in another direction, or I had increased my caution in tracing their course, I might have intrigued with a whole seraglio of women of fashion, without drawing upon me an atom of that vengeance of which I was the victim. I could not tell the true cause, as it would have increased, if possible, the irritation against me, without doing any good; and, besides, my authority would have been lighter than a feather, in the public opinion, when put in competition with the power that persecuted me:— for, religious opinions apart, the whole was an abominable persecution.

"I never felt so sensibly the inconvenience of a bad character as at this period. Impudence could do but little; hypocrisy, which is so thick a garb for half mankind, was not a veil of gauze to me; and, as for repentance, that was not in the reach of ordinary credibility. I was really in the situation of the Quaker's dog, who, being caught in the fact of robbing the pantry, was told, in all the complacency of revenge, by his amiable master, 'I will not beat thee, nor kill thee for thy thieving; but I will do worse, for I will give thee a *bad name;*' and immediately, on driving him from the house, alarmed the neighbourhood with the calm assurance that he was a *mad dog*; so that the poor animal was pursued with the unreflecting brutality usual on such occasions, which soon put an end to his existence. You may truly apply this story to your affectionate friend,

"[THOMAS LYTTELTON]."

He offended his uncle, Bishop Lyttelton, in a similar manner, according to the version of his disgrace with that prelate which he gives in a letter to a friend, of which the following is the greater and concluding portion :—

"Some years ago I had formed an unlucky plan to mortify my right reverend uncle, who had taken some authoritative liberties with me, without giving him a fair opportunity to express his resentment. This was no less than an attack upon the temporal privilege of episcopacy, in possessing a seat in the House of Lords. I had some thoughts of my own upon the subject, but I had fortunately added to their number and importance from the accidental perusal of a republished tract on the conduct of our bishops through upwards of twenty reigns, which unanswerably proved that, during so long a period, they had almost uniformly manifested themselves to be foes to rational liberty. I took up the argument in a very general view, urged it with modesty, and, what was better, with security, as, in case it had been returned with anger, I was armed with the opinion of my father, who was present, and, in his *Persian Letters*, has written to the same purpose. In short, I enjoyed all the triumph that my malicious expectation could have framed. The prelate grinned with vexation, but was forced to acquiesce in silence; and I had my revenge.

"But, not many days after, when my resentment towards this reverend relation had been lost in its fruition, a trifling circumstance happened, which his vigilant anger gladly seized, in order to heap upon me every indignity which his truly Christian spirit was capable of producing. As a family party of us were crossing the road on the side of Hagley Park, a chaise passed along, followed by a couple of attendants with French horns. 'Who can that be?' said my father. 'Some itinerant mountebank,' replied I, 'if one may judge from his musical followers.' I really spoke with all the indifference of an innocent mind; nor did it occur to me that the Right Reverend Father in God, my uncle, had sometimes been pleased to travel with servants accoutred with similar instruments.

"But evil on itself will soon recoil,"

and my recollection was soon restored to me by a torrent of abuse, which was, in length, violence, and, I had almost said, in expression, equal to any sacred anathema of popish resentment. In short, I was cursed, damned, and sent to the devil, in all the chaste periphrasis of a priest's implacability. The whole of the business was of a very singular nature: he availed himself of an inoffensive occurrence to let loose his resentment at a past offence; while I, in a state of actual innocence, sunk beneath the consciousness of past guilt.

"But, to conclude with a serious observation, be assured, my friend, that, however rich, great, or powerful a man may be, it is the height of folly to make personal enemies of any, but particularly from personal motives; for one unguarded moment—and who could support the horrors of a never-ceasing, suspicious vigilance!—may yield you to the revenge of the most despicable of mankind. From a very unpleasant experience of my own, I should most sincerely counsel every young man who is entering on the theatre of the world to merit the good opinion of mankind by an easy, unaffected, and amiable deportment to all, which will do more to make his walk through life respectable and happy, than those more striking and splendid qualities which are for ever in the extremes of honour or disgrace. Adieu!"

There is a strong resemblance between the position of Thomas Lyttelton at this period, and that of Mirabeau ten years later. Mirabeau, in 1781, plunged in profligacy and in debt, had returned to France after self-expatriation forced upon him by his misconduct, corrected and repentant, willing to amend, and longing to be reconciled to his family. But he knew not what to do with himself, nor did his father know what to do with him. The old marquis appealed to his brother, the Commander of the Order of Malta. "Have pity," he wrote, "on thy hurricane-nephew; he acknowledges, and with good reason, that the intellect and talent he employed in committing his follies are surprising; he admits this, like all the rest, for he is the greatest confessor of faults in the universe It is impossible to possess greater intelligence and facility. With every attribute, or nearly so, of the sky-rocket, he is a thunder-bolt of labour and expedition. Example, knowledge, and superiority correct him of themselves; but he has an immense want of being governed. He knows that he owes his return to you; he knows that you have always been pilot and compass to me, and that you must be the same to him; and he puts his vanity in his uncle. I tell you he is a rare subject for the future. You have all the Saturn necessary for his Mercury. But if once you hold him, do not let him go; should he even perform miracles, keep your hold of him, and pull him by the sleeve, for the poor devil requires it."

"I will not have him," replied Commander Mirabeau. "If, at thirty-two years of age, he requires to be ridden with a curb rein, his understanding will never ripen. . . . If, at his age, he is not sufficiently master of himself to avoid running his head against a post, it is madness to attempt to make anything of him."* Ten years after this correspondence, the name of Mirabeau was a potent spell to conjure with in the politics

---

* "Memoirs of Mirabeau." 1842.

of his country. Thomas Lyttelton was four years younger, when he returned to his native country under similar circumstances, than the great Frenchman was when this correspondence passed between his father and his uncle. If Mirabeau's future was not to be despaired of at thirty-two, still less was Lyttelton's at twenty-eight.

CHAPTER V.

Morals of the Eighteenth Century—Gambling and Gallantry—Mania for Card-playing and Betting—Singular Wagers—Lyttelton's Wager with Blake—Elopement of Sally Harris with Lyttelton—Letter about George Ayscough—John Courtney—Mrs. Dawson—Letter on the Passions—Mrs. Peach—Lyttelton's Account of his Courtship and Marriage—Letters to his Father on the Subject—Anecdote of Lord Lyttelton—Letter from Lord Chatham to Lord Lyttelton—Lord Lyttelton's Reply—A Contrast.

THE most superficial reader that ever skimmed the cream of Horace Walpole's letters must rise from the perusal of that interesting mass of correspondence with the impression that the Georgian era was a most immoral one. Moral debasement and political corruption seemed to vie with each other for an odious and disgusting supremacy. Court and Cabinets, Lords and Commons, were all alike tainted with corruption and immorality. Those who were pointed out as vicious men were merely worse than the others; and it was one of the greatest misfortunes of the age that its affairs had to be conducted, as a rule, by bad men, because an Administration of the virtuous was rendered impracticable by the too frequent conjunction of mental dulness with moral purity.

Gambling and gallantry were vices from which few public men were free. The social pictures painted by Hogarth had not ceased to be truthful representations of a considerable section of English life and manners, though a little—perhaps a very little—abatement may have to be made from their grossness. The passion for cards and dice, and for betting, had received an enormous development. Lyttelton and the Damers, the Foxes and the Foleys, did not perhaps seek the perilous excitement of cards and dice in such dens as Hogarth painted, where there was no ballot for the admission of gamblers with pedigrees, to the exclusion of gamblers without, and where George Barrington and Jack Rann could make a wager or throw the ivory cubes, without fear of interruption by Bow Street "runners," or those guardians of virtue, the parish constables. But high play went on nightly at all the clubs, and the best minds and hearts of the age were drawn into the fatal vortex. Fox, the school-fellow of Lyttelton and the Damers at Eton, and one day to be Prime Minister of England, equalled them in his rage for play, and exceeded them in the amount of his losses. Before he had attained his twenty-fourth year, his debts to Jew money-lenders amounted to the almost incredible sum of £100,000! He never won a large stake but once, when he gathered up £8,000 in crisp notes and bright guineas. But no loss ever ruffled his equanimity. Topham Beauclerk, a good-natured *roué* and ill-natured wit, calling upon him one morning, after a night of terrible losses at the card-table, found him calmly reading Herodotus. "What would you have me do," said Fox, on his visitor expressing surprise at the manner in which he bore his losses, "when I have lost my last shilling?"

Lord Coleraine and his two brothers squandered their patrimony at the gaming-table, and then cajoled or swindled their mother out of the £1,600 a year, which was all their demands upon his purse had allowed their father to bequeath to her, leaving her helpless and destitute, so that she became dependent upon a friend even for a bare subsistence. Then, as we learn from Horace Walpole, they sent for the poor lady, saying that her presence was necessary to some affair of business. "It was to show her to the Jews," says Walpole, "and convince them that hers was a good life, unless she is starved. You must not suppose that such actions are disapproved; for the second brother is going minister to Brussels, that he may not go to jail, whither he ought to go."

Betting ruinously supplemented the chances of cards and dice. The betting-books of White's and Brookes's contain bets on every conceivable subject—on the length of a life, the duration of a ministry, the result of an election, the sex of an unborn child, a convict's risk of the halter, or the truth about the latest scandal. Lord Nugent made a bet with Earl Temple that he would spit in the Earl of Bristol's hat; and the nasty wager was as nastily won, though it was very nearly resulting in a duel.* Lord Mountford bet Sir John Bland twenty guineas that Beau Nash would survive Colley Cibber. The same nobleman, when asked, soon after his daughter's marriage, whether she was in a condition to add to the number of his Majesty's subjects, replied, "Upon my word, I don't know; I have no bet upon it." Walpole says of him, that he "would have betted any man in England against himself for self-murder," so dominant was the passion for reducing everything to a calculation of chances. "There is a man about town," writes Walpole in 1768, "a Sir William Burdett, a man of very good family, but most infamous character. In short, to give you his character at once, there is a wager entered in the

---

* Sir Nathaniel Wraxall's "Memoirs of my own Times," vol. i.

bet-book at White's, that the first baronet that will be hanged is this Sir William Burdett."

One day, a man fell down insensible before White's, and was carried into the house, where odds were immediately offered and taken as to whether he was dead or in a swoon. It was proposed to bleed him; but those who had betted that he was dead protested against the use of the lancet as affecting the fairness of the bet! Walpole tells a story of a clergyman, who, entering White's on the morning of the earthquake of 1750, and hearing bets laid whether the shock was caused by a natural convulsion of the earth, or by the explosion of a powder-mill, went away in horror, declaring that the members of the club were such an impious set that he believed, "if the last trump were to sound, they would bet puppet-show against judgment."

"You have won both your wagers," says Thomas Lyttelton, writing to a friend. "In speaking of the inhabitants of China, I *do* make use of the word *Chineses*; and I borrow the term from Milton. As to your first bet, that I used such an expression, your ears, I trust, will be grateful for the confidence you had in them. But your second wager, that, if I did use it, I had a good authority, is very flattering to myself; and I thank you for the opinion you entertain of the accuracy of my language. My memory will not, at this moment, direct you to the page, but you will readily find the word in the index of Newton's edition of Milton."

He made a singular bet with a gentleman name Blake, touching the virtue of a young woman named Harris, who was a waitress at an inn,* and whose beauty, wit, and coquetry had gained her many admirers, among whom were both the wagerers. Blake bet Lyttelton a hundred guineas that he would induce this girl to elope with him, and offered her all the money for her compliance. The offer was refused; and the girl's reputation for virtue seems to have been so high, that the refusal excited less surprise than her subsequent elopement with Lyttelton, who was probably aware of her preference for himself, and, therefore, the least surprised of the circle in which she was known. It is Sarah Harris who is referred to, under the name of Pomona, in the following letter :—

"[Ayscough] by no means deserves your pity; and the conduct which I have of late used, and shall continue to use, towards him, arises from

---

* "Bolton's inn at Hockrel."—Preface to *The Rape of Pomona*. Thomas Lyttelton, in a letter presently to be quoted, calls the place Hocknel. It is not to be found by either name in any gazetteer.

my perfect knowledge of his character, and the remembrance of his former treatment of myself. I told you long ago, when my bulrush hung its head, that, high as this gentleman then bore himself, the time would come when he would hang his head in his turn, and bend his back for me to tread upon. All this and more is now come to pass.

"You express your surprise that he does not discover some degree of resentment on the occasion of his last journey to Hagley. The fever of that business flushed him with no small hope, and the succeeding ague shook him with disappointment; but he had the prudence to conceal his symptoms, and I left him to cure himself. He may bluster in a guard-room with new commissioned ensigns, and, in the leisure of a tiltyard duty, may weave fanciful wreaths of future fame; nay, he may venture to give his name to the world in a newspaper, or the title-page of a miserable poem; but the prowess of our hero will go farther.* If I were to bid him go to the Pomona of Hocknel for a pippin, he would not hesitate a moment, and would burn his fingers

---

* It seems probable that the word "no" has been inadvertently omitted before "farther," either by the writer or the printer.

willingly in roasting it ; and, when I had eaten the pulp, he would content himself with the core.

    "' All this my little Greek exactly knows,
      And bid him go to hell, to hell he goes.'

"If, however, your obstinate humanity should look towards such an object, have a little patience, and he will give you an opportunity for the full exercise of it. I am in the secret, but I shall not gratify his vanity by betraying it. After all, I find him convenient, and to my purpose. He is ready, submissive, and not without amusement. If he were to die, I should say with Shakespeare, '*I could have better spared a better man.*'

"At this moment, he is sitting on the other side of my table, in the act of making some of his own bad poetry worse, in which agreeable business I may, perhaps, be kind enough to give him some assistance. You would not, probably, have suspected him in so close a vicinity to me, but it is a fact; and when I have folded up my letter, he shall enclose it in its envelope, and set the seal to this certificate of his own good qualities ; nay, I will make him direct it into the bargain. Your pence, it is true, will suffer for this whim of mine, but the revenue will be a gainer—a circumstance which must satisfy you as a patriot, on the truly political idea of making follies productive to the State. You may observe, however, and with some reason, that every one should pay for his own. To such a remark I have nothing to answer, but that I am," &c.

His amour with Sarah Harris was made the subject of a ribald and indecent poem, entitled "The Rape of Pomona," which the compiler of the catalogue of the library of the British Museum attributes to him, though it is stated, in the preface, to be the production of a Cambridge student, whose passion for the beautiful waitress had induced him to locate himself under the same roof with her, in the humble capacity of a waiter. However this may be, the poem is written in the assumed character of Bolton's waiter, and edited by John Courtney, a gentleman who then represented the little borough of Tamworth in Parliament, and was probably a worthy associate of the Damers, the Foleys, the Foxes, and other tavern-haunting, dice-throwing nominees of the owners of rotten boroughs. If Courtney was not himself the author of the doggerel, it may have been written by Combe, who, having dissipated his fortune by gambling, was, in 1771, found by a friend at an inn at Swansea, in the position of waiter. Combe, however, completed his education at Oxford, not at Cambridge. There is an allusion in the poem to a lady named Dawson, who is described in a note as "a foolish widow who chose to make Mr. L—tt—n the guardian of her person and fortune, and enjoys the fruits of her credulity." It is incredible that this would have been written by Lyttelton himself, even if he could be proved to have been capable of writing, and giving to the world, such a ribald and obscene composition. The extract is given here because it fixes the date of an amour to which public attention was subsequently called by Sir Nathaniel Wraxall,* in his usual blundering manner, as will hereafter be shown.

The following letter, on the comparative influence of reason and the passions, may most appropriately be introduced in this place :—

"My dear Friend,—Your letter, which I received no longer ago than yesterday, would do honour to the most celebrated name among the moral writers of any period. It is the most sensible, easy, and concise history of the passions I have ever read. Indeed, it has never been my lot to have given any great portion of my time to such studies. These powers have kept me too much in the sphere of their own tumultuous whirlwinds

---

* " Memoirs of My Own Time." 1836.

to leave me the leisure of examining them. I have been, am, and I fear shall be, their sport and their slave; and when I shall acquire that serenity of character which will enable me to examine them with a philosophical scrutiny, I cannot tell. My expectations are at such a distance on this point, that I am almost ashamed to mention my apprehensions to you. It is, however, treating you with the confidence you deserve, to tell you that from my soul I think the very source of them must be dried up before they will lose their empire over me. In the lively expression of the poet, 'they are the elements of life,' without which man would be a mass of insensible and unintelligent matter. Now, it is that happy compound of these elementary particles of intellectual life that you so well describe, so thoroughly understand, and so happily possess, which I despair of attaining. I have the resolution to make resolutions, but it extends no farther—I cannot keep them; and to escape from the misery brought on by one passion, I have so habituated myself to bathe in a branch of the same flood, that I cannot look for any other relief.

"You very naturally ask me where all this must end? I know not!—and to similar interrogatories I have sometimes madly replied, I care not! But I shall not offend you with such a declaration;

and when I am writing to you, I do not feel disposed to do it. In answering you, therefore, I shall adopt the language of the ruined gamester, who addressed his shadow in the glass:—'*Je vous ai dit et redit, Malheureux! que si vous continuez à faire de pareil tours, vous iriez à l'hôpital.*'

"You lay great stress upon the powers of reason, and, in truly philosophical language, heightened by the most proper and affecting imagery, present this sage directress of weak mortals to my attention. I receive her at your hand; respect her as your friend; and venerate her as the cause of your superiority over me; but whether she perceives that my respect is insincere, or remembers how shamefully I have neglected her, so it is that she slides insensibly from me, and I see her no more. My bark rides steady for a moment, but it is not long ere it again becomes the sport of winds and billows. But after all, and without any blasphemous arraignment of the order of Providence, permit me to ask you, why is this principle —implanted in our natures for the wise and happy regulation of them—so weak in itself, so slow in its progress, and so late in its maturity? If it is designed to control our passions, why does it not keep pace with them? Wherefore does it not *grow with their growth, and strengthen with their strength?* And what cause can be assigned that the one are ripe for gratification before the other has scarce bursted into blossom?

"Let us, however, take a long stride from the imbecility of youth to the firmness of mature age, and we shall see that the passions have only changed their form; that reason still totters, is frequently driven from her throne, and even deserts those who have most cultivated her friendship and acknowledged her power. The contest frequently continues through life, and the superiority as often ends, where it always begins—on the side of passion. We may be said even sometimes to outlive reason; while passion of some kind, and many times of the worst kind, will preserve its influence to the last. To conclude the matter, how often does the lamp of human reason become extinct, yielding corporal nature a prey to passion in the extreme, whose tortures are rendered more fierce by the iron restraints of necessary policy and medical interposition!

"If it were possible to trace the course of reason in the mind of the best man that ever lived, from its first budding to a fulness of maturity, what a mortifying scene would be unveiled! What checks and delays, what tranquillity and tumult, what frequent extinction and renovation, what rapid flights and sudden downfalls, what contest and submission, would compose the operations of this rightful mistress of human actions? Men of cold tempers, and habituated to reflection, may cry up this distinctive faculty of man; they may chaunt its apotheosis, and build temples to its honour: such were Lord Shaftesbury and Mr. Addison; and they may be joined by those whose fortunate education and early connections have given to their warmer dispositions the best objects; in that confined but happy society I must place my friend, whose kind star preserved his youth from temptation, and blest his bloom of manhood with the ample and all-satisfying pleasures of virtuous love. You will not suspect me of wishing to diminish the reality of that merit which I so much admire, or of a desire to damp the glow of that virtue whose lustre cannot be diminished by my envy, or heightened by my praise; but, in the course of human affairs, time and chance have so much to do, that I cannot suppose even your worth to be without some obligations to them.

"To conclude this very, very long letter, I must beg leave to observe that I do not understand why reason, that divinity of philosophers, should be cooped up in the confined region of the brain, while the passions are permitted to range at large, and without restraint, through every other part of the body. I see you smile; but be assured that these two jarring powers are, for a moment, both united in me, to assure you that I am, with a real sincerity, yours, &c."

There was living at this time, at the Leasowes, that rural paradise of Shenstone, a lady named Peach, to whom had been given at her baptism the unique name of Apphia. She was the second daughter of Broome Witts, a gentleman residing at Chipping Norton; and the widow of Joseph Peach, late Governor of Calcutta. Still young, and according to contemporary accounts, as amiable as she was beautiful, she attracted the attention of Thomas Lyttelton, and seems to have encouraged it under the delusion fostered by the old adage—"A reformed rake makes the best husband." It may be gathered from the following letter, that, on his part, the preference amounted to no more than the absence of dislike; and that he was impelled to the thought of marriage by the insufficiency of the allowance he received from his father:—

"Have you ever by chance looked into a book on the science of cookery? If so, have you not observed that the culinary disciple is instructed, when certain quantities of gravy, or essence, or conserves, are prepared, to put them by for use?

Now, if we could manage our ideas in the same manner—if we could lock up our acquired thoughts and knowledge in a kind of intellectual store-room, from whence they might be drawn forth for application—we should no longer be the slaves of a capricious recollection, which at this hour offers its treasures with intuitive readiness, yields them on the morrow with sullen reluctance, and on the succeeding day may refuse them to our most arduous researches. The active events of life, however, seldom die on the remembrance: and you must certainly be mistaken in associating with me the circumstance you mention in your letter, which is at this instant before me. It is morally impossible that I should have forgotten it. My memory, perhaps, is the only faculty I possess which has not at one time or other deceived me; nay, so firm is its texture, that the oblivious hours of courtship do not affect its wonted capacities—though, to say the truth, mine is a very drowsy progress. Assiduity without love, tenderness without sincerity, and dalliance without desire, afford the miserable, the hopeless, but the faithful picture of my sluggish journey to the temple of Hymen. However, to give something of colour to the intervening hours between consent and fruition, his lordship performs wonders, and sighs and flatters for his heedless son; nay, he tunes his lyre, and sings the power of those charms which, by an anti-Circean fascination, are destined, by his fancy, to recall my vagrant footsteps to the paths of virtue. But, alas! I know not the resolution of the Greeks; I cannot resist the song of the syrens, and, partial as I may be to paternal music, it will prove, in its influence upon me, far inferior to theirs.

"But all is not torpor and inanimation, and what love could not produce, vanity has inspired. Two of the brethren of the house of my Dulcinea made her a visit last week, with the design of turning her from the expectation of a coronet, and from me. I need not tell you that they are honest, simple *bourgeois,* or they would not have meditated such a fruitless errand to their ambitious sister.. I was well assured that they would not convert her; and the fancy came across me to aim at converting them. In this business I so exerted myself in every form of attention, flattery, and amusement, that I verily believe they returned to their home at Chipping Norton, without enforcing that remonstrance which was the object of their journey.

"That Chipping Norton—in whose neighbourhood I passed with my grandmother many of my youthful days, and to which I had never associated any idea but that of pigs playing upon organs—

that chilly Chipping Norton should yield one of its former toasts to be the *cara sposa* of your friend! What can your fertile fancy deduce from the union of Hagley's genius and the widowed protectress of the more than widowed Leasowes? If offspring there should be, what a strange demi-theocrite will owe its being to such a Hymen! Alas! my friend, this is but a dream for your amusement; the reality will offer to your compassionate experience the marriage of infatuation and necessity, whose legitimate and certain issue will be a separate maintenance, and perhaps a titled dowry.

"I have many and various communications to make to you, but they must be reserved for personal intercourse. In the meantime, when you shall see me announced as being added to the Benedicks of the year, save me, I beseech you, save me your congratulations. Nothing is so absurd as the tide of felicitations which flow in upon a poor newly-married man, before he himself can determine —and much less the complimenting world—upon the propriety of them. Marriage is the grand lottery of life; and it is as great a folly to exult upon entering into it, as on the purchase of a ticket in the State wheel of fortune. It is when the ticket is drawn a prize that we can answer to congratulations. Adieu!"

There is no act of Thomas Lyttelton's life that presents so many difficulties to the biographer as his marriage. The contrast between the tone of the foregoing letter and that of the more brief epistles which he addressed to his father just before his union, and on his wedding-day—the contradiction to the suspicion of hypocrisy which is afforded by the openness and candour displayed in his acts, and in the expression of his thoughts and feelings on every other occasion—the suddenness with which the event was brought about, during his visit to the Leasowes—the agreement of the result with the dark vaticinations of the letter just given, constitute a problem in the science of the human heart which will probably never be solved.

It is certain, however, that Lord Lyttelton represented the match to his friends as the result of an ardent and reciprocal attachment, from which everything was to be hoped; and that similar representations were made to him both by his son and by Mrs. Peach. Some light might perhaps be thrown upon the matter if we knew the duration of Thomas Lyttelton's stay at the Leasowes before the marriage took place; what took place between the parties and the brothers of Mrs. Peach; and what caused the marriage to take place suddenly, and without the knowledge of

Lord Lyttelton. But upon these points we are in the dark, and the family archives at Hagley Hall have unfolded for me only the following contributions to their elucidation :—

"MY DEAR LORD,—It is unnecessary for me to tell you I am as happy as it is possible for me to be: if anything could add to my present felicity, it would be your lordship's company. Lord Temple's letter was equally agreeable to Mrs. Peach and myself. I own I ever was proud of his presentiment in my favour. My dearest little woman is everything to me—the sweetest companion, the most sensible friend, and will make the best of wives. She unites almost contradictory excellencies. Adieu, my dear lord. I remain, ever your most dutiful and most obliged son,

"T. H. LYTTELTON.

"Leasowes, *June* 18*th*, 1772."

At the back of this, Mrs. Peach wrote as follows :—

"Mr. Lyttelton persuades me that your lordship will receive, as a mark of my entire respect, this hasty and irregular assurance of the tender and unutterable affection that my improved acquaintance with the amiableness of his manners and the ten thousand dormant virtues of his heart have excited in my mind. It will be the delightful employment of my life to preserve his love and enlarge his happiness—fortunate beyond expression should I succeed—since it may secure to me the additional blessing of your lordship's approbation, and draw a veil over the many weaknesses and imperfections that the candour of your noble family does not allow them to attribute to, my lord, your lordship's most faithful and most obliged servant,

"Apphia Peach."

Eight days afterwards, on the 26th of June, 1772, they were married in the parish church of Hales Owen, the bridegroom betraying an absence of mind on the occasion, which must have been as mortifying to the bride as it was ominous of the future. The story is told by Lyttelton himself as follows:—

"If I am not very much mistaken, your library table is always furnished with an interleaved Bruyère, on whose blank pages you amuse yourself with extending the ideas of that celebrated writer, or directing them to modern applications. I am, therefore, to offer my name as an addition to your collections, and to desire that in your *scholia* on that excellent work, I may furnish a trait to his admirable character of the absent man.

"On the day of my marriage, a day—but no more of that! After the nuptial benediction was over, and we were returning to our equipage, instead of being the gallant Benedick, and conducting the new-made Mrs. [Lyttelton] to her coach, I slouched on before, and was actually getting into the carriage, as if I had been quite alone; but, recollecting myself as my foot was upon the step, I turned round to make my apology, which completed the business, for I addressed the bride in her widowed name, with 'My dear Mrs. [Peach], I beg ten thousand pardons,' and so on. This fit of absence was as strange as it proved ridiculous—an omen, perhaps, of all the ungracious business which is to follow. You may first laugh at this little foolish history, and then, if you please, apply it to a more serious purpose.

"But this species of absence is an hereditary virtue. A virtue! say you? Yes, sir, a virtue; for it is a mark of genius, and my right honourable father possesses it in a most flattering degree. I will present you with a most remarkable example, which you may also add to the composition of your modern Theophrastus. His lordship was about to pay a morning sacrifice at the shrine of M———, and a large bunch of early pinks lay upon his toilette, which were to compose the offering of the day. With those antique or professional beaux who wear the tie or large flowing wig, it appears to be convenient, in the ceremony of their dress, that the head should bring up the rear, and be covered the last. The full-trimmed suit was put on, the sword was girded to his side, the *chapeau de bras* was compressed by his left arm, the bunch of pinks graced his right hand, and his night-cap remained upon his pate. The servant having left the room, the venerable peer, forgetful of his perukean honours, would actually have sallied forth into the street in full array, and *en bonnet de nuit*, if his *valet de chambre* had not arrived, at the critical moment to prevent his singular exit. I was present, but my astonishment at his figure so totally suspended my faculties, that he would have made the length of Curzon Street before I should have recovered any power of reflection. I was accused, as you may suspect, of a purposed inattention, in order to render his lordship ridiculous; and, I was told upon the occasion, that, although this kind of occasional absence of mind might furnish folly with laughter, it generally arose from that habitual exertion of thought which produces wisdom. You may congratulate me, therefore, on the prospect of my advancement to the title of sage.

"I am already married, and what is to follow, God alone knows. Strange things daily happen *dans ce bas monde,* and things more strange may be behind. I have such a budget to open for you! but that discovery must be reserved till we meet. Suffice it to say at present—

"*Quædam parva quidem, sed non toleranda maritis.*"

This unrestrained communication of the feelings with which the writer entered upon married life evinces a state of things most unpromising for the domestic felicity of the young couple. What could be hoped for from an union of which one of the parties had, before marriage, predicted that the result would be a separation? The event was announced to Lord Lyttelton by his son on the same day, in the following letter:—

"Leasowes, 26*th June*, 1772.

"MY DEAR LORD,—I was this day so fortunate as to lead Mrs. Peach to the altar. I need not tell your lordship that the impatience and ardour of a lover was one chief cause that determined my fair bride; your Lordship's letter was another motive that operated on her gentle mind. She is a woman of exceeding generosity of spirit and principle. Nothing, my dear lord, is wanting to perfect my felicity but your company; nothing else is wanted to complete her happiness. I wait with eagerness for the moment when I shall have the honour of presenting Mrs. Lyttelton to her father. Adieu, my dear lord. In all states and circumstances of my life, believe me to be, with unfeigned affection, your lordship's most dutiful son, and most obliged servant,

"T. LYTTELTON.

"I shall again write to your lordship by to-morrow's post."

The promise conveyed in the postscript was redeemed in the following letter:—

"Leasowes, 27th June, 1772.

"MY DEAR LORD,—I promised your lordship yesterday to write to you by this day's post, as I thought you would be desirous of knowing what articles had been drawn, and what promises I had entered into. The only article settled by me previous to my marriage was the settlement of a jointure on my wife in case she survived me, so far as I was enabled to settle it, which is only from the time of your lordship's decease. This settlement is £1,000 a year, which is all that is in my power to appoint.

"I remain, therefore, exactly in the same situation as before my marriage took place, with the addition of her fortune. Concerning the disposition of it, I have entered into no agreement, but have (previous to my marriage) explained to my wife, and to the gentleman who married us, and who is an intimate friend of hers, what were my intentions. They both approved of them, and it is my desire to carry those intentions into execution as soon as possible; but my respect and duty to your lordship make me wish to lay the plan before you, and I hope it will in all particulars meet with your approbation, and that, though I am free to act as I think proper, you will find that I mean to do everything consistent both with my honour and interest, which terms, if well understood, are synonymous.

"I wait, therefore, with impatience, for your lordship's arrival to ratify and confirm my happiness, and I flatter myself I shall every day make myself more worthy of your regard and affection. Adieu, my dear father. Believe me ever your most dutiful son and obliged and obedient servant,

"T. LYTTELTON.

"Mrs. Lyttelton desires her dutiful respects to your lordship."

The Earl of Chatham conveyed his congratulations on the event to Lord Lyttelton in the following terms :—

"MY DEAR LORD,—I have a most longing wish to be able to be the bearer of my warm felicitations to your lordship and the happy pair on the completion of an union which knits you all together for life in the sweet triple bonds of paternal, filial, conjugal love and domestick happiness; may the virtues of your race guard the pious work, and fix the felicity of your family on that *fortuna domûs et avi numerentur avorum!* I could not but smile to hear that Cupid knew his Hagley for true Paphian ground, and had taught his slow brother Hymen to mend his pace in so delightful a race, and am sure your lordship has more than forgiven your flesh and blood this amiable impatience. From all I hear of Mrs. Lyttelton, I have not the least doubt that Hymen now will have his turn, and lead Love for his inseparable companion. Lady Chatham desires to be included in the same cordial sentiments with myself on whatever interests your lordship's happiness, and that of your family."

Lord Lyttelton says in his reply, after thanking his noble correspondent for his felicitations :—

"My son stole a march upon me, which I shall not complain of if he continues as sensible of the prize he was in such haste to take as he was when he took it; and I do not despair that he will. For my own part the more I see of the lady the more I esteem and love her. They both desire me to present their most respectful compliments and thanks to your lordship and Lady Chatham, and to all their amiable young friends at Burton Pynsent."

What a contrast between these letters and those of the bridegroom! The congratulations of Lord Chatham seem like the sunshine that gilds the waves, after a storm in which some noble vessel has been submerged, while the dusky sea-plants wave beneath above the corpses of the drowned mariners. While the two peers are exchanging compliments, we seem to hear, through the hum of friendly felicitations and a haze of orange blossoms and white lace, the ominous words,—" assiduity without love, tenderness without sincerity, dalliance without desire!"

CHAPTER VI.

Separation—Journey to Paris—Death of Lord Lyttelton—Letter on the Event—Return to England—Letter of Condolence from the Earl of Chatham—Correspondence with Earl Temple—Letters on his New Position—Hopes of Moral Amendment—Dissatisfaction with Hagley—Letter to Sir Richard Lyttelton—Political Views—The American Troubles—His Estimate of Public Men—Hopes and Aims for the Future.

THOMAS LYTTELTON's ante-nuptial anticipations proved prophetic. His married life was of very brief duration. After a few months' cohabitation at his father's house in Hill Street, he and his wife separated for ever. The event can scarcely have surprised those of his friends who were acquainted with the feelings he had entertained on the subject before his marriage. None of the published letters of himself or his father throw any further light on the causes of the separation, nor can the remotest glimpse of the state of affairs in Hill Street during his brief experience of the matrimonial state be found in the correspondence of Lord Chatham; while, of the unpublished letters placed at my disposal by the courtesy and kindness of the present Lord Lyttelton, only two are of subsequent date to the inauspicious honeymoon, and these relate to other subjects. But probably more is said in his own letter, just before his marriage, to account for the separation than was written by anyone else.

He left London when the rupture occurred, and proceeded to Paris, where he was staying when, in the August following, he received the news of his father's death. He does not appear to have been summoned to Hagley during his father's illness; for, though there is a passage in the letter of condolence which he subsequently received from the Earl of Chatham, which would favour the supposition that he was there at the time of his father's death, this must evidently be construed otherwise, as only his sister and her husband, Lord Valentia, appear to have been present on the mournful occasion. There is no doubt that he received the sad intelligence while yet in Paris, for he concludes a letter written on the occasion with the mention of a duel, adding: "I was very near being hampered in the affair; but my sable suit and funeral duties excused me from the employment, and I suppose the first news I shall hear of the event will be in England."

The following is the first portion of his letter,

in which he records his early impressions of his changed position:—

"I awoke, and behold I was a lord! It was no unpleasant transition, you will readily believe, from infernal dreams and an uneasy pillow, from insignificance and dereliction, to be a Peer of Great Britain, with all the privileges attendant upon that character, and some little estate into the bargain. My sensations are very different from any I have experienced for some time past. My consequence, both internal and external, is already greatly elevated; and the *empressement* of the people about me is so suddenly increased as to be ridiculous.

"Without meaning anything so detestable as a pun, I shall certainly *lord* it over a few of those who have looked disdain at me. My coronet shall glitter scorn at them, and insult their low souls to the extreme of mortification. I have received a letter from [Ayscough], that dirty parasite, full of condolence and congratulation, with a *my lord* in every line, and *your lordship* in every period. I will make the rascal lick the dust, and, when he has flattered me till his tongue is parched with lies, I will upbraid him with his treason, and turn my back upon him for ever. There are a score of bugs, or more, of the same character, whom the beams of my prosperity will warm into servility, and whose names will be left at my door, before I have been ten days in town; but may eternal ignominy overtake me if I do not make the tenderest vein in their hearts ache with my reproach! Whether the world will be converted into respect towards me, I do not pretend to determine; its anger will, at all events, be softened; but, be that as it may, I can look it in the face with less fear than I was wont to do, and make it smile upon my political career, though it may still hold a frowning aspect towards my moral character.

"Permit me, however, to assure you that, whatever change may appear in me towards others, I shall ever be the same to you. The acquisition of fortune, and an elevation to honours, will not vary a line in my regard to those whose friendship has been so faithful to me as yours has been; nor shall you ever have cause to repent of your assiduous kindness to me. There is a balance in the human passions; and the mind that is awake to a spirit of revenge is equally inspired by the sentiments of gratitude. There is a dirty crew who shall experience the former, while you may confide in my solemn assurance to you of a most ample exertion of the latter."

He returned to England immediately, and, hastening to Hagley, received there the following letter from the Earl of Chatham, which has been already referred to :—

"DEAR SIR,—The most unexpected and afflicting account of the sad event at Hagley has filled all here with deep concern. Lady Chatham and I truly feel how great a loss you, my dear sir, in particular, and all the family and friends of our departed truly virtuous friend, have sustained in the death of Lord Lyttelton. The best consolation his friends can receive is from the reflection that those virtues which endear his memory rendered his last moments tranquil and full of comfort. The melancholy news found Mr. and Mrs. Hood here, whose feelings on this unhappy occasion their own letters will express. Your presence in the mournful scene at Hagley must be of the greatest utility to your whole family, however severe the trial. Lady Chatham desires to express by me her wishes, very sincerely united with mine, that your health may receive no impression from the loss you have sustained and the sad offices in which you are engaged. I am ever, with truest esteem, my dear sir, your faithful and affectionate humble servant,

"CHATHAM."

It is to be regretted that we have not the young lord's reply to the great statesman, nor the letter, which he wrote about the same time, to Earl Temple, and which elicited the following kind response:—

"My Lord,—You do justice to my feelings in the expression of your own concerning the loss of one so justly dear to us all, and whose memory will do honour to his family and country as long as they exist. You have an hereditary right, not only to my affection, but to every real service it could be in my power to show you; the great figure you may yet make depends upon yourself. Harry the Fifth had been Prince of Wales; he knew how, with change of situation, to shake off the Falstaffs * of his age, and all those forlorn accomplishments which had so long stifled and depressed his abilities. Forgive an old man, and by affection a kind of parent, the hint he takes the liberty of giving; and be assured he ardently wishes to see what your lordship calls his partiality justified by conduct which will make him happy in calling himself, my dear lord, your most affectionate and obedient servant,

"Temple."

---

* George Bodens, who seems to have been of Falstaffian proportions and proclivities, is probably here alluded to.

Though his letters to Chatham and Temple on this occasion have not been preserved, their tone and substance may be inferred from the following epistle to a friend, whose identity has not been determined :—

"My dear Friend,—Your letter reached me with a large packet of others, which my father's death had occasioned. How altered is the language of them upon the occasion! Yours, indeed, is exactly the same, or, if anything, bears the tincture of more than usual severity. Flattery is a strain altogether new to me, and by the last two posts I have had enough to surfeit the most arrant coquette upon earth. It is true, I cannot compliment your letter with possessing an atom of adulation; nevertheless, it is the only one which has given me real pleasure, because it is the only one which bears the characters of real friendship. Though I have acted in such a direct opposition to your cautions and remonstrances, I am not the less sensible to that generous passion which produced them, and has now taken the first opportunity to give me the essence, as it were, of all your former counsels, in thus calling my attention to real and permanent honour. However I may offend you hereafter, you shall never again have cause to reproach me with a forfeiture of my word. I have at present lost that confidence in myself which would justify me in offering assurances to you: the hopes of regaining it, however, are not entirely vanished, and when they are fulfilled, which I trust they will one day be, you shall receive the firstfruits of my renovation.

"I understand the purpose of your observation, that the generality of men employ the first part of life in making the remainder of it miserable. I feel its force and consider it as an indirect caution to me not to pursue a conduct which must be attended with such a lamentable consequence. But, alas! *credula turba sumus*; though I have paid dearly for my credulity, unless it should be immediately followed by the fruits of an wholesome experience. We despise the world when we know it thoroughly; but we give ourselves up to it before we know it, and the heart is frequently lost before it is illuminated by the irradiations of reason.

"I have now succeeded to the possession of those privileges which are a part, and perhaps the best part, of my inheritance. Clouds and darkness no longer rest upon me. My exterior of things is totally changed; and, however unmoved some men's minds may be by outward circumstances, mine is not composed of such cold

materials as to be unaffected by them. Such an
active spirit as animates my frame must have
objects important in their nature, inviting in
their appearance, and animating in their pursuit.
No longer forced to drown sensibility to public
disgrace and private inconvenience in Circean
draughts, my character, I trust, will unfold
qualities which it has not been thought to possess,
and finally dissipate the kind apprehensions of
friendship. My natural genius will now have
full scope for exertion in the line of political
duty; and I am disposed to flatter myself that
the application necessary to make a respectable
figure in that career will leave me but little time
for those miserable pursuits which of late have
been my only resource. But I must desire you
not to expect an instant conversion; the era of
miracles is passed, and, besides, the world would
suspect its sincerity. It is true I am sinner
sufficient to call down the interposition of heaven,
but the present age has no claim to such celestial
notices. My amendment must be slow and
progressive, though, I trust, in the end, sincere
and effectual. But be assured that, however the
completion of your good wishes for me may be
deferred, I am perfectly sensible that there is
something necessary besides title, rank, and
fortune, to constitute true honour. With this

sentiment I take my leave of you, and am, with real truth, yours very truly,

"LYTTELTON."

The remainder of the summer and a portion of the autumn following his father's decease were passed at Hagley, in carefully investigating his financial position and forming plans for the future. The country had few attractions for him, however, and Hagley had little of his regard. In a letter which he addressed to Sir Richard Lyttelton in October, he thus describes the situation in which he found himself and the estate:—

"I thank you, my dear sir, for your three letters, for, unanswered as they have been, I must not lay the fault upon the post, but upon my own indolence, or rather *ennui*; for I have suffered great *ennui* at seeing the vast expense that Hagley runs me into, and the little pleasure it affords me. I love the country at times, but I consider it as a place for retirement, and am surprised to find myself 130 miles from the metropolis in an immense palace without company, and surrounded, like a deposed nabob, by a set of *blackguards*. I have just made up the last year's housekeeping accounts, and have signed them with an unwilling hand. Under the administration of that wise economist, Lady Lyttelton, they amounted to just *two thousand and ninety pounds sterling!*

"I hope you have made here a full stop, and have expressed marks of wonder and admiration; but you will be more astonished when I assure you that the expenses have in other years been nearly as great; nor do I see how they are to be lessened, tho' I am *fully determined they shall.* But such bills are every day brought in for pails, pitchers, perry, wine, cyder, porter, strong beer, straw, hay, oats, barley, coals, candles, liveries, rabbits, hams, hot-house, mourning, mop squeezers, tythes, tinkers, and tradesmen, that I have been forced to fly for it, and shall set out for Bath next Saturday.

"But, jesting apart, Hagley is to me a gulph that swallows up all my estate. The expense of keeping it up, together with the servants that necessarily remain there, amount to £500 per annum. Then follow the charges for journeys, transporting of servants, goods, plate, &c.; so that Mr. Bayliss was accustomed to pay away all the produce of the estate half a year before it became due. There is not at this time a shilling remaining of the Michaelmas rents, there are a great many bills unpaid, and I owe him £130. This was the state of things at the death of my poor father, by whose conduct we learn that, tho' a man be possessed of the greatest abilities, and endued with the most exalted virtues, it shall (in this world) avail him nothing without prudence.

"I fear, my dear sir, I have fatigued you with my losses and crosses; but I write to you as to my friend, and treat you with friendly familiarity. I shall be at Bath on Tuesday, and expect there a letter from you, directed to me at the hotel. Adieu, dear sir. I thank you for your news, and remain, with sincere attachment, your most affectionate and faithful nephew and servant,

"LYTTELTON."

The great abilities of Lord Lyttelton, the foretaste of his powers as a debater and orator which he had given while in the House of Commons, and his family connection with the Earl of Chatham, made the probability of his enacting a conspicuous part in the political world a matter of considerable interest. The Duke of Grafton had at this time retired, and Lord North was in the third year of a lease of power under which the American colonies were lost and a hundred millions added to the national debt. George III., for the first time, had a minister after his own heart, who required no prompting from the Earl of Bute to work out the royal will, but maintained the cause of prerogative, "the right divine to govern wrong," spontaneously and steadfastly. Whether Lord Lyttelton would give a general support to a minister whose views were, on many important questions, opposed to his own, was doubtful; and the attempts made to elicit from him an unqualified avowal of Tory principles were unsuccessful. He was inclined to an independent course, and while he expressed his own views openly and explicitly, as the following letter shows, he would not pledge himself to support Lord North before seeing his measures:—

"Without any violent exertion of my natural vanity, I can easily imagine that the eye of mankind looks towards my political career, and that, for want of a better subject, there may be some among them who amuse themselves with forming conjectures concerning it. The ministry have attempted to feel my pulse upon the occasion, but without success; though I will tell you in confidence that they have nothing, at present, to fear from me. In the great subject of this day's politics, which seems to engulph every other, I am with them. I shall never cease to contend for the universality and unity of the British empire over all its territories and dependencies in every part of the globe. I have not a doubt of the supremacy of Parliament over every part of the British dominions in America, the East and West Indies, in Africa, and over Ireland itself.

"I cannot separate the ideas of legislation and taxation: they seem to be more than twins; they were not only born, but must co-exist and die together. The question of right is heard of no more; it is now become a question of power; and it appears to me that the sword will determine the contest. The colonies pretend to be subject to the King alone; they deny subordination to the State, and, upon this principle, have not only declared against the authority of Parliament, but erected a government of their own, independent of British legislation. To support a disobedience to rights which they once acknowledged, they have already formed associations, armed and arrayed themselves, and are preparing to bring the question to the issue of battle. This being the case, it becomes highly necessary for us to arm also; we must prepare to quench the evil in its infancy, and to extinguish a flame which the natural enemies of England will not fail to feed with unremitting fuel, in order to consume our commerce and tarnish our glory. If wise measures are taken, this business will be soon completed, to the honour of the mother country and the welfare of the colonies, who, in spite of all the assistance given them by the House of Bourbon, must, unless our Government acts like an idiot, be forced to submission.

"For my own part, I have not that high opinion of their Roman spirit as to suppose that it will influence them contentedly to submit to all the horrors of war, to resign every comfort in which they have been bred, to relinquish every hope with which they have been flattered, and retire to the howling wilderness for an habitation; and all for a dream of liberty, which, were they to possess it to-morrow, would not give them a privilege superior to those which they lately enjoyed; and might, I fear, deprive them of many which they experienced under the clement legislation of the British Government.

"I do not mean to enter at large into the subject; but, if Ministers know what they are about, the matter may be soon decided: and in every measure which tends to promote such a desirable end they shall receive all the poor helps I can give them; I will neither sit silent, nor remain inactive. But if, by neglect, ignorance, or an indecisive spirit—the latter of which I rather suspect from them—they should let the monster grow up into size and strength, my support shall be changed into opposition, and all my powers exerted to remove men from a station to which they are unequal. Remember this assertion—preserve this letter—and let it appear in judgment against me, if I err from my present declaration."

In another letter, which may have been written about this time, he expresses his opinion of some of the political and literary celebrities of the day in the following terms, which show that he had opportunities of enjoying their society :—

"Charles Fox is highly gifted; his talents are of a very superior nature; and, in my opinion, Fitzpatrick is scarcely behind him; in the article of colloquial merit, he is at least his equal: but they neither of them possess that attic character which, while it corrects, gives strength to imagination, and, while it governs, gives dignity to wit. The late Earl of Bath and Mr. Charles Townshend were blessed with no inconsiderable share of it; and it is an intemperate vivacity of genius that confounds it in Mr. Edmund Burke. But the man who is in the most perfect possession of it has figured in so high a line of public life as to prevent the attention of mankind from leaving his greater qualities to consider his private and domestic character:—I mean Lord Chatham, whose familiar conversation is only to be excelled by his public eloquence. Perhaps Lord Mansfield was born, if I may use the expression, with every attic disposition; but the shackles of a law education and profession, and some other circumstances which I need not mention, have formalised, and, in some degree, repressed the brilliance of his genius. With respect to this great man, I cannot but pathetically apostrophise with Pope—

"'How sweet an Ovid was in Murray lost!'

"George Selwyn is very superior to Chase Price, but very inferior to Charles Townshend, against whom, however, he used, as I am told, continually to get the laugh; but this proves nothing, for good-humoured George Bodens would have gained the prize from them both in the article of creating laughter. I may be wrong, perhaps, but it has ever appeared to me that Mr. Selwyn's faculty of repartee is mechanical, and arises more from habit than from genius. It would be a miserable business indeed if a man who had been playing upon words for so many years should not have attained the faculty of commanding them at pleasure.

"Garrick is *himself* upon the stage, and an *actor* everywhere else. Foote is a mimic everywhere; excellent, delightful, on the theatre and in private society, but still a mimic. No one can take more pains than Mrs. Montagu to be surrounded with men of wit; she bribes, she pensions, she flatters, gives excellent dinners, is herself a very sensible woman, and of very pleasing manners; not young, indeed, but that is out of the question: and, in spite of all these encouragements, which, one would think, might make wits spring out of the ground, the conversations of her house are too often critical and pedantic, something between the dulness and the pertness of learning. They are perfectly chaste, and generally instructive; but a cool and quiet observer would sometimes laugh to see how difficult a matter it is for *la belle présidente* to give colour and life to her literary circles. It surprises me that you should leave Windham out of your list, who (observe my prophecy) will become one of the ablest men and shining characters that the latter part of this age will produce. I hazard little in such a presentiment; for his talents, judgment, and attainments will verify it.

"The gibes and jests that are wont to set the table in a roar promote the cheerful purposes of convivial society, but they have nothing to do with that *attic* conversation which is the highest enjoyment of the human intellect. Wit, believe me, is almost extinct; and I will tell you, among other reasons, why I think so :—because no one seems to have any idea of what wit is, or who deserves the title of it. To think little, talk of everything, and doubt of nothing; to use only the external parts of the soul, and cultivate the surface, as it were, of the judgment; to be happy in expression, to have an agreeable fancy, an easy and refined conversation, and to be able to please, without acquiring esteem; to be born with the equivocal talent of a ready apprehension, and, on that account, to think one's self above reflection; to fly from object to object, without gaining a perfect knowledge of any; to gather hastily all the flowers, and never allow the fruit time to arrive at maturity: all these, collected together, form a faint picture of what the generality of people in this age are pleased to honour with the name of wit."

With a brilliant career opened to him in the Senate, he prepared himself once more for oratorical triumphs, and seems to have aimed at original and lofty flights of thought. Though he regarded the Earl of Chatham and the Earl of Mansfield as the two greatest orators of the period, he was careful not to frame himself on either as a model; and, though he thought that Burke's speeches derived dignity from the application of Biblical language, he would not follow his example. "For the life of me," he says, "I cannot read sermons even with Lord Chatham; and my hands are too unhallowed to unfold the sacred volume: but I find in Milton's poems everything that is sublime in thought, beautiful in imagery, and energetic in language and expression. To attain a reputation for eloquence is my aim and ambition: and if I should acquire the art of clothing my thoughts in happy language, adorning them with striking images, or enforcing them by commanding words, I shall be indebted for such advantages to the study of our great British classic."

And so we take our leave of him on the eve of the opening of Parliament for the session of 1774, restored to society, giving hopes of moral amendment, dreaming of political distinction, and studying Milton.

CHAPTER VII.

Parliamentary Session of 1774—Appeal to the Lords in Becket v. Donaldson—Speech on Literary Property—Letter to Earl Temple—Speech on the Booksellers' Copyright Bill—Dedication of his Father's Works to him by George Ayscough—Letter on the Subject—Thoughts about Maids of Honour—Speech on the Government of Quebec Bill—Meeting of the New Parliament—Debate on the Address—Speech on the American Question—Secrecy of the Lords' Debates—Motion on the Subject—Rejection of the Motion—Successful Second Attempt—Project of Selling or Leasing Hagley.

PARLIAMENT assembled on the 17th of January, 1774. The public mind was still excited upon the question of the right of election, raised by the resolution of the House of Commons excluding Wilkes from his seat; but the Ministry adhered to its policy of regarding that matter as finally settled, and passed over in silence the protests of Whig peers and the petitions of popular assemblages. The agitation died out under this treatment, and the policy of the Government was greatly assisted by the growing seriousness of the American difficulty, which every day assumed a more grave aspect. Lord

Lyttelton had given great attention to this question, and took every occasion of making it understood that his support of the Government depended upon the firmness and vigour which they might display in restoring order, and the wisdom of the measures which they might afterwards adopt for reviving loyalty, in the disturbed colonies.

The first occasion, however, on which he addressed the House of Lords was the debate on the appeal of a bookseller named Donaldson from a decree of the Court of Chancery, by which he had been restrained from the sale of a piratical reproduction of a work published by another bookseller, named Becket. Lord Lyttelton evinced the sympathy with the literary profession which he had inherited from his father by supporting the decree, urging that literature, though intangible, was property, and must receive a very sensible shock from the reversal of the decree, should that be the decision of the House. His speech was somewhat discursive, however, much of it being occupied in tracing the arts and sciences from Greece to Rome, and their progress in this country, and in eulogising George III. and the King of Prussia as the only Sovereigns who were lovers and patrons of literature. It must be recorded to his honour, however, that no other peer displayed so much sympathy with literature and the literary profession, the question before the House being argued chiefly by the law lords, and on legal grounds, and the debate resulting in the reversal of the decree.

The next occasion on which he addressed the House was when the American question was brought before it by one of the Ministerial measures affecting it, which, as usual, called up the Earl of Chatham in opposition to it. There is no report of this speech of Lord Lyttelton's in Hansard's *Parliamentary History*; but it is referred to in the following letter to Earl Temple, dated May 17th, which indicates that the Ministry were disposed to accord him a certain degree of confidence, though as yet he held the position of an independent member :—

"My dear Lord,—I snatch this minute to tell your lordship that the Ministry seem desirous that Lord Chatham should again rise, though, as they hope, not in his fury, for, if he does, they are annihilated. It will not be possible to delay those bills that are now before the House; but there is another American bill which will serve Lord Chatham's purpose, and that they will put off on his account till Wednesday. It is of no great consequence, indeed, but, as a part of the great whole, it will be sufficient to warrant his lordship's appearance. It is a bill for quartering and regulating the troops in the colonies.

"I have the pleasure to assure your lordship that all the comments upon that part of my speech which regarded that great statesman convince me that at present all parties feel the necessity of his interference. Some great little people opened themselves very freely on that head. The politics of France are changed, and consequently the politics of England. The commonwealth calls loudly for a dictator, and you cannot be mistaken in the man. I will wait upon your lordship to-morrow at half after two, and communicate my thoughts *vivâ voce*. In the meantime, give me leave to rejoice with your lordship at the French king's death, as perhaps it will be the means of awakening, and therefore of saving, this miserable country."*

He had another opportunity of expressing his views on the question of literary property on the motion for the second reading of the Booksellers' Copyright Bill, which was made on the 2nd of June. The rejection of the bill

---

* "Correspondence of the Earl of Chatham," vol. iv., p. 344.

having been moved by the Earl of Denbigh, Lord Lyttelton supported the second reading, reminding the House that the object of the bill was not to set aside the decision arrived at in the suit of Becket *versus* Donaldson, but to relieve men who had invested sixty thousand pounds in the purchase of copyrights since 1769, and who had shown, by the prices they had paid for them, that they believed they had a common law right to the exclusive use of what they had purchased. He instanced Hawkesworth's narrative of the exploring voyages of Captain Cook, for which an unusually large sum had been paid by the publishers; and informed the House that he had received letters from Robertson and Hume in favour of the measure. The amendment of the Earl of Denbigh was carried, however, by twenty-one votes against eleven.

It was about this time that the first collected edition of his father's works was published, under the editorial supervision of George Ayscough, who dedicated the volume to his noble cousin in one of the lengthy laudations of the period, concluding as follows:—

"I must now beg leave to assure your lordship that it is my desire that this work may not only give satisfaction to the public, but also be honoured with your lordship's particular approbation. I am proud to confess that I have ever had the highest veneration for your refined taste, sound judgment, and ripened abilities; and at the same time permit me to add my most ardent wishes that those great talents, which are certainly equal to those your father possessed, may, like his, be exerted with indefatigable zeal in the service of your country, and that, like him, your lordship may hereafter prove a shining ornament of the Senate, and one of the firmest pillars of the Constitution. —*Sed quid verbis opus est?* Your lordship has already forestalled my hopes; and my wishes, even at this early period, are nearly accomplished."

How the nephew, instead of the son, came to be appointed to the task of editing the late lord's works, and what Lord Lyttelton thought of the matter, is stated in the following letter :—

"I must acknowledge, notwithstanding I am treated with some degree of civility in it, that the dedication you mention is a wretched business, and disgraces the volume to which it is prefixed.

You wonder I did not write a better for him myself: and I would, most assuredly, have done it; but among many excellent qualities which this dedicator possesses, he is a blab of the first delivery, and I dared not venture to trust him.

"The testamentary arrangement which appointed him to the honourable labours of an editor took its rise from two motives;—first, to wreak a degree of parental resentment against an ungracious son; secondly, from an opinion that a gracious nephew's well-timed flatteries had created of his own understanding; and, thirdly, from a design of bestowing upon this selfsame gracious nephew a legacy of honour from the publication, and of profit from the sale, of the volume. He is as proud of the business as a new-made knight of his title; is never easy but when he is receiving incense from booksellers and their journeymen, and loves to be pointed at as a child of science. I wish he may be contented with his present celebrity; though, if I know him aright, this editorial business will awaken ideas of his having talents for a superior character, and that he is qualified to publish his own works with as much *éclat* as he has done those of another. If he attempts to climb the ladder of ambition in any, but particularly in a literary way, he must fall. I have counselled him to be content: and the booby gives it out that I am envious of his reputation. Poor silly fool! I only wish the daw may keep the one poor feather he has got; for, if he attempts any addition to his plumage, the vanity will draw him into a scrape, in which he will be stripped as bare as Nature made him."

The following is the only letter of Lord Lyttelton in which Junius is mentioned. His disclaimer of any talent for irony, which he nevertheless indulged in occasionally with considerable success, is unusually free from any indication of the family foible; but his powers of perception and discrimination were acute, and experience was gradually correcting the mistakes of his earlier life :—

"Indeed, my dear friend, you mistake the matter: irony is not my talent. It is a fine rhetorical figure; and, if there were a chance of attaining the manner in which Junius has employed it, its cultivation would be worth my attention. But you add an harsh injustice to real error when you suppose that I have employed any powers of raillery I may possess on the subject of her most excellent Majesty. I recollect the conversation which produced this report to my disadvantage, and, if it were true, to my dishonour. I can easily despise the malice of those who understand and misrepresent me; but that ignorance which both misunderstands and misrepresents is mortifying in the extreme. I should really think it little less than blasphemy to speak ill of a princess who deserves so well. The Queen does honour to the British throne; she has a right to the place she possesses in the breast of every reflecting Englishman; and it has ever been my opinion that her character unites the royal virtues of her station with the most amiable qualifications of her sex. Nor have I ever been disposed to speak unfavourably of the ladies who attend her person or compose her suit. There are, I must own, half-a-dozen figures of her household who are objects of my pity; and the strain of commiseration which broke from me on their subjects has been represented, I find, as a contemptuous raillery of their royal mistress. My memory will serve me, I believe, to recollect the general tenour of my discourse on the occasion, which I shall offer to your candid interpretation.

"The Dowager Lady Townshend, as you well know, divides the human species into men, women, and Herveys; and where is the crime, if I parody on her ladyship's logic, and apply it to the division of her Majesty's household into men, women, and *maids of honour?* Nor will it be difficult to justify this new line of distinction, if we consider the peculiar offices which compose the duty, and the singular privileges which reward the service of these courtly virgins.

"To make up at least two court suits in a year; to dance as many court minuets in the same space; to sidle, on days of duty, through the presence chambers at the tail of a royal procession; to take her place in an established corner of the drawing-room; to say, 'Yes, sir,' or 'No, sir,' and curtsey, when she is noticed by the King; to say, 'Yes, madam,' and 'No, madam,' and curtsey, when the Queen does her the same honour; to make an occasional one of six large hoops in a royal coach, and to aid the languor of an easy party in a side-box at a royal play, compose the principal labours of a maid of honour's life. But they are not without their rewards. A moderate salary, and a thousand pounds when Miss gets a husband; an apartment in a palace, and, I believe, a dinner from a royal kitchen; in the rotation of six weeks, a seven days' possession of a royal coach, a royal coachman, and a shabby pair of royal horses, for the purpose of shopping in the City, paying distant visits, airing in the King's Road, and the being set down at the very gate of Kensington Gardens, while women of the first fashion are obliged to trip it over a hundred yards of green sward between their coaches and the place of admittance; to take place of baronet's daughters; to go to plays, operas, and oratorios gratis; to have physicians without fees, and medicines without an apothecary's bill; to chat with lords and grooms of the bed-chamber around the fire of an antechamber; to stroke the beardless face of a new-made page; and, perhaps, receive an heir-apparent's first effort at flirtation, constitute the various privileges of a maid of honour.

"This brief history, my dear friend, you well know to be founded in fact, and will, therefore, be ready to applaud the tender pity I feel for these virgin automatons. I have never seen them bringing up the rear of a royal train but each of them has appeared to bear, in legible characters, on her forehead, *who will marry me?* Nevertheless, upon the most favourable average, not one in three years, during the present reign, has been rewarded by Hymen; which, in their particular situation, is as pitiable a circumstance as can be found in the long catalogue of female mortifications. A lady of the bed-chamber is obliged only to a partial duty; and, during the short period of her attendance, is, in some degree, the companion of her royal mistress; while the virgins of honour are not admitted, as I have been informed, to stick a pin in a royal handkerchief. Even the women of the same department figure in her Majesty's cast-off gowns only on royal birthdays; but these poor persecuted damsels are the common hackneys of drawing-room parade; whether ill or well, in humour or out of humour, by day-light or by candle-light, they are obliged, through three parts of the year, to be on the continual stretch of State official exhibition.

"I remember, when I was little more than a boy, to have seen a young lady in training for this important office; and the whole of that serious business consisted in nothing more than a practical lecture on entrances and exits, the language of courtesies, and the art of conducting a large hoop in all modes and forms of possible pliancy. I laughed then as boys laugh, and had some unlucky thoughts in my head, which were not arrived at maturity; at this period I would willingly give an opera subscription to be present at a similar exercise.

"After this manner did I treat the honourable subject of her Majesty's honourable virgins; and little did I think that it would beget a long admonitory epistle from you, to warn me against speaking evil of dignities. My wit, such as it is, has never directed a single glance at the throne; and I have received the welcome testimony of your applause more than once, for exerting the full force of my understanding to support the wishes of it. You have my ready leave, my dear friend, to laugh with me, and at me—to reprove and to admonish me; but I must entreat you to relax your proneness to believe every idle tale that is fabricated to my dishonour."

The first of his speeches on the American question, which is recorded in Hansard, was made on the 17th of June, when the Commons' amendments to the Government of Quebec Bill came before the Lords, and were opposed by the Earl of Chatham. Lord Lyttelton, following the Earl of Dartmouth, said that whatever fell from Lord Chatham made the deepest impression upon the House and the country; but the noble lord's opposition to the clause excusing the Canadians from the oath of supremacy, and substituting an oath of allegiance, induced him to give his reasons for differing from him. So far from thinking with Lord Chatham that no true Protestant could give his consent to the clause, he affirmed that no true Protestant could refuse it his hearty concurrence, because it was conceived in a spirit of moderation, candour, and toleration of all religions which were not incompatible with the precepts of morality and the general welfare and happiness of mankind. To oblige Catholics to deny the supremacy of the Pope was to compel them forcibly to abjure their religion, and, in reality, to commence a persecution of them. Opposition always grew and strengthened under the scythe of persecution, and fanaticism was never formidable until it was oppressed. The Canadians had, ever, since the conquest of their country, been good and peaceable subjects of Great Britain ; and were, therefore, entitled to a beneficial code of civil policy, and to the free exercise of their religion. Though he had the greatest reverence for the Protestant faith, he had no less respect for the safety and good government of the State : and to force the Canadians to renounce errors which they had imbibed with their mothers' milk was to attempt to alter the constitution of their minds, and, by so doing, to lay the foundation for a resistance which, if it did not proceed to rebellion, would at least tend to alienate their minds from the allegiance which they had adopted, and which, under the mild government then exercised over them, would, he hoped, be strengthened and matured by 'time. It was a matter of triumph, he said, to this great and free country to treat the inhabitants of a country conquered from France with more lenity, and to give them a better form of government, than they had received from their mother country. He supported the bill chiefly for its moderation and lenity, because he deemed it sound policy for a conquering nation to lay the yoke lightly on the necks of those subjected to their dominion.

The Earl of Chatham having observed upon the inclinations of the Canadians towards France, Lord Lyttelton went on to say, that nothing would be more likely to win them over to England than the amelioration of their political and commercial situation, and, above all, the giving them liberty of conscience. In reply to the remark that, if the bill passed, the bells might be taken down from the steeples, and the steeples from the churches, he observed that, even if that were to happen, the evil would not be great; for Christians might meet in faith and charity without those things, which, to the pure of heart and the truly devout, were of little importance. They were the externals of a religion, the internals of which were charity and benevolence; and in those principles, he contended, the clause originated which the Earl of Chatham had so uncharitably censured. Having answered the religious argument, he proceeded to show why he approved the general policy of the bill, and insisted that the code embodied in it was conformable to the genius of the Canadians, and consistent with their political notions and the form of government to which they were accustomed. Forms of government, he said, must always be suited to the dispositions of the governed: the mild constitution of England would be rejected with contempt by Asiatics, and degenerate into licentiousness with the Canadians. As to the idea of the Earl of Chatham, that the political separation of Canada from the rest of the British American provinces would divide their interests, he did not apprehend such a consequence; but, if the other provinces were determined to resist the lawful authority of Great Britain, he saw no reason why the loyal Canadians should not co-operate with the rest of the empire in subduing them and bringing them to a proper sense of their duty. He thought that, in such case, the Canadians would be a check upon the intractable spirits that were bent upon the subversion of British power, and the setting up of an independent republic.

It is clear from this speech that Lord Lyttelton saw farther into the future, and had a better conception of the tendencies of the dispute between the British Government and the North American colonies, than even the veteran statesman whom he so frequently eulogised. At a later period of the contest, Lord Chatham was still unable to see the direction in which events were tending, and to which he and his party were, from various motives, consciously or unconsciously assisting the leaders of opinion across the Atlantic to guide them. The contrast shows the keenness of Lord Lyttelton's mental perception, and indicates a depth of knowledge of the actual state of affairs which could only have been acquired by an amount of inquiry and study, of which none but those who knew him best had deemed him capable.

Parliament was prorogued shortly afterwards, and on the 30th September was dissolved. The new Parliament assembled on the 29th of November, when the usual contest of those days ensued upon the vote of the address to the king, in reply to the royal speech. American affairs furnished ample materials for a stormy debate. Lord Lyttelton urged the necessity of asserting the sovereign right of Great Britain over the colonies by the most prompt and resolute measures, and declared that it was no longer the question whether the mother country should relinquish the right of taxation, but whether the commerce which had carried her through the last war should be subject to the wise and necessary regulations prescribed by the Navigation Act, and confirmed by many subsequent Acts, or be at once thrown open at the will of factious Americans, who were now struggling for free and unlimited trade, independent of the mother country, and for powers inconsistent with, and derogatory to, the honour and dignity of the Crown. He maintained that, if the Government should now in the least degree recede from the position that had been taken, all would be over, and America would give laws to England, instead of receiving them from her.

The first year of his possession of senatorial functions closed with their exercise in the cause of that publicity which he constantly advocated, as one of the best defences of civil freedom. The House of Lords had at this time been closed during four years against all who were not members of that assembly, and the exclusion of members of the House of Commons was regarded by the latter with considerable dislike. Lord Lyttelton moved for a call of the House on the 6th of December to consider a motion for dispensing with the standing order so far as to admit members of the House of Commons, and gave many excellent reasons for the concession; but the motion was lost by thirty-six votes against twenty-eight. Encouraged to persevere by the smallness of the majority, he moved, on the 15th, a resolution in favour of allowing each peer to introduce a stranger; and this proposition, which was supported by the Duke of Manchester and the Lord Chancellor, was acceded to without a division.

He seems to have had at this time some thoughts of selling his patrimonial possessions; for his uncle, Lord Westcote, wrote as follows, at the close of the year, to a gentleman named Champion: "If an Act of Parliament would have been necessary to render [valid] a sale of this fine place, this most enjoyable one to me in all seasons, I presume that my consent must have been obtained to such Act, which is a thing I should not lightly have given. *Sed nunc non erit his locus*, for the noble lord, before he went to London, authorised his attorney here to offer the place to anybody that would take it for a term at the rent of £600 per annum, which, though it may seem high, is not much so when it is considered that £300 or £400 might be made of the land to be included in the lease. I don't think a tenant will soon be found, but this is his lordship's present idea." Lord Westcote, it should be observed, was the presumptive heir.

CHAPTER VIII.

Lord Lyttelton's Speech on the Earl of Chatham's proposal to withdraw the troops from Boston—Speech on the Provisional Bill for the Settlement of the American difficulty—Strictures on Lord Camden—Complaints of the Duke of Richmond and the Duke of Manchester—Lord Lyttelton's exculpation—Speech on the Administration of the Poor Law—Debate on the Licensing of the Manchester Theatre—Speech on the Quebec Act—Strictures of Horace Walpole—Visit to Bristol—Parson Adams—Story of a Lost Sermon—The Lyttelton pudding and the Parson's cradle—Scheme for relieving Hagley of the jointures of Lady Lyttelton and the Dowager.

At the commencement of 1775 it was still hoped by all parties that the American difficulty would be adjusted without recourse being had to arms. The Ministry hoped for submission, the Opposition for the awakening of the Tories to the conviction that the Americans would not submit, and could not be coerced. Holding the mother country to be in the wrong, the Earl of Chatham, on the 20th of January, moved an address to the king, praying for the withdrawal of the troops from Boston. Lord Lyttelton on this occasion adhered to the line of independent action he had marked out for himself. He began by com-

plimenting his noble relative on his great political
wisdom and his various and extensive talents, the
fruits of which had been seen in the glorious successes of the late war, which must deservedly
crown him with immortal laurels. His arguments
against the motion were based chiefly on his
favourite idea of the legislative supremacy of the
British Parliament. He ridiculed the idea of an
inactive right as absurd, when there was the
most apparent and urgent necessity for exercising
it. It would be the extreme of madness, he said,
not directly to assert it, or for ever to relinquish
it. He could not agree with the noble lord in
his encomiums on the proceedings of the Congress at Philadelphia, and, so far from applauding
their wisdom, contended that they breathed
throughout the spirit of unconstitutional independence and open rebellion. He pointed to the
language in which some of the resolutions were
couched, and endeavoured to prove that, if the
mother country should give way on the present
occasion, from mistaken motives of presumed advantage to trade, such a concession would inevitably
defeat its object; for it was plain that the Navigation Act, and other regulatory statutes on which
those advantages rested, and the true interests
of both countries depended, would fall victims
to the interested and ambitious views of the

Americans. Every concession would produce fresh demands, and in the end bring about a state of traitorous independence, at which it was plain the Americans were aiming. He lamented the disgraceful and miserable condition of General Gage's troops, daily wasting away by sickness and desertion, destitute of clothing and rations, their spirits broken, and themselves disheartened by the insolent taunts and repeated provocations of the rebellious rabble around them. He reflected severely on the conduct of those who had placed the troops, and kept them, in such a disgraceful position. He desired to know by what secret power or overruling influence the wishes of Parliament had been defeated; and, in conclusion, disclaimed all personal connection with the Ministry, and declared that he supported them only because he believed them in the right.

The Earl of Chatham replied that, if he could believe that Lord Lyttelton was correct in his view of the ultimate aims of the Americans, none would be readier than himself to resist and crush them; but he thought that their opinions could not be known until they were treated with justice, as subjects of the king, not as aliens or traitors. The motion to withdraw the troops from Boston was lost, the division showing sixty-eight votes against it and only eighteen for it.

Lord Lyttelton had prepared himself very carefully for the speech which he made on this occasion, but the impression which it produced was not equal to his anticipations, and it satisfied himself even less than his friends. In a letter to a friend who had not heard it delivered, he says :—

"I receive your congratulations with an unaffected sensibility; but, as your applause proceeds from the partiality of a favourable representation, and not from your own immediate experience, I may, without impropriety, or any false show of modesty, to which I am not very much habituated, observe, that the part I took in the debate to which you so kindly allude would not have been so favourably mentioned if you had been one of its crowded audience.

"I will tell you, with great truth, that it was an important object with me to exert the full force of my mind and talents on the business of that day. I had directed all my thoughts to that purpose, and not only executed a very unusual industry in acquiring the knowledge necessary to give my opinions their due weight, but had laboured the dress in which they were to be clothed, and attentively composed the decorations which were to give the final embellishment. In short, I omitted no mode of study, reflection, or exercise which might enable me to force conviction and ravish applause. But I succeeded in neither; and, after a speech of some length, I sat down, oppressed with disappointment and mortification.

"Several circumstances, unexpected in themselves, and untoward in their nature, co-operated to the fall of my pride on that day. In the morning, while I was rehearsing my part to [Ayscough], by some mistake [Henley] was admitted to me, and not only interrupted my lesson, but, by the ready communication of his eccentric flights upon the same subject, threw my well-marshalled band of ideas into irretrievable confusion. But this was not all; he desired to accompany me to the House, and, in our way thither, he seized upon the bugle ornaments of my clothes as a subject for still more discomfiting singularities of thought; so that I was most heartily glad when my coach broke down in Parliament Street, and produced a separation.

"The worst, however, remains behind. It was my purpose to follow the Earl of Shelburne; and, in consequence of such a plan, I had necessarily pre-supposed the line of debate he would take, with the general turn of argument he might adopt, and had prepared myself accordingly. But all my conjectures proved erroneous; for that noble lord took a course so different from my pre-suppositions, and displayed a degree of political erudition so far beyond me, that, when I arose, the confusion between my prepared thoughts, and those which were suggested by the able discourse of the foregoing speaker, was so great that, although I was not thrown into hesitation, I got so wide of the point before me as to be called to order with great vehemence and some propriety from the opposite side of the House. This proved *confusion worse confounded*; and, though I proceeded with some degree of spirit and recovery, I sat down, at length, with much self-dissatisfaction: nor had I reason to think, from the succeeding part of the debate, that I had made any impression on those within the bar, whatever I might have done among the tribe of curious listeners without it.

"This is a true unvarnished state of the case; and, from the circumstances of it, I have formed a resolution, which I trust you will approve, to make no more such studied preparation. I will give the announced subjects all the consideration they deserve, acquire all the knowledge of them in my power, form my general principles, and leave their particular arrangement, with the necessary shape, dress, and delivery, to the circumstances and impressions of the moment. When a senator is to take the lead in a debate, in order to introduce a projected motion of his own, or is engaged to second that of another, he may enter upon his task with the most minute verbal preparation; but when he is to take his casual turn, he must trust to his feelings of the moment, operating upon the knowledge of the moment. If a man, with the common gifts of speech, possesses a good store of the latter, he may be soon habituated to yield himself to the former, with a certain assurance of acquiring an important political reputation.

"In American affairs I have ever possessed a perfect uniformity of opinion. My doctrine has ever been that legislation involves in it every possible power and exercise of civil government. For this principle I shall never cease to contend; though I am forced unwillingly to acknowledge that the Ministerial means of supporting it have, at times, been very erroneous. But you may be assured that, if some better plans for reinstating Great Britain in the full dominion of her revolted colonies be not pursued (an event which humanity at first, succeeded by misinformation and later indecision, has so unfortunately delayed, but which is still practicable), Ministers shall hear the deep-toned energy of my reproach. I will lift up my voice against their timid and indecisive counsels. My political career, at least, shall not be marked with dishonour."

On the 1st of February the Earl of Chatham's provisional bill for settling the troubles in America was read the first time, and a motion made by the Earl of Sandwich for its rejection. Lord Lyttelton, seeing no prospect of wiser measures on the part of the Government, supported the measure. He again warmly complimented the Earl of Chatham, observing that the noble lord's knowledge was as extensive as his intentions were good and great, and that, "in a most trying situation, when the nation was nearly reduced to despair, he stood forth alone, and rescued it from ruin." For these reasons, as well as for the merits of the bill, he thought it deserved a more favourable reception. He could not agree with Lord Chatham in some points, particularly with regard to the Quebec Act; but he thought it extremely improper to summarily reject a proposition which carried on its face a plan of reconciliation, and made an opening for substituting negotiation for the sword.

His views as to the supremacy of the British Parliament had undergone no change, but he would gladly see all the substantial fruits of that supremacy enjoyed through the submission of the Americans, instead of being wrested by force and violence. He animadverted in strong terms on the conduct of the Government in sending an insufficient force to Boston, and was called to order by the Earl of Sandwich, who, however, was himself called to order by the Duke of Richmond, who insisted that Lord Lyttelton ought not to have been interrupted. Proceeding with his speech, he reminded the House of the remark of Augustus, when a Roman general, leading an inadequate force against a German host, was defeated, that the blame rested upon those who had sent an insufficient force into the field. The Ministerial amendment was carried by sixty-one votes against thirty-two, and the Earl of Chatham's bill was consequently lost.

On the 7th, when an address to the king on the state of affairs in the American colonies was moved, Lord Lyttelton repeated his arguments for the unity and universality of British empire, and was very severe upon Lord Camden for his legal disquisition upon the different kinds and degrees of treason. "Those little evasions and distinctions," he observed, "are the effects of professional subtlety and low cunning. It is absurd to the last degree to enter into such flimsy observations on words and phrases, to draw from them deductions equally puerile and inconclusive, that the colonies are not in rebellion. For my part, I shall not abide by such far-fetched interpretations, but be guided by common sense, and consult only the papers upon the table. What! will any noble lord in this House rise and tell me seriously that a country is not in rebellion when it openly disclaims all obedience to the laws, all dependence on the legislature?—when they offer to appropriate public monies to the means of resistance,—when they prevent the courts of justice from assembling, and the counsellors of the Crown from acting? Will any noble lord pretend to say that any or all of these are not manifest acts of rebellion? —or that it is not treason in every obvious, substantial, and legal sense of the word to attack one of the king's fortresses, make his troops render it up, and convert the king's stores to the direct purpose of resisting his lawful authority by force of arms? Are these acts of most flagrant treason and rebellion, or are they, according to the ingenious argument of the noble and learned lord, to be construed as mere misdemeanour?" He then entered upon a very spirited defence of the Earl of Mansfield, bestowing the highest encomiums on his talents, integrity, and political conduct, and charging his accusers with being weak and evil counsellors, no less in their general sentiments than in their personal attacks.

His speech was severely animadverted upon by the Duke of Richmond for its remarks upon Lord Camden, which the Duke of Manchester, at a later period of the debate, stigmatised as "indecent and unprecedented." Lord Lyttelton endeavoured to exculpate himself, alleging that his language was hypothetical. He added that the more he heard upon the subject, the more he was convinced that the Americans were in rebellion; and referred to the statutes relating to treason, and to the authority of Lord Chief Justice Foster. The address was carried by a hundred and four votes against twenty-nine.

As the session proceeded, it became evident that Lord Lyttelton had not merely mastered the American question for the purpose of making an oratorical display on great occasions, but had prepared himself by diligent study to take an useful part in the debates upon every important question, political or economical, which might be brought under the notice of the House. On the 4th of May he made a very able speech in support of a bill for relieving and employing the poor of the hundreds of Mitford and Launditch, in Norfolk. The Act of Elizabeth for the relief of the poor was, he said, a very excellent and useful measure; but the neglect and abuses which had crept into its administration were as deplorable as they were shameful. He dwelt with great energy on the vast sums wasted in parochial litigation about the settlement of paupers, and on the corruption, cruelty, and interested conduct of parish officers. "There is," he said, "above three millions of money annually raised in this country for the support of the poor; and I solemnly believe that, with the vast sums of money thrown away in suits relative to parish settlements, and squandered by churchwardens and overseers in their feasts and revellings, with several other species of misapplication and fraud, not a million and a half is applied to the purposes for which it is granted." The abuses of the system of pauper relief were too gross, however, to be dealt with by sectional measures, and the time had not come when a comprehensive measure of reform could be brought forward with any prospect of success. The amendment of the Poor Law awaited that enlargement of the popular representation which was not effected until more than half a century later.

There was at this time a bill before the House for licensing a theatre in Manchester, which had been brought up from the House of Commons. Of this bill Lord Lyttelton had undertaken the charge, and the Earl of Radnor had, for reasons incomprehensible at the present day, determined to oppose it to the utmost of his power. The episcopal bench was canvassed, and promised, without exception, to give the bill an uncompromising opposition. Lord Radnor moved the rejection of the bill on its first reading, but, on the previous question being put, he found himself alone, all the bishops dividing against him! He thereupon recorded a strongly-worded protest against the bill, in which its supporters were stigmatised as encouragers of vice, immorality, and profaneness. This was the extraordinary position of the question when, on the 12th of May, Lord Lyttelton moved the second reading of the bill. It would strike the present generation as something odd—more odd even than Lord Radnor's protest—that the Earl of Carlisle supported the bill, on the ground that theatres were an antidote to Methodism; and that the Bishop of London opposed it, not because he thought, with Lord Radnor, that theatres were necessarily conducive to vice and immorality, but because the "Beggar's Opera" tended in that direction.

Lord Lyttelton contended that the Bishop of London, in admitting that theatres, properly conducted, might serve to promote the cause of virtue, had pleaded powerfully in favour of the bill, though he would prohibit the representation of Gay's opera. "I am pleased," he continued, "to find that the right reverend prelate has given me so fair an opportunity of satisfying him on that head, and informing him that the intended manager has given me the fullest assurances that the 'Beggar's Opera' shall never be played there. The right reverend prelate likewise tells your lordships that, if custom and the current prevailing opinion of mankind had not forbidden it, he could with pleasure be present to see the English Roscius appear in some of his capital characters. I applaud the wish, and I am sorry to observe that nothing but prejudice and ignorance could lay the foundation of a distinction which is to preclude any set of men from enjoying the fruits of so pleasing, instructive, and solid an entertainment. The right reverend prelate endeavours to make a distinction between places where entertainments of this kind ought or ought not to be permitted, by which he would exclude all trading and manufacturing towns. But here I must beg leave to dissent from him, and to draw the direct contrary conclusion; for, in my opinion, there is no place under proper regulation in which they should be more encouraged, as people who labour intensely require a proportionate recreation, and the sixpence spent at the theatre is much better laid out than at the alehouse."

He then turned to the protest of the Earl of Radnor. "It gives me great pain," said he, "but my duty as a member of this House will not permit me to pass over in silence a matter of no small consequence which has been mentioned during this day's debate; I mean the protest signed a few days since by a noble earl near me, which, give me leave to say, when properly and seriously considered, has a much more direct tendency to corrupt the morals of the lower orders of the people than all the theatrical exhibitions ever represented in this country. The right reverend bench, who are the great protectors of the interests of religion, the known promoters of virtue and morality in their respective dioceses, who in their own persons enforce by example what they teach by precept, who are the only set of men in the Christian world of the same description that follow the rigid doctrines of primitive Christianity, and show themselves true disciples of the Saviour,—this very respectable body are not only held out to the present generation, but their names are handed down to posterity, as the encouragers of vice, immorality, and profaneness; and, still more to aggravate the charge, their own words on a former occasion* are quoted and contrasted with their recent conduct, in order to convict them of hypocrisy, and surcharge the picture.

"This is the substance of the noble lord's protest. Now, what will be the probable consequence, as operating on the people? First, to increase that levelling spirit and contempt of the higher orders of the State which I am sorry to see is already too prevalent, and which is known to be so destructive of all subordination, order, and good government; and, secondly, to persuade mankind that religion and morality are no more than empty words, taken up and echoed for personal interested purposes, when it is proved that the very protectors and guardians of both have deserted their charge as unworthy of their care and attention. This, my lords, will be the

---

* In 1771, when they protested against a bill for licensing a theatre in Liverpool.

certain effect of the noble earl's protest in its present form; and it is on this ground that I now presume to contend that it is highly incumbent on his lordship to withdraw it, or to modify it in such a manner as to prevent the manifest evils it must otherwise be productive of.

"I know the noble earl's candour; I am satisfied of his love of truth and justice. His religious tenets are too well known: indeed, his ecclesiastical—I should say, his episcopal—character for sanctity of life and purity of doctrine are already so notorious that his lordship wants no essential quality but a mitre and a pair of lawn sleeves to make him a perfect bishop. I therefore entreat that his lordship, from those united motives, will undeceive the public, and disabuse the public mind, by erasing the exceptionable parts of the protest, or consent to withdraw it entirely. The explanation of the right reverend prelate, the sentiments of the whole bench, show beyond question that justice rigidly demands what is now asked; for surely the noble lord could not wish to have it go abroad that the right reverend bench voted for the bill when the fact was confessedly otherwise, and that the cause of virtue, morality, and religion should suffer by means of any such misrepresentation?

"On the whole, my lords, I appeal to the candour and justice of the noble lord; I trust to his care of the morals of the people, and his love of truth, that he will devise some method to set this matter on a right footing; and I press him more earnestly to the execution of this request, because, otherwise, I must be under the disagreeable necessity of moving to expunge from your lordships' journals what truth will not permit to remain there—what is in its nature so very injurious to the personal character of so respectable a part of this House—and, finally, what may be so destructive to the morals of the people, and the civil and religious interests of this country."

Some further debate ensued, the Earl of Radnor explained, and the bill was read the second time, and committed by a majority of thirty-three votes against twenty-five.

On the 17th a bill was introduced by Lord Camden to repeal the Government of Quebec Act, and was opposed by Lord Lyttelton, who showed himself as well acquainted with the past and the present condition of the Canadians, who were at the time almost entirely of French descent or birth, as he was with the state of affairs in New England. Lord Camden having said that the Act was "abhorrent to the British Constitution," Lord

Lyttelton reminded him that it was not framed for the meridian of England, but for the conquered subjects of France, consonant to the faith of treaties, and to stipulations agreed upon by the conquerors, which were part of the solemn pact between Great Britain and France, covenanted for and ratified by both nations at the conclusion of the war.

"And then, my lords," he continued, "I will go a step further. I will meet the noble lord on his own ground, and will uphold that the general principles and policy of the Act were founded on wisdom,—that the principles of it, which his lordship affirms to be repugnant to Christianity, emanated from the Gospel, and are coeval with the religion of our Saviour,—that they breathe forth the spirit of their Divine Master; for they are neither principles of Popery or servitude. They are principles, my lords, of toleration, unrestrained by prejudice, and unfettered by absurd and odious restrictions. The inhabitants of Canada were Catholics before they were conquered by England; they are Catholics now, but under the jurisdiction of a Protestant Parliament, and the cognisance of Protestant bishops, who form part of that Parliament, and who, I believe, were unanimous in allowing them the free exercise of their religion. In regard to the policy of the Act, I cannot but think it to be indisputably excellent, because it tends, by the beneficence of its aspect, to remove those rooted prejudices which are carefully instilled into the minds of all the subjects of France against the laws and constitution of England. This Act, my lords, has more effectually opened their eyes than the perusal of all our statute books; it has given them, with the mild code of our criminal law, a share of those blessings we derive from freedom; it has abolished the torture, it has raised the people from the oppression and tyranny under which they crawled, and has perpetuated in their hearts that dominion which has so recently been acquired by our arms.

"But, says the noble lord (and here he seems to press triumphantly his argument), you have by this Act affected the interests of commerce,— those interests that ought to be most dear to Great Britain. They ought to be so indeed, my lord; and so far are those interests from being hurt, that it has been the chief purpose of the Act to improve them; they have flourished under it, even beyond the most sanguine expectations; for, my lords, since the non-importation agreement has been entered into by all the other provinces of America, who but the Canadians have opened a channel for British manufactures? Who but Canadians have kept alive your drooping commerce, by taking prodigious quantities of goods from England, which, by their spirit and diligence have, notwithstanding the unlawful combinations of the Americans, penetrated and pervaded every part of the continent? Notwithstanding the factious resolutions of the assemblies—notwithstanding the inflexible enmity of Congress—the Canadians have opened a way for the English trader: by their means he has found a passage into America for his various sorts of merchandise; they have been carried into all the provinces—they have even crossed over the peninsula of Boston. These, my lords, are the consequences you have derived from this Act; reprobated, indeed, by the noble lord, but most cordially received by loyal Canadians, who take every occasion to show how sensible they are of its utility, and how desirous of testifying their gratitude.

"But the noble and learned lord has not confined his opposition to the general principles and policy of this Act; he has, with the designing subtlety of a lawyer, attacked the law part of the bill. He has told your lordships that the intention of it was to throw an unlimited power into the hands of the Crown—that the design was manifest, because they were denied the *habeas corpus*; he has assured you that, by excepting the Canadians from the salutary influence of that excellent provision for the liberty of the subject, you have altered the tenor of that wholesome policy which has always induced, and should always compel, Great Britain to give to all conquered countries the full and perfect system of English freedom in return for their allegiance. The noble lord has instanced the case of Jamaica, of Barbadoes; but, above all, of Ireland. Has the noble lord forgotten, then, that Ireland, though in possession of the criminal law of England, has not the *habeas corpus?* That Act, which is a special privilege monopolised by Great Britain, is not even extended to Ireland; but Ireland has what is in fact equivalent to it, and so has Canada.

"Would the noble lord desire, then, that those new conquered subjects of England, against whom he shows such strong and irreconcilable hatred, should be indulged with a privilege which even liberty herself seems to be jealous of, and which has hitherto been denied to the loyal inhabitants of Ireland? My lords, he does desire it; he would do anything to answer his purpose, to increase storms, to perplex, to distress the Administration. Animated by these views, I am not surprised that he hates the nobility of every country; they stand in his way; he would rub them out of his system of government; he has told your lordships that it is the *noblesse* and the priests of Canada that are alone benefited by this Act, and that it would be better for the province if both prelates and nobility were whipped out of it. These are his lordship's sentiments—republican sentiments, my lords—which, with less impropriety, might have come from the mouth of a factious burgher of Geneva, but which are foreign to the genius of the British constitution."

He concluded by asking the Ministry for information as to the intentions of the Spanish Government in preparing armaments the magnitude of which forbade the idea that they were designed to act against Morocco, as had been represented. The Earl of Rochford replied so lightly and complacently to this question that the Earl of Bristol endeavoured to impress its gravity upon the House, and Lord Lyttelton rose again.

"I did not," he said, "press the noble earl in office to betray the secrets of it, nor to divulge matters of state. I wished only to give His Majesty's Ministers, if they thought proper, an opportunity of averting part of the censure which might be deservedly thrown on them in case an unexpected blow should be struck, and to prevent the fraud and imposition people might be liable to from a few among them who might have better or earlier intelligence than the rest. I have, it is true, no great opinion of Spanish politics, yet I must abide by my former assertion, that I am convinced that, however conscientious his Catholic Majesty may be, and desirous of propagating the Christian faith, and extirpating the enemies of the Cross, His Majesty, much less his Ministers, would not put the nation to the enormous expense of the present armaments merely to make proselytes in the wilds and deserts of Africa. The Spanish Cabinet is composed, like those of other princes, of men of different abilities and dispositions, and business is transacted in it, as it is in all others where there is no Prime Minister, by plurality of voices. I can never, therefore, be persuaded to think that a majority of men trained up to public business could ever be led to adopt so preposterous a measure. The noble earl in office seems to place too great a reliance on the assurance given by the Spanish Cabinet, and I will tell your lordships why I think so. It is because I am well informed. I know it to be the current language of the several branches of the House of Bourbon that they do not look upon themselves as bound to give us any previous information of their hostile intentions, either by declaration of war or otherwise, on account of our capture of the French ships before the commencement of the last war. I therefore call upon the noble earl at the head of the Admiralty to inform the House what force we have immediately ready to put to sea, should the first accounts from that quarter bring us intelligence that Gibraltar was attacked by the Spanish fleet?"

The Earl of Sandwich said that he did not think he was obliged to give the information, or that Lord Lyttelton was authorised to ask it; he condescended, however, to inform the House that the naval force ready to put to sea immediately was superior to any that could be brought against Gibraltar by Spain and France combined. The House divided on the Earl of Dartmouth's motion to reject the bill, when the amendment was carried by eighty-eight votes against twenty-eight.

Lord Lyttelton printed the speech delivered by him on this occasion, and its publication served Horace Walpole as a peg for one of those ill-natured remarks which, from hereditary hostility, he missed no opportunity of making.* The

---

* "Thank my stars, I have done both with authorship and noble authors, for my Lord Lyttelton has printed a speech. It is a poor affair, void of argument, and grossly abusive on Lord Camden.

Parliamentary session usually extended, at that time, from the beginning of October to the end of May or beginning of June, so that legislators were in town, as well as in the country, during the months when each was most enjoyable. It was in the summer of 1775 that Lord Lyttelton made the sojourn in Wiltshire, and the subsequent visit to Bristol, which are related in the following letter :—

"We all of us grew suddenly tired of our Wiltshire rustication; and, without a dissentient voice, voted a party to Bristol, where I ate such excellent turtle, and drank such execrable wine, that, with the heat of the weather into the bargain, I was suddenly taken ill at the playhouse, almost to fainting, and was obliged to hurry into the air for respiration. Believe me, I did not like the business. Cold sweats and shiverings, accompanied with internal sinkings, gave me a better notion of dying than I had before, and made me think so seriously of this mortal life that, on my return home, I shall take the opportunity of the first gloomy day to make

---

It will be as difficult for the Court to uphold his oratory as his character, if he has recourse to the press."—*Letter to the Rev. William Mason.*

my will, appoint executors, and harangue my lawyer into low spirits on the doctrine of death and judgment.

"I exhibited myself—for none of the party would accompany me—at a public breakfast at the Hot Wells, and sat down at a long table with a number of animated cadavers, who devoured their meal as if they had not an hour to live; and, indeed, many of them seemed to be in that doleful predicament. But this was not all. I saw three or four groups of hectic spectres engage in cotillions: it brought instantly to my mind Holbein's 'Dance of Death,' and methought I saw the raw-boned scarecrow piping and tabouring to his victims. So I proceeded to the fountain; but, instead of rosy, blooming health, diseases of every colour and complexion guarded the springs. As I approached to taste them, I was fanned by the fœtid breath of gasping consumptions, stunned with expiring coughs, and suffocated with the effluvia of ulcerated lungs. Such a living Golgotha never entered into my conceptions; and I could not but look upon the stupendous rocks that rise in rude magnificence around the place as the wide-spreading jaws of an universal sepulchre.

"Lord Walpole told me he was there in attendance upon a daughter. I was glad to turn my back upon the scene; but I had not yet come to the conclusion of it, for, as I was waiting for my chaise, two different persons put cards into my hand, which informed me where funerals were to be furnished with the greatest expedition, and that hearses and mourning-coaches were to let to any part of England. I immediately leaped into my carriage, and ordered the postillion to drive with all possible haste from a place where I was in danger of being buried alive.

"After all, this tenancy of life is but a bad one, with its waste and ingress of torturing diseases, which, not content with destroying the building, maliciously torture the possessor with such pains and penalties as to make him oftentimes curse the possession.

> "Man's feeble race, what ills await!
> Labour and penury,—the racks of pain:
> Disease and sorrow's mournful train,
> And death, sad refuge from the storms of fate.

"If I continue this kind of letter any further you will tell me that I shall repent, found hospitals, and die a Methodist, and that Rochester's funeral sermons and mine will be bound up in the same volume, to the edification and comfort of all sinners of every enormity. Adieu, therefore, and believe me very truly yours,

"LYTTELTON."

Lord Lyttelton was not partial to rural sports, and neither hunted or shot; but he liked to retire occasionally from the gaieties of London society and pass a few weeks in the country, at the houses of his friends. As he seldom dated his letters, and never with the year, and the names of the persons to whom those collected by Combe were addressed were suppressed at their particular request, they cannot always be assigned to the year in which they were written, nor can his correspondents always be conjectured; but the foregoing letter is stated, in the preface to the collected edition of 1806, to have had the date of the summer of 1775 assigned to it by the person to whom it was addressed. Few of the letters bear internal evidence of later date, and it is to the latter part of that year, therefore, that those must be assigned which describe in so amusing a manner the convivial gatherings assisted at by the jovial clergyman whom he calls Parson Adams, and whose true patronymic cannot now be discovered.

"I take the opportunity of a sober hour, while everyone of the society here, except myself, is happy in the delirium of a fox-chase—to tell you where I am, what I am about, and with whom engaged. The spleen of a gloomy day seized upon my spirits, so I ordered my chaise, and sought the enlivening hospitality of this mansion. To increase our satisfaction, who should arrive, an hour after me, but your clerical friend, whose blunt simplicity and rough, unpolished benevolence afforded them unusual entertainment. Parson Adams—for he has no other name within these walls—came on Thursday to dinner, and continued with us, in much joy and heart, till Saturday afternoon, when, suddenly awaking from a kind of snoring doze, he made a most vociferous and unexpected demand if it was not the last day of the week, and receiving, after some pause of astonishment and laughter, an answer in the affirmative, he arose in haste, examined his pockets with a most anxious vivacity, and then broke the cordage of the bell in the violence of ringing it. Being requested to explain the meaning of all this agitation, he observed, in a tone of voice which betokened no small disappointment, that as, in truth, it was Saturday, the morrow must, in the natural order of time, be Sunday; and, as Sunday was the Sabbath day, it was fitting he should immediately return home, to prepare himself for the duties of it. The night approached, and threatened darkness; it was, therefore, proposed to him to retake the possession of his arm-chair, nor to think of business till the next morning.

"'My good friends,' replied the doctor, 'it becomes me to inform you that my habitation is fourteen miles distant, and that the church where I am to officiate to-morrow morning is exactly in the mid-way; so that, if I remain here till the time you propose, I must ride fourteen miles to fetch a sermon, return seven of the same miles to preach it, and then go over those individual seven miles for the third time to preach the same sermon again, which I take, according to common arithmetic, to be no less than twenty-eight miles; and all this riding, with double duty, will be too much both for man and beast. I really thought,' continued our divine, 'that I had equipped myself with a sermon, in order to make the first church an half-way house on my return to my own parish; but I have either forgot to clap my divinity in my pocket, or I took it out accidentally with my tobacco-box in my way, and have unfortunately dropped it in the road.'

"He then emptied all his pockets, one by one, not forgetting the side-pockets of his breeches, turned them inside out, covered the floor with a quantity of dry crumbs of bread and cheese, looked into his tobacco-box, took his watch from his fob, poked down two of his fingers, examined the lining of his coat, and at length, with a deep sigh, and a huge expectoration upon his handkerchief, which he had thrown upon the ground, he gave it up for lost. 'It was,' said he, 'the best discourse I had to my back, and as pretty a piece of supernaculum as ever was enclosed in black covers. It was divided,' continued he, 'into three parts; the first was taken from Clarke, the second from Abernethy, the third was composed by myself; and the two practical observations were translated from a Latin sermon, preached and printed at Oxford in the year of our Lord 1735.'

"On my observing that his discourse had as many heads as Cerberus, he grew warm, and told me it was much better to have three heads than none at all. 'But,' added the doctor, 'if you wish to know more of the matter, it had four beginnings and seven conclusions, by the help whereof I preached it, with equal success, on a Christmas Day, for the benefit of a charity, at a florists' feast, an assize, an archdeacon's visitation, and a funeral, besides common occasions.' On this account, F. observed that it put him in mind of the mention made in 'Tristram Shandy,' of a text which would suit any sermon, and a sermon which would suit any text. This the zealous preacher loudly declared was a false insinuation, for that his text was steady to its post, nor had ever deserted it; and that whoever took him for a man who would hold out a false flag, or change his colours, on any occasion, mistook his character, and did him a very sensible injustice.

"At this period the master of the house returned from a quiet, but fruitless examination of his book-case, for the purpose of finding, perchance, some old printed sermon which might have served the doctor's purpose, prolonged the pleasure of his society, and saved him his dark and dangerous journey. On this disappointment, I ventured to remark that, as he had given us so many agreeable specimens of his ready eloquence, it was certainly in his power to treat his flock with an extempore discourse; and I strongly recommended him to adopt my idea, when he struck me dumb by hinting to me, in a loud significant whisper, that I was mistaken in supposing it to be as easy to preach a sensible discourse on a divine subject, extempore, in a pulpit, as to talk a precipitate hour of flowery, frothy nonsense, on a political one, in the Parliament House. At this moment of superiority his horse was announced, and we all attended to hear, rather than to see, him depart, which he did with much horse language, and in a night of triple darkness.

"It was now seven o'clock; our spirits were fled with the parson: we gambled a little, but not with sufficient spirit to keep us awake, till at length supper fortunately arrived to change the scene; and I had scarce dissected the wing of a capon, when we were all alarmed by a voice from the court, which repeated the cry of 'House! house!' with uncommon vehemence. We left the table, and hurried to the hall-door, when the same voice demanded, in the same tone, whether that was the road to Bridgnorth? On a reply in the negative, it continued, 'I suppose, then, I am at Davenport House.' On a second reply in the negative, 'Then where the devil am I?' returned the voice, for we could see nothing; but, the candles arriving, who should appear but our unfortunate doctor, who, after wandering about the commons for upwards of three hours, had, by mere chance, returned to us again.

"We received him in triumph, placed him at the head of the table, where, without grace or apology, or indeed uttering a single word, he seized on the best part of a fowl, with a proportionable quantity of ham, and left us to laugh and be merry, while he voraciously devoured his meat, and held his tongue. At length, observing that his clay wanted moistening, and that punch was a fluid the best adapted of any other to his soil, he did not delay an instant to quench his thirsty frame from a large bowl of that refreshing beverage. The cords of his tongue were now loosened, and he informed us that Providence having, as he supposed, for wise and good purposes, intimated to him, by a variety of obstructions, that he should not discharge his usual functions on the morrow, it became him to show a due resignation to the will of heaven, and, therefore, he should send his flocks to grass on the approaching Sabbath. In a similar strain he continued to entertain us, till, weary with laughter, we were glad to retire. The next morning it was hinted to him that the company did not wish to restrain him from attending upon the divine service of the parish; but he declared that it would be adding contempt to neglect if, when he had absented himself from his own churches, he should go to any other. This curious etiquette he strictly observed; and we passed a Sabbath contrary, I fear, both to law and gospel.

"In the fulness of his heart our divine has given us an invitation to dine with him at his parsonage, on Thursday next. I expect infinite entertainment from the party; and you may depend, by the succeeding post, to receive the best hash of it which the cookery of my pen can afford you."

Lord Lyttelton fulfilled his promise, as the following letter, evidently addressed to the same person, shows :—

"The visit is paid, and more than answered the warmest expectations which could be formed in its favour. Our reverend host had insisted, not *à la mode de Scarron,* that each of his guests should bring his dish, but that they should individually name it. This easy preliminary was readily complied with, and it was my lot to give birth to as excellent a plumb-pudding as ever smoaked upon a table ; which, from my adoption, he is resolved in future to call a Lyttelton. You see what honours wait upon me, and to what solid excellence my title is assimilated. F—— had named a goose, which he immediately christened after its godfather, who did not quite relish the joke, and could hardly force a laugh, when the rest of the company were bursting. The whole meal was a very comfortable one ; and the doctor produced us no small quantity of very tolerable wine : his punch was grateful to the nostrils, but he had made it in a large pewter vessel, so like a two-handled chamber-pot, that my resolution was not equal to the applying of it to my palate.

"On its being observed that he must have taken no small pains to procure all the good things before us, he declared that no trouble had attended any one article but the pudding, which, he said, had almost destroyed a pair of black plush breeches, in riding round the country to learn how it should be made in perfection. 'You cannot be ignorant, my lord,' continued our divine, addressing himself particularly to me, 'that a plumb-pudding is nothing more than a pudding, however it may be composed, with plumbs added to other ingredients; but, apprehensive that the ordinary skill of our homely kitchens, in this particular, might not be agreeable to such refined palates as yours, I resolved to traverse the whole neighbourhood, in order to obtain all necessary intelligence. Every learned person to whom I applied agreed, as your lordship may suppose, in the essential articles of flour and water, milk and eggs, suet and plumbs, or raisins; but the variety of other articles which were severally recommended filled two pages of my memorandum-book, and drove me almost to despair. In the multitude of counsellors I did not, according to the proverb, find wisdom, but confusion. I was successively, alternately, and separately advised the addition of rum, brandy, wine, strong beer, spices of every sort, chopped liver, and Hollands gin. With this load of multifarious intelligence, I hastened to the market-town, furnished myself with every ingredient my own little store-house did not possess, and returned home jaded, fatigued, and my pockets laden with the produce of all quarters of the globe. But another important labour,' added the doctor, 'succeeded, in the consultation about the choice and due mode of applying the hoard of grocery and variety of liquors which were displayed in form on the kitchen-dresser: it was a solemn business, for *the Lord had commanded it*. Consultation, however, begot difference of opinion, and difference of opinion brought on dispute; so that I was at length obliged to interpose my authority; and, to shorten the business, I ordered all the various articles, consisting of more than a dozen in number, to be employed without favour or affection. The motley mixture was accordingly made; and, as every person consulted seemed to agree that the longer it boiled the better it would prove, I ordered it to be put into the pot at midnight, and sent for a famous nurse in the neighbourhood to sit up with it, and, with a vestal's vigilance, to keep in the fire till the family arose. In this state of concoction the pudding remained till after the arrival of this good company, who, I hope, will be so prejudiced in its favour, from the Herculean labour which produced it, as to attack its circumference with Herculean appetites.' Here ended the culinary oration, and, as I before observed, the subject of it contained unrivalled excellence; and, though we laughed at it and over it, we did not fail to cause a very apparent diminution of its ample dimensions.

"Thus, my dear friend, we ate and laughed, and drank and laughed, till night stole imperceptibly upon us; when our hospitable host informed us that he had two beds and a cradle in his own house, and that he had prepared three others at two neighbouring farmers: so that we might be at rest as to our lodging, nor, like him, encounter the perils of a darksome night. 'The squires,' added he, 'must sojourn to my neighbours; my two beds will serve the peer and the baronet; and I myself will take the cradle.' Now, this cradle, which caused us no little mirth, and will, I presume, have a similar effect upon you, who are acquainted with the huge figure which was to occupy it,—this cradle, I say, is a most excellent moveable for a small house. It is made of sufficient size to hold an infant six feet in length, can be placed anywhere, and will enable an hospitable spirit to supply a friend with a lodging when his beds are engaged. If I had not been fearful of affronting our divine, I should have indulged my curious fancy by going to roost in it; but the best bed was prepared for me, and the fine Holland sheets, which, probably, had not been taken out of the sweet-scented press for many a month, were spread for my repose : nor would my slumbers have been suspended for a moment, if the linen had not produced so strong an effluvia of rosemary that I almost fancied myself in a coffin, and wrapped in a winding-sheet. But fatigue soon got the better of fancy; and I awoke the next morning to life and spirits, but not to immortality.

"Before I bid you adieu, permit me to add a singular example of complimentary repartee, which our friendly host very unexpectedly addressed to me, previous to our departure. As I was looking out of the parlour window, from whence nothing is to be seen but a black dreary heath, he asked me how I liked the prospect. I answered that, from its wild appearance, if Nebuchadnezzar had been doomed to pasture in his environs, he must have died for hunger. 'And if that prince,' replied the doctor, 'had been sentenced to have passed his savage years in your park at Hagley, he need not have regretted the loss of a throne, or wished a return to the enjoyment of his human functions.' At this period of self-importance, which, in the very description, returns upon me, you cannot be surprised if I take my leave. Adieu."

There was probably a trip to the metropolis between these rural visits and Lord Lyttelton's return to Hagley, for which place he had little affection. A brief sojourn in London may be inferred from the fact that he won a large sum of money at cards, which, after due consideration of the matter, he determined to devote to the relief of his estate from the jointures of his wife and his step-mother. The following letter, in which he communicated this intention to the friend to whom the two preceding letters were addressed, is the only one in which his love of play is alluded to :—

"It gives me no small satisfaction to be assured that my two last letters have afforded you the satisfaction it was their office to communicate. The rural divine plays a most admirable part in the jovial interludes of provincial society. It is a pleasant circumstance to meet occasionally with a man whose humour, sense, and foible are so blended that, while he possesses the pleasant mixture of simplicity and vanity which bars him from distinguishing when you laugh with him or at him, you may give a loose to the whole of your mirthful dispositions without any restraint from the fear of giving offence. Our reverend friend told B—— that he is in no small disgrace with his parishioners for entertaining so great a sinner as I am, and that one of them, who had seen me at Kidderminster, declares throughout the neighbourhood that I have a *cloven foot*. I am not without my expectations that equal vouchers will be produced for my tail and horns, and then the devil will be complete.

"At length the grave and anxious occupations of worldly wisdom succeed to mirth and jollity. The interest of money and the value of lives, together with trusts and securities, are the subjects of my present meditations. To explain myself, I am considering a plan for easing my estate of the jointures to the two Dowager Lady Lyttletons —for they are both so, in fact—by making a purchase of equivalent annuities for their *valuable* lives. Fortune has been kind to me, and I will, for once, win your applause by applying her gifts to sensible purposes. To use a newspaper species of portraiture, what think you of the picture of a young nobleman offering the favours of Fortune on the altar of Wisdom, by the present

Lord Lyttelton? If this idea should be completed—and I assure you the dead colouring is disappearing apace—will you place the painting in the cabinet of your mind, in the room of the picture you designed, and have so often retouched, of that self-same nobleman sacrificing the gifts of nature to folly, vice, and intemperance?

"I trust and believe that a sordid thirst after money will never be added to the catalogue of my failings. It is true that the love of play proceeds from the desire of gain, and is, therefore, said to be founded on an avaricious principle. If this be fact, avarice is the universal passion; for I will venture to affirm that, more or less, we are all gamesters by nature. But the desire of winning money for the sake of spending it and increasing the joys of life is one thing, and the ardour of acquiring it in order to lock it up and render it useless is another.

"Mammon, the least-erected Spirit that fell
From Heav'n: for e'en in Heav'n his looks and thoughts
Were always downwards bent, admiring more
The riches of Heav'n's pavement, trodden gold,
Than aught divine or holy else enjoy'd
In vision beatific."

It may appropriately be mentioned here, though it would be unnecessary if Lord Lyttelton had been less systematically abused, that he was never suspected of playing otherwise than fair. "Scrupulously honest" are the words used in reference to this point by the friend who wrote the sketch of his character, which was prefixed to the posthumous volume of poems which was published by his friend and executor, Roberts, in 1780.

CHAPTER IX.

Opening of the Parliamentary Session of 1775-76—Debate on the Address—Speech of Lord Lyttelton—Speech on the Introduction of Foreign Troops without the Consent of Parliament —Change of Relations with the Ministry—Appointment as Chief Justice in Eyre, north of the Trent, and a Privy Councillor—Letter on his Appointment—Opposition to the Duke of Grafton's Motion for Return of Troops in America— Defence of the Prohibitory Bill—Vindication of his Conduct against the Duke of Richmond—Calumnies of Horace Walpole—Trial of the Duchess of Kingston.

PARLIAMENT re-assembled on the 26th of October, actual hostilities having commenced in America during the recess by the attack of the rebel colonists on the troops at Concord, near Lexington, followed by the engagement at Bunker's Hill, in which the former gained the advantage. Amendments to the Address having been moved by the Marquis of Rockingham and the Duke of Grafton, Lord Lyttelton condemned both the address and the Rockingham amendment. Having resented what he deemed an implied censure on the Earl of Chatham in the speech of the Earl of Sandwich, and eulogised his noble relative with his usual warmth, he turned to the Address, and, while maintaining the sovereignty of Parliament to the fullest extent, strongly condemned the conduct of Ministers. They had, he said, totally failed in their promises, and were no longer to be trusted or supported with safety. He alluded to his conduct the preceding year, when he had voted with them, how strenuously he had recommended vigorous measures, and how frequently he had pressed them on this head. Though he could not vote for the amendment, because it did not declare the Americans to be in rebellion, he totally disapproved of the Address, and of the measures recommended in it.

He described the situation as being now entirely altered. Boston, he said, was turned into a hospital, where more died by famine and neglect than by the sword in the field. Great Britain had probably not a foot of land in her possession on the American continent. The expense and hazard of reducing the rebels, and the little dependence to be placed in men who had either been misled themselves or had purposely misled others, operated so strongly on his mind that he could no longer give his support to the Government, and he must consequently unite in opinion with the Duke of Grafton in wishing that all Acts relating to America which had been passed since 1763 might be repealed, as a ground for reconciliation, the restoration of public tranquillity, and the return of the Americans to their wonted obedience and subordinate dependence on the mother country.

The Duke of Grafton's amendment was rejected, however, by sixty-nine votes against twenty-nine; and the Address was carried by seventy-three votes against thirty-three. It was as evident to Lord Lyttelton as to the leaders of the Opposition that the Ministry, supported by such a majority, could carry whatever measures they might propose; but he was determined to support no Administration that would not act with vigour against the rebellious colonists. He was sufficiently free from party considerations and influences to have accepted office under the Earl of Chatham, if he could have converted that statesman to his own views on the American question; but such a conversion was not to be expected, and, while Lord North would neither make concessions to the Americans, nor act with vigour against them, he felt himself constrained by his conscience and his political principles to maintain an independent position.

The Government having made arrangements at this time for raising troops in the Electorates of Hanover and Hesse, the Duke of Manchester, on the 1st of November, moved a resolution, declaring the introduction of foreign troops into any part of the British dominions, without the consent of Parliament, to be dangerous and unconstitutional. The Earl of Rochford met this attack by moving the previous question, on the ground that Lord North would ask Parliament for an Act of Indemnity ; and, in the course of his speech, showed a desire to fritter away the Bill of Rights by fine-drawn distinctions, that drew from Lord Lyttelton a warm rebuke. He should prefer, he said, under the circumstances, an Act of Indemnity to a vote of censure ; but the arguments of the noble earl surprised and alarmed him.

"Is," he asked, " our glorious Revolution, the only sure foundation of all our liberties,—is the Bill of Rights, a compact entered into at that glorious period,—as well as the acknowledged sense in which that modern Magna Charta has been received for nearly a century,—to be done away with by distinctions and explanations repugnant to the intentions of its framers, to the letter and the spirit, to both its legal and its constitutional construction ? I was willing to make every reasonable allowance,—to grant something for expediency, more for necessity,—in short, was willing to accede to the propriety of anything or everything which might be urged in justification of the measure; but that it is legal or constitutional, is a proposition I can never assent to,—a doctrine which, as an Englishman, I will never endure. Though a young man, I am old enough to remember the conduct of a great Minister, a steady friend to his country,—I mean the Earl of Chatham,—upon a similar occasion. I venture to call it a similar occasion, but I believe that no noble lord in this House, however sanguine for the present system of measures, will assert that the present urgency equals the one I am going to mention.

"It was in the very heat of the war, when we required to recruit the army and navy with from fifteen to twenty thousand men annually, that that great statesman, feeling the necessity of having recourse to foreign levies, resolved to raise a certain number of foreigners to serve in America. How did he carry the measure into execution? In the midst of a war, the widest in extent, the most interesting in its consequences, the greatest in its immediate importance, the heaviest in point of expense,—when our coasts were daily expected to be invaded by dangerous and inveterate enemies,—while the war, even in America, was yet doubtful,—the Earl of Chatham, instead of pleading the great and justifiable motive of necessity,—instead of cavilling about this or that word,—in the full spirit of the Constitution, in the full spirit of an Englishman, came to Parliament for its sanction. So very careful was that great man, so tenacious of everything that might be construed into the most trifling infraction of the Act of Settlement, that he inserted two clauses in the Act that enabled the Crown to take those troops into its pay:— one, that they should serve in America only; the other, that no foreign officer should hold a higher rank than that of lieutenant-colonel."

Sir James Lowther moved, in the House of Commons, a resolution in the same terms as that of the Duke of Manchester; but it was rejected in both Houses. Six days afterwards, when the Duke of Richmond proposed to call Penn, the governor of Pennsylvania, to authenticate the petition of Congress to the King, Lord Lyttelton opposed it, on the ground of the inconvenience that would result from such a course becoming a precedent, and a long debate ensued. The motion to examine Penn at the bar of the House was rejected by fifty-six votes against twenty-two; but it was finally resolved, on the motion of the Earl of Denbigh, that the governor should be examined on the 10th, it being thought that the information he could give would be useful in guiding the House to a decision upon the petition. Between the two debates there seems to have been a rumour current in political circles that Lord Lyttelton had taken office under the Government, or would shortly do so; and on the 10th, after Penn had been examined, the Duke of Richmond, supporting the petition as a basis for reconciliation, said: "Where are the troops to come from that are to conquer America? We have heard of twenty thousand Russians. It may be a mere report; but Ministers give no information, and there are such fluctuations of men, without any change of measures, that nobody knows who to apply to. Whether the noble lord in red (Lord Lyttelton) was now a Minister of the day could not with certainty be pronounced; if he was in the secrets of the Government, he might possibly indulge the House with some information concerning the set twenty thousand Russians to be sent to America."

Lord Lyttelton rose as the duke sat down, and said that he should not be prevented from doing his duty by the insinuations which had been thrown out. He repeated his former arguments that the Americans were in rebellion, and guilty of treason; commented on Penn's evidence as affording proofs of the situation being as he described it; and contended that the effect of the Duke of Richmond's motion, if adopted, would be to transfer authority from Parliament to Congress. The Earl of Sandwich censured the Duke of Richmond for his insinuations, and denied that there was any intention of employing Russian troops in America. The motion was rejected by eighty-six votes against thirty-three.

During the interval of five days between this debate and the next occasion on which he spoke, Lord Lyttelton was appointed to the sinecure office of Chief Justice in Eyre, north of the Trent, and admitted to the Privy Council. He was much gratified by this elevation, which had been an object of ambition with his father, and, in the fulness of his elation, wrote as follows to a friend :—

"I thank you most sincerely, my very dear friend, for your obliging congratulations on my late promotion; and I have no better way to answer the friendly counsels which accompany them, but by opening my heart to you upon the occasion, and trusting its sentiments with you.

"You knew my father, and I am sure you will applaud me in declaring that his character did real honour to his rank and his nature. A grateful fame will wait upon his memory, till, by some new change in human affairs, the great and good men of this country and period shall be lost to the knowledge of distant generations. In the republic of letters he rose to a very considerable eminence; his deep political erudition is universally acknowledged; and, as a senator both of the lower and higher order, his name is honoured with distinguished veneration. In his private, as well as public life, he was connected, and in friendship, with the first men of the times in which he lived; and, as a character of strict virtue and true piety, he has been universally held forth as the most striking example of this age. The idea of uncommon merit accompanies all opinion of him; and to mention his name is to awaken the most pleasing and amiable sentiments. As you read this short and imperfect outline of his character, fill it up, and do it justice.

"Now it will, perhaps, surprise you when you are informed that the post in Government which this great and good man most desired, and could never obtain, was the Chief Justiceship in Eyre, &c. &c. The reverse of the picture is as follows: that your humble servant and his *gracious* son, whose character you perfectly know, has been appointed to this very post, in the infancy of his peerage, without

P

any previous service performed, hint given, or requisition made on his part, and without the proposition of and conditions on the part of the Minister.* When I was surprised by the offer, I was surprised also by a sudden and unusual suffusion on my cheeks at the contrast of mine and my father's character, of mine and my father's lot. Indeed, so big was my heart on the occasion, that when the Ministerial ambassador had left me the sentiments of it burst forth upon the first person I saw, who happened not to be a very proper receptacle for the reflections of virtue.

"There is a very great encouragement in this world to be wicked, and the devil certainly goes about in more pleasing shapes than that of a roaring lion.† In the name of fortune, my dear friend, how and why are these things? Is it the increasing corruption of the times, or the weakness of Government, that gives to dissolute men the meed of virtue, or do Ministers think it

---

* There seems a typographical error here, as the letter stands in the edition of 1806, and that the sentence should read, "the proposition of any conditions on the part of the Minister."

† The allusion is to the words of Peter, chap. v., v. 8, of the first general epistle: "Be sober, be vigilant; for your adversary the devil, as a roaring lion, walketh about, seeking whom he may devour."

expedient to give a sop to the mastiff whose growl might make them tremble? You, who have made men and manners your study, who have looked so deeply into the volume of the heart, and have acquired such a happy art of reconciling the apparent inconsistencies of human affairs, must instruct me. I wish you could improve and convert me. I am not insensible to what is good; nay, there are moments when the full lustre of virtue beams upon me. I try to seize it, but the gleam escapes me, and I am re-involved in darkness. The conflict of reason and passion is but the conflict of a moment, and the latter never fails to bear me off in triumph.

> " ' *Video meliora proboque,*
> *Deteriora sequor.*' "

There seems no reason to doubt the accuracy of the statements contained in this letter, and the inference of Lord Lyttelton from his appointment. He was a very young man for a Privy Councillor, being only in his thirty-second year. But the evidence which he had given of superior bailities and attainments had already made him a noteworthy man in the Senate, and men of such brilliant oratorical and debating powers were not so numerous on the Treasury benches that the Government could afford to neglect and disregard him. Even if they had been slower to discern, or less willing to recognise his talents, the pertinacity and energy of his attacks must have convinced them that he was a man of whom account must be taken, whether they liked him or not. The only post at their disposal at the time which could be offered to a man of his position was, therefore, placed unconditionally at his acceptance; and, to make amends for its being a sinecure, a seat in the Privy Council was coupled with it. There seems to have been no correspondence on the subject; the offer was conveyed to him verbally by a supporter of the Government, and Lord Lyttelton, after receiving explanations as to the American policy of the Cabinet, accepted it.

His first Ministerial speech was made on the 15th, two days after he received the appointment, when the Duke of Grafton moved for a return of the number of troops in America, and Lord Lyttelton opposed the motion, on the ground that the return would be the means of conveying information to the rebels. He commented severely on this occasion on the conduct of Lord Camden, whose speech he characterised as at once a libel upon Parliament and an encouragement to the rebels. "The noble and learned lord," said he, "while he sets up for an advocate of liberty, says something which I do not well comprehend, unless its object is still further to blacken and vilify this country. His lordship tells you, as an overbearing and domineering Englishman, he should like to trample on the liberties of America. I do not pretend to say what his native impulses may be, but I will venture to assert that he thinks very differently in this respect from the majority of this House and this nation, neither of which want to invade the rights of the Americans, much less to trample on their liberty." He concluded by expressing the hope that Great Britain would never desist until she had obtained full submission and obedience to the exercise of her constitutional power. The motion of the Duke of Grafton was negatived without a division.

There is nothing in this speech, as reported in Hansard's "Parliamentary History," to indicate that the relations of the speaker towards the Government had undergone any change; there is no deviation whatever from the views and sentiments on the American question which he had constantly expressed from the day on which he first took his place in the House of Lords. Yet Horace Walpole, writing two days afterwards to Horace Mann, speaks of Lord Lyttelton as "this hopeful young man, who, on being refused a place, spoke for the Americans, and in two days, on getting one, against them." The speeches themselves would be a sufficient reply, if any were needed, to this libel, which is conceived in the characteristic Walpolean spirit. There is just as little reason for the statement that Lord Lyttelton asked for a place, and was refused, as there is for the assertion that, within two days, he spoke for and against the Americans. But political independence was so rare in those days, that few politicians could understand the propriety of opposing the Government on one day, and supporting it on another, without supposing the acceptance of a place or a pension in the interval; and Walpole, though not a politician himself, must have heard enough in his own family to have made him specially incredulous as to the existence of honest placemen and independent members.

On the 15th of December, when the Prohibitory Bill was before the House, Lord Lyttelton supported it, and defended the Government against the charge brought against them by the Duke of Manchester, of having introduced it at an improper time, and desiring to hurry it through Parliament. "On the contrary," said he, "it is well known, and it is now confessed on all hands, that the Administration have delayed, instead of hurried, the necessary measures for reducing this obstinate and rebellious people to obedience, from motives of lenity, and a wish to prevent the effusion of blood and the horrid devastation consequent on civil war. And I am not certain that all the mischief which has since happened may not, in a great measure, be attributed to a mistaken motive of humanity." He replied to the Duke of Manchester's charge, that the measure was a violation of the Bill of Rights, by the allegation that the Americans were in a state of rebellion, and repeated his former arguments in support of that proposition.

Then, replying to the Duke's warning, that war was imminent on the continent of Europe, and would soon afford occupation for the British fleet, he said: "Would that be a motive for submitting to rebels in the present contest? I think it would not: I am sure it ought not. France and Spain would conclude that a nation which had not the power to control its own members would be no longer a formidable enemy. They would look upon you as an abject, tame, mercenary people, who, from mere love of lucre, would consent to sacrifice all pride, dignity, and the superior interests of yourselves and posterity, rather than suffer temporary inconvenience, or forego for awhile the advantages derived from commercial intercourse with your colonies. They would look on you as a nation of merchants, from whom nothing was to be feared, devoid of that martial ardour, native prowess, and thirst of fame which have hitherto rendered you formidable to your enemies.

"Therefore, I contend, my lords, that it is doubly incumbent on you to exert yourselves, even as a means of keeping ambitious neighbours in that state of awe and reverence which will always be one of the best bulwarks of national safety and domestic tranquillity. My lords, though I wish sincerely that America, should she persist obstinately to resist the constitutional and equitable claims of this country, may be compelled to acknowledge them, yet I do not desire that the people of that country should be abridged of their ancient privileges. Whenever they return to a proper sense of duty, I shall very readily give my support to any plan which may be most likely to heal the unhappy wounds that have already been given, and for receiving them once more into the bosom of the mother country." He denied the contention of the Duke of Manchester that the Government had abandoned the right of taxation. He would not, he said, pretend to say in what manner, or to what extent, America should contribute to the imperial exchequer; but he contended that the principle should be insisted upon, and that America should share the burdens of the mother country equally with the advantages she derived from the connection.

The Duke of Richmond accusing him of having changed his views after accepting office, he rose again to exonerate himself from the charge. He recapitulated what he had said on the question of employing foreign troops in America, and asserted that, as regarded the general policy of the Government, he had uniformly spoken as he had done that day. On the first day of the session he had opposed the Government, because they seemed unwilling to give information. "There," he continued, "the matter rested until his Majesty's servants thought proper to give me the information I thought necessary to direct me in my future conduct. They were pleased to repose a confidence in me which I hope and trust I shall never abuse, and which perfectly satisfied me that their views were founded in wisdom, and were directed to such objects as promised to ensure the most happy and desirable termination of the present unhappy dispute. Thus convinced of the rectitude and wisdom of the Administration, I accepted the place I now enjoy; but on no other terms than those I have mentioned.

"I have always acted, and shall continue to

act, on the most conscientious motives, and on reasons of the most perfect conviction. I have never swerved from my integrity in a single instance. I received the place I have been appointed to as a mark of his Majesty's most gracious inclinations towards me. I have always looked upon it, in point of emolument, as a matter of very trivial consideration. My fortune is too considerable for me to regard it in any other light. I did not seek it; I did not act the servile part of stooping to beg for it; and I think I have a right not to be included among such as do, for I shall never sacrifice my opinions to any personal or private consideration." He then commented strongly on the speech of the Duke of Richmond, and concluded by saying: "I perfectly coincide in the opinion of Cicero, who was an actor in the scenes immediately preceding the destruction of the liberties of Rome, that a licentious use of liberty is totally destructive of its essence. His expression was extremely applicable to the present occasion—*immoderata licentia conscionis.*" The Earl of Denbigh supported him, the Duke of Richmond made an exculpatory reply, and a stormy debate was closed by a division, which resulted in the second reading of the bill being carried by seventy-eight votes against nineteen.

The part taken by Lord Lyttelton in the preliminaries to the famous trial of the Duchess of Kingston for bigamy, and the ill-natured, if not untruthful, remarks of Horace Walpole thereon, render desirable a brief sketch of that lady's remarkable career. She was the daughter of Colonel Chudleigh, who died while she was very young, and at the age of eighteen obtained the appointment of a maid of honour to the Princess of Wales. Her beauty, accomplishments, and agreeable manners procured her many admirers, among whom was the Duke of Hamilton, who pressed his suit with so much fervour that she consented to become his wife on his return from a Continental tour, for which he started in 1741. During his absence Miss Chudleigh became acquainted with Captain Hervey, son of the Earl of Bristol, and, though she at first disliked him, she was induced to accept him by the warmth and assiduity of his intentions, and the base conduct of an aunt named Hanmer, with whom she was then living, and who intercepted the letters of the Duke of Hamilton. Hervey, being dependent on his father, it was agreed that the marriage should be a secret one, and the occasion of a visit made by the parties to the house of a friend named Merrill, near Winchester, was availed of for its performance by the rector of the parish, whose name was Ames, in the presence of Mrs. Hanmer, a gentleman named Mountney, and a servant of the former named Ann Cradock. Hervey joined his ship a few days afterwards, and the bride, returning to London, plunged into a vortex of pleasure with such indifference to appearances and consequences that her reputation soon became questionable.

On the return of the Duke of Hamilton from the Continent, an interview took place, which led to the discovery of Mrs. Hanmer's treachery, greatly to the anger and mortification of Mrs. Hervey. The duke soon afterwards married one of the celebrated Misses Gunning, and the mortified and disappointed Mrs. Hervey, between whom and her husband mutual disgust had arisen, participated in the gaieties and dissipation of the fashionable world more recklessly than ever. Burning to release herself from the bonds of marriage, and living in continual fear of dismissal from her appointment at Court, she was not long in finding the means of accomplishing her purpose. Having ascertained that Ames was dead, she obtained permission to inspect the register of marriages, and, whilst the clerk's attention was temporarily diverted from her, she tore out the leaf containing the entry of her marriage. The fraud had not been committed long before she had reason to regret it. Her husband succeeded to the title and estates of his father, and she found that, after losing the chance of becoming a duchess by the wrong-doing of another, she had deprived herself of the rank of countess by a fraudulent act of her own. Her mischances in this respect did not end here, for she had no sooner bribed the clerk to re-insert the leaf she had torn from the register than she received an offer of marriage from the Duke of Kingston.

After failing in several attempts to procure the mutilation of the register a second time, she cohabited for several years with her ducal lover, observing, however, all the outward appearances of decorum and propriety. These relations were so irksome to both parties, however, that the duke, having been made acquainted with the lady's position, used every effort to induce the Earl of Bristol to become a consenting party to proceedings for the purpose of annulling the marriage. For some time the earl hesitated, but at length he consented, and, after eminent lawyers had been consulted, a jactitation suit was instituted. The earl purposely failing to substantiate the marriage, the Ecclesiastical Court pronounced it null and void, and the parties were advised that this decree could not be disturbed. Under this impression, the marriage of the Duke of Kingston and Miss Chudleigh was publicly solemnised, and, for a few years, the lady was one of the most brilliant stars of the fashionable world.

Her husband died in 1775, bequeathing the income of his estates, which were not entailed, to the duchess during her life, if she remained unmarried; and the reversion to a younger nephew, to the exclusion of an older one. About this time, Ann Cradock, being in pecuniary distress, applied to the duchess for relief, and, being refused any assistance, went to the late duke's eldest nephew, and communicated to him all she knew of the dowager's secret marriage in 1744. A bill of indictment for bigamy was immediately preferred against the duchess, and, being found a true one, notice was given to her solicitor, and sent through him to Rome, whither she had gone immediately after her husband's funeral, calling upon her grace to plead to the indictment, or suffer a judgment of outlawry. The duchess immediately returned to England, where, owing to her rank, and the position she had long held in society, the charge against her had created an extraordinary degree of excitement.

The House of Lords determined that she should be tried by that assembly, but there was a difference of opinion among their lordships, as to whether the trial should take place in the Parliament Chamber or in Westminster Hall. The Earl of Mansfield stated that there was no precedent for such a trial in a case of felony, and opposed it on the grounds of its inconvenience and its costliness, at the same time expressing the opinion that the offence of the duchess was as venial as the consequences of the trial would be unimportant. Lord Lyttelton held a very different view of the matter. "I think," he said, "that the offence is one of the most atrocious nature, tending directly to dissolve the bands of civil society." He contended that the duchess should be tried with every possible solemnity.

"His lordship," he said, referring to the Earl of Mansfield, "seems of opinion that the solemnity of the trial cannot operate by way of example on persons of inferior rank. I think that it will. I think that it will teach the public at large, that the highest are not exempt from punishment, if they transgress the laws; and it will likewise convince them that, as the laws of their country are their common security, so are they the common avengers of every species of guilt and injustice, be the rank or fortune of the offenders what it may. The learned lord, in speaking of the suit instituted in the Chancery Court, says that that

Court is restricted in its judicial proceedings by the Ecclesiastical Court, which has declared the marriage void. Now, my lords, if that sentence should come out to have been procured by collusion and imposition, that is another cogent reason for sifting the matter to the bottom; for what would be the probable consequences of leaving it in the power of parties to dissolve the marriage by such collusive management as this? That, by previous agreement, instituting a cause of jactitation, where only such evidence appears as the parties think fit to produce, the Ecclesiastical Court gives sentence, and the parties are at liberty to marry again. If the lady, in such a case, should have children, the law is defeated, the true line of legal descent broken, and the next heir robbed at once of his honours and estate, by the introduction of spurious issue. This, my lords, is a matter that requires your most serious consideration. For anything that your lordships know, or can venture to foretell, if this matter be not now properly scrutinised, in twenty years it may again present itself in a different form. We may be called upon to decide on the rights of different claimants for those honours." He concluded a very telling speech as follows: "On the whole, my lords, I most sincerely wish that this affair may be fully and fairly investigated;

that the trial may be in the most public manner, accompanied with every possible solemnity; and that it may not prevail in general that this House, departing from its duty, and its known love of justice, should choose to huddle the affair up by having no, or very few, witnesses to their proceedings, and the grounds of their determination."

The Earl of Mansfield replied that the Marriage Act would obviate such inconveniences as Lord Lyttelton apprehended; but, on this view being opposed by the Earl of Sandwich, he acknowledged that the Marriage Act would be a safeguard only as a general rule to which there might be exceptions. The result of this debate, which took place on the 12th of December, was that the House decided that the Duchess of Kingston should, on surrendering to her bail, be taken into the custody of the Usher of the Black Rod; but dissented to the proposition that she should be conveyed to the Tower at the close of each day's proceedings. On the 14th a resolution was moved by Lord Dudley that the trial should take place in Westminster Hall.

This was opposed by the Earl of Marchmont, and supported by Lord Lyttelton. "I think it incumbent on your lordships," the latter observed, "to make the trial as public as possible. Places where justice is administered should be open to the eye of the public. What would be the case here? There would be room for only twenty or thirty persons. This, in my opinion, would be establishing a very dangerous precedent, which might materially affect this House, your lordships' posterity, and the whole body of the British peerage. A time might come when a peer might be brought to trial at this bar, when only the same number would be admitted, and care might be taken to occupy the room with persons admitted on purpose to misrepresent what took place, which would deprive the peerage of the privilege of a fair, indifferent, and open trial. The noble earl, who has produced so many precedents, has drawn them from times very unfavourable to public liberty and true constitutional government. He has taken them from the time of Charles I. I trust that the principles of the Parliament in those times were as opposite to the present as the disposition of that mistaken tyrant was to that of his present Majesty."* He concluded by suggesting a verbal amendment of the

---

* The first portion of this sentence seems to have been badly reported. The extract is given as the passage stands in Hansard's "Parliamentary History." The speech, as there reported, does not support the assertion of Horace Walpole, in a letter to Horace Mann, that "Lord Lyttelton, as bashful as herself, said that, as she

resolution, and, Lord Dudley consenting thereto, the motion was agreed to by the House.

So much was the public mind excited by the forthcoming trial—the trial of a duchess for bigamy being without a precedent in our criminal records—that Foote, then lessee of the Little Theatre in the Haymarket, conceived the idea of making the Duchess of Kingston figure in "A Trip to Calais," under the name and style of Lady Kitty Crocodile. He probably thought that its suppression would serve his purpose as well as its production, for he read the play to the duchess, and met her expressions of indignation with an offer to abandon the idea on condition of receiving from her Grace the sum of two thousand guineas! The magnitude of the demand staggered the duchess, as it well might; but, rather than be held up to public scorn and ridicule, she offered the comedian a cheque for sixteen hundred guineas. Encouraged by this offer to persist in his scandalous demand, Foote refused to abate a single guinea; but his resolve to produce the play was rendered nugatory by the refusal of the Lord Chamberlain to sanction

---

could not pretend to chastity or modesty, there was no room for compassion." It is exceedingly unlikely that Lord Lyttelton used such language; but Walpole often repeated as facts the gossip that reached him at Strawberry Hill.

its performance. He threatened to print it; but, finding that he would, by so doing, render himself liable to an action for libel, he abandoned that design also. He then offered to compromise the matter for the sum offered by the duchess; but her Grace, having, in the meantime, consulted her legal adviser on the subject, refused to comply with the extortionate demand, and turned the tables upon the actor by publishing the whole of the correspondence.

The trial came on in Westminster Hall on the 15th of April, 1776, the accused having petitioned the House of Lords for delay, on the ground of indisposition. Lord Lyttelton presented the petition, which was supported by the certificate of her Grace's physician; and this fact, which is recorded by Hansard, would be sufficient ground of presumption, if any such evidence could be needed, that his lordship was guiltless of the coarse and unfeeling remark attributed to him by Horace Walpole. The Queen, the princesses, and other members of the royal family, many of the foreign ambassadors, and a great number of the nobility, were present during the trial. Ann Cradock was the principal witness for the prosecution, proving the first marriage and its consummation; but admitted that she had been influenced by pecuniary considerations in accusing the duchess. A gentleman named Hawkins deposed that the accused had, on one occasion, informed him that she was very unhappy, on account of a jactitation suit which she had instituted against Captain Hervey, and which would oblige her to disavow her marriage upon oath. On a subsequent occasion she informed him that she had obtained a decree in her favour, and upon his asking her how she had got over the oath, she replied that the circumstances of her marriage were so blended with falsities that she had easily reconciled her conscience to the matter, since the ceremony was of such a loose and scrambling character that she could as safely swear that she was *not* as that she *was* married.

The duchess conducted her defence personally, reading a statement that she considered herself a single woman when she married the Duke of Kingston; that, influenced by her love for him, she had instituted a suit in the Ecclesiastical Court, which had decreed her supposed marriage with Captain Hervey to be null and void; and that she had since experienced every mark of esteem from her late mistress, the Dowager Princess of Wales, and been everywhere received and recognised as Duchess of Kingston. After calling some witnesses to rebut the evidence of Ann Cradock, in which she did not succeed, she was removed from the bar, and the peers deliberated. Then she was recalled, and informed that their lordships had found her guilty. Upon being asked if she could allege any reason why judgment should not be pronounced upon her, she handed in a paper containing the words: " I plead the privilege of the peerage."

After some further deliberation, the Lord High Steward informed her that their lordships admitted the plea, and that she would be discharged on payment of the usual fees. The duchess, who had been calm and self-possessed throughout the trial, thereupon fainted, and was carried out of the hall by her chaplain and physician, and the ladies who attended her. She retired to Calais with the title of Countess of Bristol, and resided in France until her death in 1796, remaining in possession of the large income bequeathed to her by the Duke of Kingston, whose will was confirmed by the Court of Chancery, notwithstanding all the efforts made to set it aside.

CHAPTER X.

Speech on the Proposal of the Duke of Richmond to Countermand the March of the German Troops—Debate on the Duke of Grafton's Motion for Conciliatory Measures—Lord Lyttelton's Speech—Letter on the American Question—Visit to the "Justitia" hulk—Anecdote of David Hume—Letter on his Political Position—Lord Lyttelton's Double Life—His Opinion of Literary Ladies—Mrs. Montague and Miss Carter—Gambling Debts of the Damers and the Foleys—Suicide of John Damer—Letters of Horace Walpole, the Earl of Carlisle, and Lord Lyttelton on the subject.

It will probably surprise most of the readers of this biography to learn that, during the years 1774-75, Lord Lyttelton spoke more frequently in the House of Lords than any other member of that assembly, with the single exception of the Duke of Richmond. This statement may, however, be readily substantiated by reference to the pages of Hansard. During the third year of his peerage he spoke less frequently. Besides those which he made on the trial of the Duchess of Kingston, he made only two speeches, according to the Parliamentary chronicler just mentioned;

and both were on the interminable subject of the American difficulty.

On the 15th of March he opposed the motion of the Duke of Richmond for countermanding the march of the Hanoverian and Hessian levies, whose employment, without the consent of Parliament, had been the subject of animated debates in both Houses in the preceding year. He argued that Great Britain must be prepared to relinquish America if she was not determined to use every means to compel the rebellious colonists to submit. "I do not pretend," he said, "to decide, in the present situation of both countries, how far it may be expedient to insist on taxes for the purpose of raising revenue; but we are fully competent to demand them, and able to compel their payment."

On the 14th the Duke of Grafton made another proposition of conciliatory measures, when the Earl of Hillsborough offered an explanation of his share in the measures of the preceding Administration, and especially with respect to the understanding of 1769—that the Americans should not be taxed for revenue. The speech made by Lord Lyttelton on this occasion was chiefly directed to this understanding. "I cannot agree," said he "that any engagement made by any Administration can be binding on your lordships. I cannot conceive that it is in the power of any set of Ministers, however able, to compliment away the inherent rights of the British Parliament. If the power be in Parliament, as I am sure it is, they cannot even themselves surrender it without a manifest breach of trust. I take it to be an original and inalienable right. If so, how much less can Parliament and the nation at large be bound by engagements of this nature made by Ministers? I allow that the right of taxation, which is the leading point in dispute, may, from motives of expediency, be suspended or abstained from; but I contend that it can never be abandoned entirely, because it is essential to the very nature and exercise of civil government." He concluded by repeating what he had said a few days previously — that America must be relinquished or compelled to submit, and that the abandonment of our colonies must not be thought of. The Duke of Grafton's motion was rejected by ninety-one votes against thirty-one.

The American provinces declared themselves independent on the 4th of July, but they were still militarily inferior to the forces sent against them, which now included the Guards and the German levies. Lord Lyttelton informs one of his correspondents, in a letter of this period, that "the Guards are ordered to cross the Atlantic;" but he does not mention George Ayscough's resignation of his commission, in order to avoid accompanying his regiment, which probably had not then been announced. The rumours then in circulation of a project of alliance between France and the United States, concerning which Lord Lyttelton seems to have had good information, are commented upon in this letter as follows:—

"I cannot yet fancy the suspected preliminaries of alliance between France and America, and I will tell you why: because I think it will not be the mutual interest of either of them to engage in such a treaty. The French finances are not in a state to justify the risking a war with England, which an open alliance with America must immediately produce. M. Maupouz and M. Necker, if I am rightly informed, are of the same opinion, and, I believe, from nobler motives and better reasons, are in opposition to those proposals which the Americans are said to have offered to induce France to give an avowed support to their cause. My information goes somewhat farther, and assures me that the opinions of the two statesmen mentioned are supported by all the graver men and old officers in the kingdom.

"America, at present, makes a very powerful and extraordinary resistance, and there seems to be a spirit awakening in her people which will wofully prolong the period of her reduction. The contest is, at present, between a child forced into resistance by what it calls tyranny, and a parent enraged at filial ingratitude, who is resolved to reclaim his offspring by force and chastisement. In such a state, though a mad spirit of rebellion may instigate revolted children to act against the parent, and the brethren of the house of their parent, the latter will go very reluctantly to the business of bloodshed, and many a brave man will consider the duty of the soldier and the citizen as incompatible, and let the former sink into the latter. But the moment that America flies for protection to the arms of France, the case will be changed; every tie of consanguinity will then be broken; it will be impossible to distinguish between them and their allies, they will be all the object of one common resentment, and the Americans must expect, as they will surely find, an equal exertion against them as will be employed against their insidious supporters."

About this time Lord Lyttelton visited the "Justitia" hulk for the purpose, it seems, of observing personally the working of the system of penal servitude which it exemplified, and of

which he had conceived an unfavourable opinion.
What he saw there shocked him very much,
and confirmed his preconceived opinion of the
results of the system. He had an idea of
endeavouring to ameliorate the condition of the
convicts, if not to procure the abolition of the
system, and he communicated his impressions
and notions of the subject to a friend in the
letter from which the following passage is extracted :—

"I have been to see the 'Justitia' hulk, where,
among many other miserables, I saw poor Dignam
wear the habit of a slave. He seemed disposed to
speak to me, but I had previously desired the
superintendent to request him, since it was not
in my power to do him service, to waive all appearance of his having known me. This mode of
punishment offers a very shocking spectacle, and,
I think, must undergo some alleviation, if it be
not entirely abolished. If it were to come again
before Parliament, I should give the subject a
very serious consideration, and the measure a
very serious opposition. Is it not extraordinary
that the first public exhibition of slavery in this
kingdom—for so it is, however the situation may
be qualified by law—should be suggested by a
Scotchman, and that the first regulator of this

miserable business should be from the same country? I do not mean to throw out any unpleasant ideas concerning anyone whose lot it was to be born on the other side of the Tweed, but merely to state a fact for your observation.

"I have known many of my northern fellow-subjects, and esteemed them. David Hume possesses my sincere admiration; but, though the object of his writings was to remove prejudices, he himself possessed the strongest in favour of his country, and was, as is the great weakness of Scotchmen, so jealous of its honour that I gave him great offence at Lord Hertford's, at Ragley, by asking him at what time of the year the harvest was housed in Scotland. My question arose from an innocent desire of being satisfied in that particular, but he conceived it to convey a suspicion that there was no harvest—or at least no barns—in his country, and his answer was slight and churlish.

"Fare you well! If you hear anything on the Continent that at all concerns the present state of public affairs, I beg you will not fail to favour me with the most early communication."

It was thought, by the best friends of Lord Lyttelton, that he was not yet in the position to which his talents entitled him, and that his succession to a post of active duties would at once serve the State, and withdraw him more completely from pursuits and associations which still prevented him from rising above the fog of an ill repute, into the purer and brighter region in which both his talents and his many good qualities so eminently qualified him to shine. It was urged upon him, by one of these friends, that he should resign the sinecure office of Chief Justice in Eyre, on receiving a Secretaryship, which there can be no doubt would have been offered him, if he had chosen to intimate his disposition to accept such an office. But he was not at that time so disposed, and in the following letter he states his reasons for his indisposition to public business very fully and clearly, and in a manner that throws considerable light upon his character :—

"You must confess, as I am sure you very well know, that one of the great arts, if not the principal one, in acquiring a reputation, as well as preserving it, is to know the extent of our genius, what objects are most suitable to it, in what track its propensities should be conducted, and what point to place the limits beyond which it must venture with caution, as well as the *ne plus ultra*, whose barriers it must not venture to pass. The man who possesses this knowledge, and acts according to the dictates of it, will not fail to make a respectable figure in any station, and with any talents; but in a high station, and with great talents, he may be secure of familiarising his name with future ages.

"Ambition, an ardent and specious child of self-love, continually urges men to pursue objects beyond their reach. Avarice, an horrid unnatural cub of the same origin, and a disgrace to it, takes a track which reason disdains and honour must condemn to satisfy its desires. Envy delights itself in obstructing the prosperous career of others; and folly, dreaming of what it cannot possess, will aim at the wreath of wisdom. In short, an ignorance of ourselves, from whatever cause it may proceed, whether from passion or want of reflection, is the origin of all our mistakes in private as well as public life. In the former, the mischief may be of the narrow extent; but in the latter the evil may affect, not only the people, but every quarter of the globe. The grand source of that glory which shone, and will continue to shine, on Mr. Pitt's administration of this country, till the annals of it are no more, was a right application of means to ends, and, among others, of employing men according to the nature and tendency of their characters and talents. You must perceive the drift of my argument; that it leads to the defence of my public political conduct since I have succeeded to my office in the Constitution.

"You tell me of application to business, and of throwing aside a golden sinecure, as disgraceful to a real patriot. You counsel me, in the most flattering manner, to claim an arduous post of Government, and, by a vigilant attention to its duties, to make a better return for the emoluments of office than half-a-dozen flowery orations in Parliament during a winter's session, which are, in your opinion, sufficiently rewarded by the gratifications of my own vanity. This, I must acknowledge, is coming at once, and without ceremony, to the point; but think for a moment, and ask yourself, what kind of figure I should make at the desk. Can you imagine that it is in my nature, and of course in my capacity, to bear the oppression of such multifarious and eternal business as must claim the attention of an eminent official statesman?

"The admirable structure of the British Constitution, its commerce, its interests, and its alliances, have been the objects of my serious inquiry and attentive consideration. I take continual occasion to watch the changing scene of its political movements. I form, with much thought, my opinions upon them. I deliver those opinions, in my senatorial capacity, to the world—not from the suggestions of a giddy hour or from the spur of momentary vanity, but from curious research, ardent reflection, and deliberate preparation. To this point my talents, such as they are, must be directed; and by having given them, in some degree, their natural direction, I have acquired a political reputation which would be lost in contempt and derision were they to be employed in the routine of official employment and the perplexities of Ministerial duty. Besides, if there be anything which requires a more than vestal's vigilance, it is the guidance of a principal wheel in the machine of our Government; and such a continual attention is foreign to my nature. I might, perhaps, possess it for a certain time, and apply it with zeal—may I not add with reputation?—but my existence would be insupportable, if the intervals of relaxation did not frequently relieve me, when I might retire

> "'To sport with Amaryllis in the shade,
> Or with the tangles of Neœra's hair.'

"There is a certain degree of phlegm absolutely necessary to the well-being of society; but I possess not an atom of it. There is also an ardour of mind that leads to national as well as personal greatness, nor am I without an active flame of it; but it burns by flashes, and possesses me only in common with other contending passions, which, in their turn, command my obedience, and are obeyed. Suffer the stream, I beseech you, to flow in those channels which nature has designed for it: let it pass on, sometimes in foaming eddies, and sometimes with a tranquil wave; be content to watch its progress; and, though it may now force its angry passage through the divided mountain, your eye may soon behold its crystal surface reflect the golden harvests and flowery meadows. But, should its natural course be changed, it would be quickly lost in bog and morass; nor ever grow into that extent and grandeur of waters which many rivulets attain before they reach the ocean.

"Is there not, in my own family, an immediate circumstance of ridicule which comes in aid of my argument? My father, who made a respectable figure as a senator in both Houses of Parliament, and possessed that theoretic political erudition which constituted him an able counsellor of the State, was incapable, as you very well know, of *counting twenty pounds*, if thrown in a promiscuous heap of the different British coins—nevertheless, he was appointed to preside at the

Exchequer, to contrive ways and means, and to run through the combinations of finance, without the knowledge of arithmetic which is necessary to an overseer of the poor. And what was the consequence? The whole nation was upon the titter during his short-lived administration; nor does any visitor of Hagley House pass through the room which is adorned with the Exchequer strong-box but beholds the empty badge and sad memorial of his Ministerial honours with a significant look of wonder or shrug of disappointment.

"The sage physician endeavours to meliorate, but not to change, the constitution of his patient, and infuses, by degrees, those wholesome aids which may help to lessen its infirmities. The same wise conduct should be pursued in the case of mental health; and to aim at turning the natural bent of genius is an application of moral quackery which will destroy all fervour of ability, administer an opiate to the faculties of the mind, bring on apathy and torpor, and destroy all intellectual nerve for ever. Adieu."

This seems to be the proper place in which to offer some remarks upon the double life which Lord Lyttelton lived during the three years which, at this time, had elapsed since the death of his father. He was in his thirtieth year when that event occurred, and the greater part of the preceding ten years of his life had been passed abroad. The cloud of paternal displeasure and social proscription covered him, with only two or three brief glimpses of moral sunshine, such as he was favoured with on the occasion of a speech in the House of Commons, on his return from his second Continental tour, and on his marriage. His family, and society in general, regarded him as a reprobate, from whom nothing better was to be expected than that he would break his father's heart, gamble away his patrimony, and die " in the worst inn's worst room," if not in a prison. In a letter which seems to be of that period he mentions some of the prophecies concerning him which were then indulged in :—

" I cannot bring it within the compass of my belief that H—— has escaped your recollection; however, I shall be able to restore it to its proper tone in a moment, by mentioning an ode addressed by him to me on the subject of gaming. You admired it too much to have forgot the author; and it now occurs to me, that you, or some one in the company, rehearsed on the occasion a long string of laughable Eton and Oxford anecdotes concerning him; nay, the very last time we were together you sarcastically repeated to me some of his vaticinations on my impetuous attachment to play, and kindly foretold the completion of them. After all, I believe you are either laughing at me, or pretending ignorance of my bard, in order to have an hash of the same dish which you are pleased to say delighted you so much in my last letter.

"Was it not you, or do I dream, who was so charmed with that part of his poem where he describes my being so reduced by gaming as to be obliged to sell Hagley, and supposes the estate to be bought by the descendant of some felon who was reprieved from death to transportation by my ancestor the judge, whose picture he tears down from the wall, as a sight disgusting to him? I am not certain as to the correctness of my recollection, but the lines are, I believe, to the following effect:—

> "'Shall some unfeeling stranger reign
> Within that blest domain?
> Some convict's spawn, by thy forefather's breath,
> Perchance, reprieved from death?
> Whilst thou, self-banished, self-enslaved, shalt roam,
> Without a friend or home!
> Still shall he tremble at the judge's frown,
> And, fraught with spite, tear down,
> From the repining wall, his venerable shade!"

None of the prophecies of that period were fulfilled. Lord Lyttelton neither broke his father's heart, gambled away his patrimony, or ended his days miserably. The first period of his life—the period during which he did most to earn the censure of the world—came to an end with his succession to rank and wealth; and the interval between his father's death and the time to which his biography has now been brought down, constituted the dual existence to which attention has been invited.

There were two spheres in which, at this time, Lord Lyttelton moved and shone. One comprised the best society of the day, whether with regard to the moral character or the intellectual capacity of the individuals of whom it was composed. With Earl Temple and the Earl of Chatham, with Fox, and Burke, and Windham, with Mrs. Montagu and the more celebrated Elizabeth Carter, he was on terms of the warmest friendship. "I am not," he wrote in a letter to a friend, "very partial to literary ladies; they are, generally, of an impertinent, encroaching disposition, and almost always bring to my mind the female astronomer, who, after applying her nocturnal telescope for a long series of months, and raising the jealousy, as well as the expectations, of the male star-gazers, declared her only object was to discover if there were *men* in the moon." But of Mrs. Montagu and Miss Carter he always spoke in the highest terms of praise, and it will probably surprise those whose estimate of his character has been formed from the gossip of his own day, as recorded in the letters of Horace Walpole and the memoirs of Sir Nathaniel Wraxall, to learn that, of those two ladies, so similar in some points of their character, and so dissimilar in others, he preferred the latter.

"The one," said he, "is an highly instructed, accomplished woman, possessed of great affluence, who indulges herself in a chaste display of fashionable as well as literary elegance, makes her drawing-room the Lyceum of the day, maintains a luxurious hospitality for the votaries of the science which she loves, and patronises the learning which she has herself adorned. The other, in a state of contented mediocrity, is humble as though she knew nothing, while she is not only the most learned woman of any age, but one of the most learned persons of that in which she lives. The pure, sublime genius, which never swerves from virtue, accompanies her in her path of rigid discretion, and is contented to slumber while its favourite votary is employed in the daily, habitual exercise of domestic duties."

Pennington says that Elizabeth Carter admired Lord Lyttelton's talents as much as she deplored his vices, of which neither the lady nor her reverend biographer are likely to have known more than was rumoured, and which Rumour's hundred tongues multiplied and exaggerated. His private life does not appear to have been at this time worse than that of any other celibate of the age, though he incurred the remonstrances of his friends by continuing to admit to his intimacy men forming the lower circle, in which he had what has been alluded to as his second life. His reply to a letter of remonstrance which one of his friends addressed to him on this subject reveals the motives by which he was influenced in allowing his house to remain open to men whose intimacy with him had been the subject of Earl Temple's friendly hint to him three years previously. Few of the letters received by Lord Lyttelton have been preserved; probably the greater part were destroyed by his executors, if, indeed, they were in existence at his death. The names of the persons referred to in the following letter are therefore unknown, they cannot even be conjectured, for Chase Price and William Combe cannot be said to have been "outcasts from all other society." The former associated, on terms of intimacy, with Charles Townshend and George Selwyn, and the latter is mentioned by Rogers and Moore, in their diaries, as among the guests at the evening party at which Lord Lyttelton is said to have insulted Lady Archer.

"My dear Sir,—Your letters to me are those of friendship. Under the impression of this sentiment I at all times receive them; nevertheless they are attended with this disagreeable circumstance, that in my answers to them I am so often obliged to make myself the hero of my own tale.

"Your last charge has a foundation in truth; and the persons you name as being in the circle of my intimacy are received at my house and admitted to my table. You tell me it is not only a dishonour but a crime to herd with such men as familiar associates, and that it is beneath a rational being to receive these outcasts from all other society into mine, merely to be flattered by their submission, to have base engines of my pleasures, or objects for that raillery which will not be returned. It is too true that I cannot altogether combat the force of these very severe observations, but let me persuade you to bestow any small portion of your leisure on the volume of human nature, to take a short review of human failings, and then to cast your eye upon that page whereon my name is written. You will there discover that my character is divided between an ardent desire of applause and a more than equal love of pleasure; and, on this discovery, your considerate regard will look with less severity upon me.

"When you have done me this justice, proceed, I beseech you, one step farther; examine the world upon my subject, and you will know what confirmed prejudices it possesses against me,—that I am the continual victim of its injustice, and that, not contented to blazon forth my defects and follies into a false, unnatural magnitude, it seems pleased with the malignant task of fabricating tales to my dishonour. Public opinion aims at excluding me from a familiar intercourse with men of virtuous life and women of chaste manners: so that when I appear, even in general society, mothers seem to be alarmed for their daughters, husbands for their wives, and fathers for their sons: nay, the very impures of the town have refused my most generous offers, from an apprehension of my capacity for mischief. I will freely own that my life has been marked with an extravagance of dissipation; but neither the force of my passions, &c., nor their success, though, viciously speaking, I might be vain of the latter can justify these violent and continual fears of me.

"But let us suppose for a moment that this

most prodigal of all prodigals should meditate a reformation, and begin the salutary work with the favourable omen of shutting his doors against those vagabonds, to use your own expression, whom you accuse him of suffering to enter them. If, in the arduous task of winning the forfeited esteem of mankind, I should begin with paying my court to the lights of the Church, and beg their sanction to my infant repentance, those holy men would not only suspect the sincerity of my declarations, but do my effrontery the credit to believe that, under the semblance of contrition, I was meditating some unholy impertinence to the sacred lawn. Permit me to continue the singular idea, and suppose me commencing my round of episcopal visits with one of the first characters of this age and nation, the present Bishop of London. After some hesitation on the part of my coachman, you may imagine me at his lordship's gate, where it cannot be supposed that I should find admittance. But this is not all. Mrs. Lowth would probably throw my visiting-card into the fire, and forbid the porter to enter my name in his book; while the right reverend prelate would determine to take the opportunity of some debate in the House of Lords, wherein I might be engaged, to satisfy his politeness as a gentleman by leaving his name at my door, without any apprehension of being admitted within it.

"What! would you have me wander, a solitary being, through the world, too bad for the good, and too good for the bad? My whole nature shudders at the idea, and I should perish in the attempt. I love superiority, flattery, and ease; and the society which you condemn affords me the threefold gratification. You will tell me that it consists of dishonourable men: in the common sense of the term, you may be right; but *dulcibus abundant vitiis*; and, as bad instruments in the hands of agreeable performers make a pleasant concert, so these characters compose an amusing society. With them I am under no restraint; they know the history of the day; some of them also are well accomplished; and, while they play upon one another, I can play upon them all. Besides, coffee may be ordered at whatever hour I please, without an opposing look; and, while I confer honour, I enjoy convenience.

"You will, perhaps, be disposed to inquire if I think it worthy of me, in the phrase of vulgar tongues, to enjoy the character of *king of the company*? The love of rule, my dear sir, is, more or less, the inmate of every breast; it is allied to all the pre-eminent virtues, and the greatest men have owed their greatness to it. Cæsar declared that the first office of a village was preferable to the second station in the Roman world. Whitfield, I believe, would not have exchanged his tabernacle for a metropolitan diocese. Zinzendorf, amid the submission of his Moravian followers, looked down with pity on despotic empire; nor, in the government of my Pandemonium, do I envy all the didactic honours of your Lyceum.

"It may be an opinion which proceeds from a dissolute refinement, but it is mine, that pleasure is not pleasure, if difficulties are necessary to its enjoyment. I wish, as it were, to have it brought home to me, without my stirring across the threshold. My taste for gratification is like their piety who erect chapels in their houses; it makes a domestic priesthood necessary to me, and, while the persons who compose it are zealous in their functions, I shall look no farther. The circumstances of my past life have produced the colour of the present moment; a future period may receive another hue. The events in every passing hour, in characters such as mine, as well as in others which are supposed to be much better, must furnish the tints. Experience may do something in my favour, your friendly oracles may do more; the calls of public duty may have their effect. To conclude, *time and chance happen unto all men*; and, through their influence, the hour may arrive when prelates will eat my soup without fear of contamination, and modest women admit me to their society without apprehending a loss of reputation. Do not be angry with me, I beseech you; it is impossible to treat the subject otherwise: and, if I might add another petition to the many you have already so kindly granted, let me entreat you to give our correspondence a more pleasing and profitable subject than the failings of your very sincere and obliged friend,

"LYTTELTON."

It will be observed that, in this letter, Lord Lyttelton refers to his "extravagance of dissipation" in the past tense; we seem to be approaching the turning-point of his life. Occupation, experience, observation, all tended to bring about amendment. If a frightful example was needed, a warning was given him in the case of John Damer. This gentleman — his schoolfellow at Eton, and his companion in Italy—had married, in 1767, the only daughter of General Conway, without being weaned by marriage from the moral aberrations of his bachelorhood. Horace Walpole, in a letter to Sir Horace Mann, sounds the first note of the overture to the tragedy which made the great sensation of the fashionable world in the summer of 1776.

"I have been much alarmed lately," writes the gossip of Strawberry Hill, "about General Conway, who, by a sudden cold, had something of a paralytic stroke in the face; but, as it did not affect his speech or health, and is almost disappeared, I am much easier. He is uneasy himself, with reason, about his daughter. Her husband and his two brothers have contracted a debt—one can scarcely expect to be believed out of England—of seventy thousand pounds! Who but must think himself happy to marry a daughter with only ten thousand pounds to a young man with five thousand a year rent-charge in present, and twenty-two thousand a year settled? And yet this daughter at present is ruined! Her behaviour is such as her father's would be; she does not only not complain, but desires her very own jewels may be sold. The young men of this age seem to have made a law among themselves for declaring their fathers superannuated at fifty, and then dispose of the estates, as if already their own. How culpable to society was Lord Holland for setting an example of paying such enormous, such gigantic debts! Can you believe that Lord Foley's two sons have borrowed money so extravagantly that the interest they have contracted to pay amounts to eighteen thousand a year? I write the sum at length, lest you should think I have mistaken and set down two or three figures too much."

Only four days after this letter was written, John Damer committed suicide, and Walpole communicated the intelligence of the sad and startling event to the Countess of Ossory in a letter, from which the following is an extract :—

"To-day I have heard the shocking news of Mr. Damer's death, who shot himself yesterday, at three o'clock in the morning, at a tavern in Covent Garden. My first alarm was for Mr. Conway, not knowing what effect such a horrid surprise would have on him, scarce recovered from an attack himself; happily it proves his nerves were not affected, for I have had a very calm letter from him on the occasion. They have sent for me to town, and I shall go to-morrow morning. Mr. Charles Fox, with infinite good nature, met Mrs. Damer coming to town, and stopped her to prepare her for the dismal event. It is almost impossible to refrain from bursting out into commonplace reflections on this occasion; but can the walls of Almack's help moralising when five thousand a year in present and twenty-two thousand in reversion are not sufficient for happiness, and cannot check a pistol!"

The terrible story was continued by the writer a few days later in a letter to Sir Horace Mann:—

"He and his two brothers most unexpectedly notified to their father that they owed above seventy thousand pounds. The proud lord, for once in the right, refused to pay the debt or to see them. The two eldest were to retire to France, and Mrs. Damer was to accompany them without a murmur, and with the approbation, though to the great grief, of Mr. Conway and Lady Ailesbury. She was luckily gone to take leave of them, and to return to town last Friday morning. On Thursday, Mr. Damer supped at the 'Bedford Arms,' Covent Garden, with four common women, a blind fiddler, and no other man. At three in the morning he dismissed his seraglio, bidding each receive her guinea at the bar, and ordering Orpheus to come up again in half an hour. When he returned he found dead silence, and smelt gunpowder. He called, the master of the house came up, and found Mr. Damer sitting in his chair dead, with a pistol by him, and another in his pocket! The ball had not gone through his head, nor made any report. On the table lay a scrap of paper, with these words—'The people of the house are not to blame for what has happened, which was my own act!' This was the sole tribute he paid to justice and decency.

"What a catastrophe for a man of thirty-two, heir to twenty-two thousand a year! We are persuaded lunacy, not distress, was the sole cause of his fate. He has often, and even at supper that night, hinted at such an exploit—the very reason why one should not expect it. His brothers have gamed—he never did. He was grave, cool, reasonable, and reserved; but passed his life as he died, with troops of women and the blind fiddler —an odd companion in such scenes! One good springs out of this evil: the leeches, the Jews, and extortioners will lose very considerably. Lord Milton, whom anything can petrify and nothing soften, will not only not see his remaining sons, but wreaks his fury on Mrs. Damer, though she deserves only pity, and shows no resentment. He insists on selling her jewels, which are magnificent, for discharge of just debts. This is all he can do; she must have her jointure of two thousand five hundred a year."

The suicide of John Damer created a profound sensation. It did not, like the trial of the Duchess of Kingston, a few months before, merely provoke curiosity, and gratify the lovers of scandal; it impressed the votaries of pleasure, and all the gay world of fashion and frivolity, with a feeling which caused the event to be spoken of with bated breath and paled cheeks. For several days the terrible story was in everyone's lips. The Earl of Carlisle wrote of it to George Selwyn as follows:—

"What were Mr. Damer's motives for so dreadful an act? There was no man more indifferent to me, but the account shocked me extremely. It is a bad example to others in misery. It makes people think of having recourse to that method of finishing their calamities, without which perhaps it had never entered their heads. If it were not so selfish an action, it would be difficult, I think, to condemn it in some cases. There never appeared anything like madness in him, yet the company he kept seemed indeed but a bad preparation for eternity."

How Lord Lyttelton received the intelligence of Damer's death may be inferred from the following letter, which probably does not, however, express all that he felt :—

"I shall expect you with impatience, and am much flattered that you can leave the society of your friend C—— for the sake of yielding to my solicitations. Is it beyond the reach of your influence to persuade him to accompany you? I am apprehensive that he may have some scruples in being a guest of mine; but, if he will accord me that honour, I will assume the virtue, though I have it not, and he shall find nothing *chez moi* which shall give the least offence to the tranquil purity of his character. Perhaps you will be my guarantee on the occasion. We were at Eton together, though not in any particular intimacy; and since that time I had once the pleasure of dining with him. I happened, by chance, to be present when he proposed to give an Etonian dinner: his politeness led him to invite me, and the party was most pleasant and classical. A particular circumstance of it I shall never forget.

"One of the company, who had done honour to his table by indulging a very voracious appetite, when the dessert was served, thought proper to recollect the deficiency of a dish of fish which had been promised him, and, in the true vein of gorged disappointment, reproached your friend for his forgetfulness. The reply was singular, affecting, and, to the best of my recollection, as follows: 'When I met you this morning,' said Mr. C——, 'I was proceeding to Temple Bar for the purpose of expending an allotted trifle on a turbot; but, a few minutes after, I received an unwilling application from a very distressed person, to whom a guinea was far more necessary than the addition of one particular dish to a plentiful dinner would be to you, and you very well know the strict regulations of my exchequer. It is true,' continued he, 'that you have lost your fish; but it is equally true that, from the same cause, a poor unfortunate fellow-creature has lost his despair. Besides, the relish of the turbot must have long been superseded on your palate, and I have added a pleasure to my heart which will last for ever.' He expressed himself with much more ease and simplicity than I have done; and I was so affected that, had I then enjoyed my present affluence, I should have instantly subscribed to hospitals, and gone about in search of doing good. But, alas! these thoughts, morally speaking, of my better days have been rendered fruitless in the succession of evil habits;

and I know not where I shall find a restorative, unless the society of your friend shall renew its former influence over me."

"Another circumstance of a very different nature occurs to me from the recollection of that day's pleasure. Poor John Damer was one of the company. He has made a strange exit in a stranger manner. We were at Eton and in Italy together, and at subsequent periods, in the habits of friendly connexion. Few of those who knew him have been more gloomily affected by the melancholy event than myself. I have been informed that the King has exerted his royal influence to prevent the publication of David Hume's posthumous treatise in defence of self-murder. I am well convinced that his Majesty has acted with his accustomed regard to the welfare of his people in procuring the suppression of a work dangerous to society and in direct opposition to evangelical precept; but, for my own part, I cannot conceive that any man, in this period of the world, could ever be argued into putting a willing end to his existence, unless some circumstance of ill-fortune, some malady of the mind, or some torturing disease of the body, more than co-operated with the arguments of the reasoning fatalist. Montesquieu does not write like himself upon the subject; and Rousseau, who seems purposely not to answer his own arguments in favour of suicide, defends it with sentiment instead of reason.

"Many examples are given, in the works of different authors, of amazing coolness in the act of self-destruction, which represent the stroke as having been given in youth, health, and prosperity. I cannot trust to appearances in these or any similar examples; nor can I believe that the *mens sana in corpore sano*, with the comforts of life, ever could submit to an act of such dreadful uncertainty. I have sometimes taken up the argument in favour of self-murder, by way of supporting an opinion, exercising a talent, or convincing a fool; but I will honestly acknowledge that the weakest of my antagonists have ever got the better of me on this subject, though I might not, perhaps, publish my conviction. Virgil's picture of the after misery of those whose hands have given a prematurity to their end would stagger the utmost sophistry of erring reason—

"'Quam vellent æthere in alto
Pauperiem pati et duros perferre labores!'

"Despair, as it arises from very different and opposite causes, has various and distinct appearances. It has its rage, its gloom, and its indifference; and while, under the former, its operations acquire the name of madness, under the latter it bears the title of philosophy. Poor John Damer was no philosopher, and yet he seems to have taken his leap in the dark with the marks both of an epicurean and a stoic. He acted his part with coolness, and sought his preparation in the mirth of a brothel.

"This is an awful subject, and, in casting my eyes over what I have hastily written upon it, I observe some inaccuracies which I should be glad to correct. But it is not my office, nor is it in my pretensions, to instruct you. When you are here, I will amuse you with a pamphlet which, without that particular view, is a complete physical, or rather anatomical, reply to those who defend the right of self-murder. It is a treatise on the 'Ganglions of the Nerves,' by a Dr. Johnstone, a physician in my neighbourhood. It is written with the pen of a scholar, and possesses throughout a most perspicuous ingenuity. This gentleman attended my father in his last illness, and was not only his physician but his confessor."

The last few words of this letter are an

allusion to the fact that it was to Dr. Johnstone that the first Lord Lyttelton, when on his death-bed, acknowledged that he had once held sceptical opinions on the subject of revealed religion.

CHAPTER XI.

Lord Lyttelton's Moral Amendment—Testimony of his Friends—His Thoughts on Scepticism and Revealed Religion—Satirical Reflections on Credulity and Incredulity—Stormy Debate on the Earl of Chatham's Motion against the War—Lord Lyttelton's Profession of Whig Principles—Letter to Lord Westcote—Opposition to raising Troops without Consent of Parliament—Speech on the State of the Country—Defence of the Conciliatory Bills—Speech on the Duke of Richmond's Proposal to withdraw the Troops from America—Strictures on the Earl of Sandwich—Death of the Earl of Chatham—Letter on the Subject—Speech on the Annuity Bill.

LORD LYTTELTON had, shortly after his father's death, desired one of his truest friends not to expect an instant amendment of his life as the first fruits of the opening to him of a public and honourable career. "My amendment," said he, "must be slow and progressive, though, I trust, in the end, sincere and effectual." That this progressive amendment did go on during the three years following his succession to the peerage may be inferred from his active political life during that period, his improved position in society, and the tone of the letters written by him to his most intimate friends. That he was a very different man in 1777, and subsequently, to the gambler and profligate who, prior to his succession to rank and wealth, had been almost an outcast from society, is a fact to which testimony is borne by those who were the most competent to form a judgment upon the matter. The author of the "character" prefixed to his poems testifies to the amendment of his private conduct during the latter years of his life; and Roberts, who says that he "knew him both in his convivial hours and in those which were more rationally employed," assured the world, in the preface to the same work,* "that the goodness of his heart for the last three years of his life became as conspicuous as the excellency of his head."

He had his attention called, about the commencement of what may be termed the third phase of his life, to the arguments of a French deistical writer; and, after an attentive perusal of the volume, wrote as follows to the friend who had recommended it to his notice:—

"I have obeyed your commands, and read,

---

* "Poetical Works of the late Lord Lyttelton." 1780.

with a very continued attention, 'Des Recherches sur le Despotisme Oriental.' The author is a person of considerable erudition, active thought, and lively imagination. He steers his vessel with no common address on the ocean of conjecture, and I have beheld his course with much admiration. But though he may help to forward an advanced progress in infidelity, I cannot flatter him with the supposition that he alone has ever made an infidel. The paradox of primitive theocracies, I believe, is not a new one, though he may have given it a novelty of examination, and branched it forth into a variety of new ramifications. A writer who strikes at the very root of sacred history, which has been an object of faith to so great a part of the more enlightened world for such a course of ages, and possesses the support of collateral tradition, as well as a supernatural strength of internal evidence—such an author, I say, should produce something more than hypothesis, though supported by the most colossal strength of human erudition. Nay, it may not be the least among the many arguments in favour of the sacred writings, that nothing but hypothesis can be brought against them. A faith of some thousand years is not to be destroyed by the elaborate, but artificial, conjectures of a modern infidel. I will oppose to your ingenious Frenchman the learned Mr. Bryant, of our own country, whose late splendid publication* is an honour to our age and nation. The Gallic infidel must sink into nothing before the veteran abilities of our English believer. These casual thoughts, my dear friend, are my own; and you may be assured that I have not stolen them from any pious page of my father's manuscript lucubrations."

To another friend who had written to him on a similar subject, he addressed a letter which contains the following satirical remarks upon the credulity of the age, as a jocose reply to the charge of scepticism:—

"You are pleased in your last letter to charge the present age with the crime of scepticism, and you have abandoned yourself to a more than common energy on the subject. To tell you the truth, I do not very clearly perceive the tendency of your accusation. If it alludes to religion, you would, I think, find some difficulty to maintain your position; if it should glance at politics, our national submission is certainly against you;

---

* "Vindication of the Testimony of Josephus concerning Jesus Christ." 1777.

or, leaving the higher concerns of the world, if you should apply your assertion to the ordinary intercourse and common transactions between man and man, you are truly unfortunate, as an extreme gullibility seems to be one of the leading features of the present times. The age in which we live does not possess so great a share as former centuries of that faith which is able to remove mountains; blind credulity, by the insults it so long offered to reason, has, in a great measure, destroyed itself, or is, rather, become modified into that sobriety of belief which is consistent with a rational being. The gaudy, awful, and presuming phantom of papal authority has long begun to disappear; that blazing meteor, which for so many ages dazzled the superstitious world, verges towards the horizon, and grows pale before the steady embodied light of liberal unimpeded science.

"But I cannot believe, although luxury and dissipation, with their concomitant depravities, have made such enormous strides among the higher orders, that infidelity in religious matters is a leading characteristic of our times. If we turn from the Church to the State, the firm confidence of a very great majority of the people in a Government which, I am forced to confess, does not possess all the wisdom that such a Government ought to possess, is a circumstance which, were I to enlarge upon it, you would be perplexed to answer. In the ordinary transactions of life, the wantonness of commercial credit is well prepared to give the lie direct to any charge of incredulity. Ask Foley, Charles Fox, and a thousand others what they think of modern infidelity, and they will tell you that the Jews themselves, that unbelieving race, have deserted from the standard of scepticism, and, having borne the stigma of spiritual unbelief for upwards of seventeen hundred years, are, at this moment, groaning beneath the effects of temporal credulity.

"*Credula turba sumus*—We are a credulous race of beings; and the most steady professors of scepticism are deceived by others, and deceive themselves, every hour of the day. Religion, which commands, among its evident truths, the belief of matters which we cannot entirely comprehend, will sometimes so habituate the mind of its submissive disciple to acts of faith, that he does not know how to withhold his assent to the most improbable fictions of human fancy; and the *credo quia impossibile est* of Tertullian is readily adopted by his yielding piety. I shall confirm the truth of this observation by a story which I have heard related, and is not more extraordinary in its nature than the tone, look, and language of belief which accompanied the relation.

"A traveller, benighted in a wild and mountainous country (if my recollection does not fail me, in the Highlands of Scotland), at length beholds the welcome light of a neighbouring habitation. He urges his horse towards it; when, instead of a house, he approached a kind of illuminated chapel, from whence issued the most alarming sounds he had ever heard. Though greatly surprised and terrified, he ventured to look through a window of the building, when he was amazed to see a large assembly of cats, who, arranged in solemn order, were lamenting over the corpse of one of their own species, which lay in state, and was surrounded with the various emblems of sovereignty. Alarmed and terrified at this extraordinary spectacle, he hastened from the place with greater eagerness than he had approached it; and arriving, some time after, at the house of a gentleman who never turned the wanderer from his gate, the impressions of what he had seen were so visible on his countenance, that his friendly host inquired into the cause of his anxiety. He accordingly told his story, and, having finished it, a large family cat, who had lain, during the narrative, before the fire, immediately started up, and very articulately exclaimed, 'Then I am king of the cats!' and, having thus announced its new dignity, the animal darted up the chimney, and was seen no more.

"Now, the man who *seriously* repeated this strange and singular history, was a peer of the realm, had been concerned in the active scenes of life, and was held in high esteem and veneration among mankind for his talents, wisdom, and Christian piety. After this information, which I give you as a serious fact, what have you to say? It is impossible but you must immediately withdraw your charge of infidelity against a period which could produce one such implicit believer."

Returning to Lord Lyttelton's Parliamentary career, we find him, on the 30th of May, 1777, making one of his greatest speeches, the occasion being the stormy debate which arose upon the Earl of Chatham's motion for an address to the King, praying that the war might be brought to an end by conciliatory measures. Lord Lyttelton acknowledged the services and talents of the originator of the motion, but expressed surprise at his tone, observing that he remembered his holding very different language on a very similar occasion, which had inspired him, in common with the nation, with the most exalted and heroic ideas. Dwelling for a brief period upon the state of affairs in America, of which he drew a vivid and impressive picture, he turned to the Opposition, and reminded them of the time when they asserted that France would not interfere in the struggle, and that the Americans had no thought of independence, and pledged themselves to support the Government if the result should prove otherwise.

"The event," said he, "has actually taken place, and what is their conduct? Instead of recommending vigorous measures, we are told that France does not intend to interfere, but, lest she should, it is proposed to open negociations with declared and open rebels. Our rights are to be abandoned, or conceded, lest France should go to war when our strength and resources are exhausted. This is strange language, and equally pusillanimous as unworthy the attention of this House." He then proceeded to show that France was not prepared for war, and contrasted her financial position with that of Great Britain. Dismissing this branch of the subject, he turned to America, repeating his arguments as to the effects of misplaced lenity in the first instance, and reminded the House of his frequent warnings on that point.

"He took great pains," says the standard chronicler of the debates, "to show that the measures of the Government were popular, and to point out the abilities of the Minister who had so judiciously planned taxes that would scarcely be felt, and yet would be so very productive. He spoke of the country gentlemen as supporting the present war almost unanimously, passed great encomiums on their consequence and integrity, and affirmed that, while measures were so strongly supported and approved of, both within and without doors, by such decisive and respectable majorities, we had every reason to expect a happy issue to the rebellion; but that, if we should be interrupted by any Power whatever, we were both able to defend ourselves and to make our enemies repent their rashness."*

The motion of the Earl of Chatham was rejected by ninety-nine votes against twenty-eight. Time proved Lord Lyttelton to have been well informed as to the unpreparedness of France for war, for it was not until two years afterwards that, having entered into an engagement with the United States to that end, that country, which had never forgiven us the humiliation of the peace which had been forced upon her in 1763, ven-

---

* Hansard's "Parliamentary History," vol. xix.

tured to declare war. His sanguine expectations of an issue of the struggle that would restore the supremacy of Great Britain over the American provinces, though not fulfilled, were warranted by the actual position of affairs at that period. The rebels were always and everywhere at a disadvantage, and the mother country had only lately begun to put forth her strength.

The appointment of Lord Westcote to Lordship of the Treasury at this time elicited from Lord Lyttelton the following letter, which is the only one relating to politics, and hitherto unpublished, that the family archives at Hagley Hall contain:—

"MY DEAR LORD,—Nothing could give me more sincere pleasure than your advancement to an office worthy of your abilities, as an appointment to the Treasury certainly is. I have ever had the highest opinion of your talents, and Lord North, in preferring you, has, in my judgment, done himself great service. I hope you will next session take a more leading part in Parliament. You are one of the very few *graves viri* left in this country. The public voice gives full credit to your integrity, your experience, and steady systematic policy. You know my interest at Bewdley, my dear lord, is yours; and this declaration is a full testimony of my hearty and earnest wish that every friend I have in that borough may give you their vote and interest. Adieu, my dear lord. May you be unanimously chosen as you was last election, is the desire of, my dear lord, your most affectionate and faithful humble servant,

"LYTTELTON.

"Hill Street, 9th June, 1777.

"My best respects to Lady Westcote, and love to the handsome little gypsey, her daughter."

It was not until towards the close of this year that anything occurred to shake the confidence of the Government in their ability to force the Americans to lay down their arms, and acknowledge the supremacy of the mother country. The surrender of General Burgoyne, with all his army, to the insurgent forces at Saratoga was the first event that created any doubt in the minds of the Ministry as to the issue of the struggle. Lord North's tone, in announcing the event to the House of Commons, was one of extreme dejection. Lord Lyttelton, however, spoke as confidently as ever on the subject on the occasion of the Earl of Chatham's motion for a return of the orders and instructions given to General Burgoyne by the Government. He began by lamenting the disaster, and eulogising General Burgoyne as an officer and a man, but he objected that the news was mere rumour, and was not properly before the House.

It was in this speech that he made a profession of Whig principles, while disclaiming the name. "I am as genuine a Whig as the noble earl," said he. "I have been bred in the principles of Whigism from my earliest days, and shall persevere in them to the end. I love Whig principles as much as I despise those of anarchy and republicanism. But, if the bare name of Whig is all that is meant, I disclaim it. If impatience under every species of constitutional government, if resistance to legal restraint, if abetting of rebels, is the test of modern Whigism, I beg leave to be excluded as one not holding such doctrines. I would much rather share the odium which has been unjustly cast upon another set of men, and be accounted a Tory."

He then entered into the general consideration of the question of right between Great Britain and her revolted colonies, repeating his former arguments, and especially enlarging upon the supremacy of the British Parliament. "Would America," he asked, "do as Ireland had done? Would she give support in return for protection?

If she would, that might be proper ground to go upon; but no step could be taken, consistently with the rights and dignity of this country, until the supreme right of Parliament was first acknowledged." In reply to the Earl of Chatham's denial that he had ever officially authorised the employment of Indians against the French, he asserted that Indians were employed, and in great numbers; and though, perhaps, not by the express direction of the Minister, the measure was his, since the officers, so far from being censured for raising Indian levies, were at least tacitly justified. And in what respect, he asked, was the tomahawk a weapon the use of which was more to be reprobated than that of the bayonet? As to abandoning the idea of subduing the rebels on account of one misfortune, the proposition was disgraceful. What would France think of such pusillanimity? Would she not conclude us an exhausted nation, and the moment a fit one for her to wreak her vengeance on us? He wished as heartily as any noble lord for a happy and honourable end of the contest, and perhaps General Burgoyne's misfortune might make it proper to offer terms to the Americans. He hoped, however, that it would not induce the country to withdraw its forces from America, as such a step would give the rebels an advantage which we could never hope to regain. The debate resulted in the rejection of the Earl of Chatham's motion by forty votes against nineteen.

On the 23rd of January, 1778, the Earl of Abingdon made a motion respecting the legality of raising troops by private subscription, without the consent of Parliament, a meeting of the merchants and traders of London having been convened at the London Tavern for that purpose, and it being known that several of the large provincial towns were prepared to follow the example. The debate was adjourned to the 4th of February, when the Earl of Suffolk moved an amendment, declaring such subscriptions to be legal and meritorious. Lord Lyttelton pointed out that there was no other evidence of an intention to raise troops in the manner indicated than the advertisement convening the meeting, and suggested that the House should reject both the original resolution and the amendment. The Earl of Suffolk thereupon withdrew his amendment, and the House rejected the Earl of Abingdon's resolution by ninety votes against thirty.

In the meantime, on the 2nd of February, the Duke of Richmond had made a motion against the sending of any more of the old corps out of the country, and thereupon had arisen an animated debate on the state of the country. Lord Lyttelton said that the resolution, if it should be carried, would be a public acknowledgment that the country was unable to prosecute the war in America any farther, or to maintain the rights of Parliament over the colonies. It would be an actual declaration on the part of Great Britain that she was neither able to defend herself or to chastise her rebellious dependencies; and of course a direct invitation to France and Spain to attempt an immediate invasion of the kingdom. He condemned the impolicy of disclosing our means of defence, observing that such a course would both defeat our claims over the colonies and show them how unequal we were to the task of reducing them to obedience, or securing ourselves against the designs of our enemies. He trusted, however, that the affairs of the nation were not in the desperate situation in which they were attempted to be shown to the public. The resources of the country were great: its spirit was correspondent to them; there remained one man (alluding to the Earl of Chatham) who would not consent to render America independent of this country. He concluded with the expression of his opinion that the Earl of Chatham was still equal to conducting the war to a successful issue ; and maintained that its effect, thus conducted, would answer the most sanguine expectations of the real friends of the country. The motion of the Duke of Richmond was rejected by ninety-four votes against thirty-one.

There is no doubt that the return of the Earl of Chatham to power was a contingency to which Lord Lyttelton often directed his thoughts, notwithstanding that statesman's advanced age, he being now in his seventieth year, and rapidly declining in health and physical vigour. He had always the Earl of Chatham in his mind as a model minister, and was never tired of eulogising his patriotism, his administrative ability, and his past services to the country. The earl had declined in popularity since he had ceased to be "the great commoner," but he was still the pilot to whom Lord Lyttelton turned mentally in every trial and trouble to which the nation was exposed. At this time the Earl of Chatham was approximating to the views of Lord Lyttelton with regard to America; and the latter was beginning to despair of his colleagues, and to rise above them. The contrast between his speech on the Saratoga disaster, and that of Lord North in the House of Commons, is remarkable ; and his confidence remained unabated when the news of that event was officially confirmed, as was shown by his speech on the last motion of the Duke of Richmond.

Lord North, irritating when he should have been conciliatory, weak when he should have been firm, dilatory when energy was imperatively required, became conciliatory when it was too late for such a policy to be effective. The surrender of General Burgoyne was followed by the introduction of the Conciliatory Bills, which the Americans, elated by their first great success, regarded with contempt and derision. Lord Lyttelton, supporting the third reading of these bills, was compelled to acknowledge that the exigencies of the situation had rendered necessary a change of measures; but he denied that there was any inconsistency of these measures with the former policy of the Government. They only expressed the desire of the Government to do, at that time, at less cost, what they could accomplish within the next two years, at a greater sacrifice of money and of human lives.

But his confidence in the Administration was waning, and when, on the 23rd of March, he rose towards the close of the debate on the Duke of Richmond's motion to withdraw the troops from America, his tone strongly resembled that which he had held four years previously. He listened in silence to the attacks of the Opposition on the policy of his colleagues in office, and was, except one, the last peer who addressed the House. After portraying the state of affairs as one of increasing gravity, England, with her revolted colonies still unsubdued, being threatened with a foreign war, for which she was ill prepared, while the prospect in India and the West Indies was deplorable, he turned to the Earl of Sandwich, and expressed surprise at the noble lord's language, which seemed to imply that the country was not so well prepared for a naval war as he had so often declared it to be. The earl did not reply; it was enough for him that the Duke of Richmond's motion was negatived without a division.

The infirmities of the Earl of Chatham must have convinced Lord Lyttelton that there was no hope left that he would ever again stand at the helm of the State. He made his last appearance in the House of Lords with his legs swathed in flannel; he was pale and emaciated, and was led into the House between his son, William Pitt, and his son-in-law, Lord Mahon, all the peers standing up to receive him, and making a clear passage for him to reach his accustomed place. The Duke of Richmond had just sat down, after moving an address to the king on the state of the country. The Earl of Chatham proceeded immediately to express the indignation which he felt at the idea, which he understood had gone forth, of yielding up the sovereignty of America.

"My lords," said he, "I rejoice that the grave has not closed over me, that I am still alive to lift up my voice against the dismemberment of this ancient and noble monarchy. Pressed down as I am by the load of infirmity, I am little able to assist my country in this most perilous conjuncture; but, my lords, while I have sense and memory, I will never consent to tarnish the lustre of this nation by an ignominious surrender of its rights and fairest possessions. Shall a people, so lately the terror of the world, now fall prostrate before the House of Bourbon? It is impossible! In God's name, if it is absolutely necessary to declare either for peace or war, and if peace cannot be preserved with honour, why is not war commenced without hesitation? I am not, I confess, well informed of the resources of this kingdom, but I trust it has still sufficient to maintain its just rights, though I know them not. Any state, my lords, is better than despair. Let us at least make one effort, and, if we must fall, let us fall like men."

The Duke of Richmond, in reply, declared

himself to be totally ignorant of the means by which Great Britain was to resist with success the combination of America with the House of Bourbon. He urged the Earl of Chatham to point out, if he could, any mode of forcing the Americans to renounce their independence, adding that, if he could not do so, no man could. The Earl of Chatham, who had listened to the duke's reply with impatience and restlessness, staggered to his feet on the conclusion of his speech, but was unable to stand, and fell back on his seat, exhausted and fainting. He was carried into an adjoining apartment, and the House immediately adjourned. Medical assistance being summoned, he in some degree recovered, and was conveyed to his favourite country residence, Hayes Place, near Bromley, where he died about a month afterwards.

Lord Lyttelton was profoundly moved by this event, and a letter which he wrote to a friend shortly after the great statesman's decease, expressed both his appreciation of the loss which the country had sustained, and his opinion of the Opposition as a party.

"I will endeavour to obey your commands, and, if possible, to compress my unprepared reflections into the compass of this paper. The Opposition is respectable for rank, property, and abilities; but it is feeble and unimportant, from the narrowness of its plans, as well as the want of a sincere confidence, a firm union, and, as I shrewdly suspect, a general political integrity in the parts that compose it. They all readily accord in opposition to the measures of Government, but differ, not only in the manner, but in the time, of exertion. They all agree to go forth against the enemy; but each distinct body follows its own leader, and chooses its own mode of attack; they never unite but for the purpose of the moment, by which means that strong-compacted, lasting force which, directed to one point, and at one instance, would scatter alarm through any administration, is frittered down into a variety of desultory operations, which would disgrace the meanest Ministerial apprehension.

"The warmest friend of Government cannot deny that in the minority there are men of sound principle and proved integrity. They are, indeed, but few in number, and may be easily distinguished from those who are influenced by the demon of disappointed ambition, the fury of desperate faction, and the suggestions of personal rancour. It has been a matter of surprise to many sensible, reflecting persons that the Opposition did not use every possible means to obtain the aid and countenance of Lord Chatham's abilities, and concentrate, as it were, their scattered rays in the focus of that great man's character. Under such a leader they might have acted with effect, and knocked so loudly at the door of Administration as to have made every member of it tremble, even in the most secret and guarded recesses of the Cabinet. But such a coalition was wholly impracticable, even if the veteran statesman had been free from those bodily infirmities which so seldom permitted him of late to step forth to any public exertion.

"If we except Lord Camden, there is not one of the leading actors of Opposition who has not, at some time or other, calumniated, deceived, deserted, or, in some manner, mis-treated this great man. Lord [Shelburne's] oratorical echo made his first entrance into the House of Commons notorious by flying, as it were, at his very throat; and yet this man has been proud to bear the armorial banner at his funeral. The first day on which the Earl of Chatham took his seat in the House of Peers, the Duke of [Richmond] was forced to bow beneath its reproof for insulting him. The Duke of [Grafton], who, to use his own words, had accepted the seals merely to trail a pike under the command of so distinguished a politician, when advanced to a higher post, turned an angry face against the leader whom he had deserted. Even the Marquis of [Rockingham], when at the head of his short-lived Administration, was vain enough to affect a refusal of Mr. Pitt's assistance.

"The conduct of such men, though it might be despised, could not be entirely effaced from his mind by all the submissive homage they afterwards paid him; and though he may have since lived with some of them in the habits of occasional intercourse, you may be assured, if his health had permitted a re-entrance into the public service, that he would never have engaged in the views of men whom he could not trust. The Ministry, I believe, sent somewhat of an embassy to him,* which he treated with contempt; and if Lord [Shelburne], in an occasional visit to Hayes, undertook a similar business on the part of Opposition, I doubt not but the answer he received, though, perhaps, more softened, had its concomitant mortification. During the last years of his venerable life he seemed to stand

---

* Overtures to join the Cabinet of Lord North were twice made to the Earl of Chatham, the second time through the Marquis of Granby.—See Jesse's "Life and Times of George III," and Lord Brougham's "Statesmen of the Reign of George III."

alone, or made his communications to no one but Lord Camden, whom

"'He faithful found among the faithless,
Faithful only he.'

"The grave is now closed upon that illustrious statesman, and his splendid orb is set for ever. There was that in his character which gave him a very distinguished superiority over the rest of mankind. He was the greatest War Minister this kingdom ever knew; and the four years of his Administration form the most brilliant period that the British annals, or perhaps those of the world, can produce. They who aim at the diminution of his glory, and that of his country, by attributing the rapid change of affairs under his Administration to chance, and the fortunate circumstances of the moment, must be slaves to the most rooted prejudice, the foulest envy, or the darkest ignorance. To the more brilliant part of his life let me add, that he was a minister who detested the arts of corruption, set his face against all Court as well as Cabinet intrigues, and quitted his important station with unpolluted hands.

"It is a great national misfortune that the mantle of this political patriarch has not been caught by any of his successors. We are not deficient in men of genius, and both Houses of Parliament give daily examples of eloquence, which Rome and Athens never excelled; nevertheless, there does not appear to be a man in the kingdom with that power of understanding, depth of knowledge, activity of mind, and strength of resolution sufficient to direct our harassed empire. There are many among us who are capable of being second in command, and filling all the subaltern departments with adequate ability; but the State as well as the army wants a commander-in-chief. The truncheon is become little more than an useless trophy, as a hand fit to grasp it is no longer to be found.

"In bearing my poor testimony to the manes of Lord Chatham, I have yielded to the impulse of my very soul. In this imperfect act of veneration I can have no interest, for the object of it is gone where the applause of this world cannot reach him; and, as I ventured to differ from him when alive, and delivered the reasons of my difference to his face, what motive can there be for me to flatter him now he is no more? To oppose the sentiments of that venerable statesman was an undertaking which shook my very frame. My utmost resolution, strengthened by a sense of duty, and the laudable ambition of supporting what I conceived to be right against the proudest names, could not sustain me. You, I believe, were present when I sunk down and became silent beneath the imposing superiority of his abilities; but I did not feel it a defeat to be vanquished by him—

> "'Nec tam
> Turpe fuit vinci, quam contendisse decorum est.'"

The last occasion on which Lord Lyttelton addressed the House during this session was the debate on the third reading of the Earl of Chatham's Annuity Bill, when he was called to his feet by a remark of the Earl of Radnor—that there had been only one occasion on which the conduct of the deceased earl had lessened the country's obligation to him—namely, when, while in office, he had set the authority of a proclamation above that of an Act of Parliament. Lord Lyttelton warmly defended the deceased statesman's conduct on the occasion referred to, when, the harvest having been deficient, and corn being largely exported from the country, an Order in Council had been issued prohibiting the exportation of corn, Parliament not being sitting at the time. Lord Lyttelton maintained that the circumstances justified the act complained of by the Earl of Radnor, and pronounced an eloquent eulogium on the departed statesman, whose like the House was not soon to look upon again.

CHAPTER XII.

Lord Lyttelton's Occupations at Hagley—Views on the Game Laws—Speech on the American War—The Earl of Bristol's Motion against the Earl of Sandwich — Lord Lyttelton's Speech—His Political Status in 1779—Relations with the Earl of Shelburne—Pitt Place—Reasons for preferring it to Hagley—Discussion on the Locality of the Soul, and the End of the World—Death of George Ayscough—Letter on the State of Public Affairs—Visit to Ireland—The Irish Volunteers—Agitation in Ireland for Free Trade.

EVERY line of evidence that can be gathered concerning the habits and pursuits of Lord Lyttelton during the latter years of his life confirms the view which has been taken in the preceding pages. He withdrew himself more and more from vicious associates, and, when Parliament was not sitting, passed the greater part of his time in the country, studying politics and political economy, when not engaged in visiting or entertaining his friends. In reply to a friend, who seems to have been curious as to his occupations at Hagley, he wrote as follows:—

"I neither hunt nor shoot; the former is a

diversion which requires sacrifices that I cannot grant, and shall not enumerate; the latter suits me better, but is as little pursued as the former. The business and form, not to say tyranny, of preserving game, which is necessary to establish a certainty of sport, is not to my way of thinking. The laws concerning game form a very unconstitutional monopoly: but that is not all; the peace and society of provincial vicinities are more or less disturbed by jealousies and disputes arising from game, in every part of the kingdom. My country employments are better than you imagine. I am reading, with great care and observation, the works of the Chancellor D'Aguesseau. Many years ago, my father gave a volume of them to me, desiring me to study it with attention, and consider the contents as his own paternal counsels. At that time I did neither one nor the other; however, I am now making ample amends for former neglect. The magistrate, the statesman, the lawyer, the man of the world, the orator, and the philosopher, will find delight and instruction in these volumes. I can say no more; and what I have now said will add them to your library, if it does not already possess them.

"You must know that I am angry with you for writing to me; or rather, for not coming, instead of writing. Delay not to visit a place you so much admire, and to see a friend who loves and values you. We will study together in the morning, and court the Muses in the evening, and you shall visit Pope's urn by moonlight, and I will promise not to laugh at you. I propose to remain here a fortnight longer; but, if you will come to me, the time of my departure shall be prolonged to your pleasure."

He returned to London on the reassembling of Parliament, deeply impressed with the gravity of the political situation, and resolved to support the Government no longer than he could consistently and conscientiously defend their acts. His view of the American question appears never to have changed. Regarding it from the standpoint of a firm conviction of the constitutional supremacy of the British Parliament, he considered that concession would be surrender, and that it was better to lose the American provinces than the British Constitution. If the Americans could not be beaten into submission, it would be better, he thought, to let them go than to purchase their obedience by degrading concessions; but, until this resolve was taken, the war should, in his opinion, be prosecuted with the utmost vigour.

Accordingly, when, on the 7th of December,

the Marquis of Rockingham moved an address to the king, strongly condemnatory of the manifesto issued at New York by the British Commissioners, for the severities with which the Americans were threatened, in the event of their rejecting the proposals for peace, Lord Lyttelton defended the manifesto, and contended that, at such a crisis, all parties should unite to support the Government, instead of carping at its language. The propositions which had been made were, he said, proper to be offered, but he was glad that they had been rejected, because, he was free to say, he did not approve of them. He maintained that it was sound policy, when America was driven into the arms of France by the machinations of ambitious demagogues, for Great Britain to dismantle her fortresses, spoil her harbours, destroy her resources, and render her of as little military use to France as might be possible. This view prevailed, and the motion of the Marquis of Rockingham was rejected by seventy-one votes against thirty-seven.

There can now be no doubt that the position assumed by Lord Lyttelton at this period of the struggle in America was a more tenable one than was held either by the Ministry or the Opposition. The former sued for peace in the same breath that they fulminated threats; the latter harassed the Government with propositions for conciliation, and yet were inimical to the independence which the Americans had declared to be the sole condition on which peace was possible. The Ministry was weak and pusillanimous, the Opposition inconsistent, and often factious. The day was near, therefore, when Lord Lyttelton would have to take a course of action independently of both Tories and Whigs.

It has been seen that he was induced to support the Administration of Lord North by the assurance of the Earl of Sandwich that the naval force of Great Britain was equal to any that could be sent to sea by France and Spain combined. The fact of Admiral Keppel's withdrawal from before Brest, on the ground that the force under his command was inferior to that of the French, staggered the honest and conscientious supporters of the Government, and furnished the Opposition with a new weapon of offence. On the 23rd of April, 1779, the Earl of Bristol moved an address to the king, praying for the removal of the Earl of Sandwich from the post of First Lord of the Admiralty. In the course of the debate, Lord Stormont took occasion to condemn what he termed the indiscretion of discussing delicate affairs of State in a public assembly. This called Lord Lyttelton to his feet, and prompted one of the greatest speeches ever made by him:—

"I enjoy a place," he observed, "which ministers are welcome to if they think it a crime in a man to declare his mind when the dearest and most vital interests of the country are at stake. Nothing shall prevent me from speaking my mind; and, even upon the most sordid motives, I appeal to every noble lord present to say whether, when the fall of stocks, the decreased value of landed property, and the accumulation of new burdens are taken into consideration, it is worth the while of any man of property to partake of the favours of the Government, when it is considered that what he receives as a placeman is no more than he loses as a landowner. I see no reason for the delicacy talked of by the noble lord who spoke last; the subject is important, and it ought to be met fairly. Spain either will or will not join France; to temporise is to lull the country into a state of doubt, and may incur the danger that will attend the interference of the Court of Madrid whenever it takes place. I hope, therefore, that ministers will insist upon an explicit answer from that Court.

"The noble viscount has compared private

friendships with the faith of nations and the
friendly assurances of one sovereign State to
another. Surely he is not serious. I cannot
imagine that any noble lord can be weak enough
to adopt that position. The cases are widely different.
Private friendships arise from similarity
of mind, similarity of principles, similarity of
views, and often from consanguinity and relationship;
and even in the latter case, your lordships
have had instances of the slight hold of that tie.
Can it be said that Spain and England have the
same views, the same principles, or ties of consanguinity?
Does not the Family Compact stare
us in the face? Is it not a notorious fact that
the separate branches of the House of Bourbon
are bound by treaty to assist each other when
either is attacked? It was but the other day
that the argument was as good regarding France.
Was it not the language of ministers that France
was the friend of England? Was it not the
language of the throne itself? Were not both
Houses of Parliament told, in the most direct
and strong terms, that France had made such
assurances of friendship as put her sincerity beyond
all doubt, and rendered every idea of her
assisting America ridiculous? And yet what has
France done?

"In the midst of those friendly assurances,

she has formally received ambassadors from America, and has been, for a considerable time, furnishing the Americans with military stores, and with the means of carrying on the war, which has cost this country so vast an expenditure of men and money. At length she has thrown off the mask, and we find the French Minister come with his famous rescript, notifying to the British Government that the King of France, out of his abundant love and friendship for Great Britain, has thought proper to enter into a treaty with America, a treaty offensive and defensive, and such as will enable America still further to resist, and to assert her independence. Let noble lords hold these well-known circumstances in view, and then let them judge of the weight of the noble viscount's argument, that private friendship and public amity are synonymous."

He then turned to the warlike preparations of Spain, stating that twenty-five ships of the line were lying in the harbour of Cadiz, ready for sea, with the flags of three admirals flying; and asserting that she had virtually stopped the entrance of the Mediterranean, and prescribed to England the bounds of her navigation. If the British Government humoured the Court of Madrid, and ceded Gibraltar as the price of its neutrality, she would be our friend in May, and, with

Gibraltar at her back, our foe in August. He next directed attention to the charge against the Earl of Sandwich, of sending Admiral Keppel to Brest with an inadequate force, and expressed surprise at the refusal of the First Lord to answer the question put to him by the Duke of Richmond, as to whether he had asserted that the force sent to Brest was equal to the French fleet it would encounter there.

"I waited," he continued, "with some anxiety, hoping that the noble lord, or some other minister, would reply. Does the noble lord recollect that he has declared that Admiral Keppel's orders were, to retire if he found the French fleet apparently superior to his own? Does the noble lord see the difficulty in which the whole matter is involved, for want of a satisfactory answer? Surely he does not mean to confess that he sent Admiral Keppel out with orders to run away from the French fleet; and yet that is the appearance of the matter as it now stands. Either Admiral Keppel was culpable for returning; or ministers are to blame for having sent him out with an inferior force. No position could be more obvious. Blame must be somewhere, and where is it to be imputed, or how are your lordships to know in what manner to vote, if no explanation is given?"

He then related what he had heard concerning the Brest affair, and repeated what Admiral Keppel had said on the subject, in describing the struggle in his mind when he found himself obliged to turn his back to the French—"A back," said Lord Lyttelton, "that had never been turned to the enemies of his country before." The admiral said that he sacrificed his feelings and his pride of heart to a painful sense of the duty he owed to his country. "The expression," said Lord Lyttelton, "is a strong indication of the conflict in his breast; and, while it does him honour, makes every man who heard him feel for the dilemma in which he was involved. It makes their hearts beat quick with the glow of applause, and makes them execrate those who placed a commander of distinguished reputation and ability in the dilemma of risking the safety of his country, or doing injury to his own feelings as a man, an officer, and a citizen.

"No officer in the navy stands higher in the opinion of seamen than Admiral Keppel; the very circumstance of his having broken orders, and returned home when he discovered the superiority of the French fleet, gained him the greatest honour from his own profession. He went out, not merely to fight for a few ships, but to defend our docks and arsenals, to defend Portsmouth and Plymouth, the city of London, the navigation of the Thames, your lordships' seats in this House—in short, to preserve the whole British empire; no less was the object he was sent to defend, and no less would have been the loss had he been defeated. Either the minister who gave the orders, or the admiral who failed to execute them, was in the wrong; but which? The admiral has not only been acquitted by his proper judges, but by the acclamations of the people of England. The conduct of the minister has not been inquired into, nor justified; and the intention of the Government appears to be, if possible, to slobber it over.

"It is not long since Admiral Keppel was sent with those twenty ships to meet a force so much superior, that the First Lord acknowledged that he was justified in avoiding it. Not long before that, the noble lord asserted, from official accounts laid before this House, that we had a naval force superior to the combined fleets of France and Spain, and that every minister who administered the British navy ought to maintain such a force—an assertion of the greatest weight, of the most material importance; for who could doubt what the First Lord of the Admiralty, who must, from his office, have the best intelligence concerning the navy, declared to be true? Who could controvert an opinion founded on official intelligence? What was the effect of this declaration, coming from such an authority? It was admitted as true; it stopped inquiry; it suspended the vigour of our operations. Much might have been done by Parliament, if Parliament had been sensible of the weakness of the country; but, the statement being false, how did it operate? It hoodwinked the House, blinding your lordships where you ought to have seen clearest; and, by giving you false hopes and expectations, deluded you to the very brink of destruction.

"With regard to myself, the First Lord's declaration respecting the state of the fleet altered my opinion immediately; it dissipated my dread of commencing war with France with an unequal fleet, gave me the hope of a successful contest, and induced me to reply to the late Earl of Chatham in defence of the First Lord, whose conduct that able statesman had attacked on the ground that he had not more than twenty ships of the line ready for sea. But mutilated accounts from office are always dangerous; in the present case, the deception was a two-edged sword, which wounded both friends and foes; but the point was turned against the breast of the nation."

Lord Lyttelton then turned to the state of the country. "The kingdom," said he, "is destitute of resources, and without allies. Our trade is declining, our manufactures perishing. The First Lord of the Treasury has confessed in his place that he could raise only seven millions when he wanted eight, and that he was forced to bribe the monied men by ruinous bargains to get the seven. We are engaged in a double war with France and America. As to the American war, however justifiable in its principles, which I think were constitutional principles, it has been in its conduct, from the time when General Gage was shut up in Boston down to the more fatal period of the surrender of Saratoga, when that brave officer, General Burgoyne, was forced to submit to the mortification of surrendering his army into the hands of the Americans, one black era, pregnant with the direst mischiefs, the most cruel fortune, the bitterest calamities, the most inexpiable evils that this country ever endured; and so it will be marked by latest posterity.

"It is now said that there is good news: Colonel Campbell has arrived from Georgia with news of a victory, and in the same breath requires reinforcements. Let noble lords consider the state of the American business as it really stands. After a contest of five years, we are reduced to little more than half a province; then what is the object of the war? America, if ours on the terms of the Commissioners, would be a burden, rather than an acquisition. To what purpose, then, are we exhausting ourselves? What object are we pursuing? It is not taxation; Mr. Vyner* is now the only man in the three kingdoms that has any idea of taxing America. It is not supremacy, it is not legislation; all that has been given up by the Commissioners, who have changed places with the Opposition. Lord Chatham's Bill was Toryism in comparison with what the Commissioners offered. They have gone in concession beyond the noble lords near me; they have even outshot the noble duke.† They have given up everything, and even proposed to pay the debts of America, incurred by her military resistance to Great Britain! Then what is the object? That is a question which must be answered. At present a general lethargy prevails; people come

---

* Robert Vyner, M.P., who had just before made a speech in the House of Commons strongly defending the Government, and maintaining the right and the policy of taxing America.

† The peers alluded to are indicated in Hansard's "Parliamentary History" as the Earl of Shelburne and the Duke of Richmond. It seems, therefore, that Lord Lyttelton spoke on this occasion from the Opposition benches.

to the bar of this House, gaping for intelligence, listening with greedy ears to the debates, hearing unmoved the recapitulation of their own wretchedness and the accumulated miseries of their country, and go away with perfect composure, like men who leave the theatre after seeing a tragedy, in the incidents of which they have not the smallest concern, and by which they are not at all affected. If the people do not soon rouse themselves, they will be put to death in their sleep."

After dwelling at some length on the condition of the country, with its languishing trade and industry, and the accumulating pressure of taxation, Lord Lyttelton went on to say that, in a crisis so alarming, party should be forgotten, and men of ability consulted, without reference to their political sentiments. He indicated the Earl of Bristol as a firm friend of the country, whose ability in his profession was undoubted, and whose counsel, especially in naval matters, might be invaluable. He called attention to the Earl of Shelburne, as possessing talents which did him great honour, and might be employed with infinite advantage to the State. He reminded the House that the Duke of Grafton had discharged official duties with credit to himself and to the country. He disclaimed personal pique or rancour in the course he had taken, assuring the House that he bore no ill-will to the Earl of Sandwich, or to any other lord in the House. He was far from condemning the First Lord; but in cases like the one they were considering it behoved every man to speak his real sentiments. The interests of every individual were at stake, because the interests of every individual were involved in the general interests of the kingdom.

He suggested that the charges against the Earl of Sandwich should be investigated in committee, day by day, until they were established or disproved. The Earl of Bristol had said that he had papers that would substantiate them; and these, if laid on the table of the House, might assist in the inquiry. He declared that his support of the Government, in pursuing the contest in America, had been based entirely on principle; but the case was materially altered when they abandoned every one of its avowed objects. There must be some known and declared object to justify the continuance of the war with America, which had proved so ruinous and disastrous; but, as regarded France, every man capable of bearing arms ought to be forced into the field before a hollow truce was patched up with her, for fear of the intervention of Spain.

The Earl of Sandwich did not reply. He had declined to do so, when called upon by the Duke of Richmond, unless it should be the will of the House, in which he well knew that the Ministry had a large majority. The Earl of Bristol's motion was rejected by seventy-eight votes against thirty-nine; and Lord North and his colleagues continued for some time longer, with gradually diminishing majorities in both Houses of Parliament, and increasing difficulty of wringing the taxes from an impoverished people, to pursue the hopeless task of subduing the Americans with one hand, and vanquishing the old Continental enemies of England with the other. The king was obstinately bent upon coercing the Americans, if it should be possible, at all hazards and any sacrifice; and upon retaining Lord North in power, as the most convenient instrument of that coercion. Lord North was too complaisant a minister to offer any objection to being merely the private secretary of the sovereign; and there were few of the crowd of placemen and pensioners who swelled the ministerial majority who possessed either the honesty or the enlightenment of Lord Lyttelton.

For the present, no change of Ministry, no new political combination, was practicable; but Lord Lyttelton had indicated in his speech the most promising one that could, by any possibility, at that time have been formed. The Duke of Grafton was a disciple of Chatham, and had been premier during the two years immediately preceding the accession to office of Lord North. The Earl of Shelburne, though a Whig, held the same position towards that party as Lord Lyttelton held towards the Tories, and favoured the idea of a Ministry of upright and enlightened men, independent of party, such as was indicated by Lord Lyttelton. Neither had a very exalted opinion of Charles Fox. The subordinate position assigned to him by Lord Lyttelton has been seen; and the Earl of Shelburne, when entrusted with the formation of a Ministry, on the death of the Marquis of Rockingham, eliminated Fox and his friends, and chose for his lieutenant William Pitt, then the most promising of the young men in the House of Commons, and brooding over a great scheme of Parliamentary reform, which, however, was not destined to fructification. Lord Lyttelton would, it may fairly be assumed, have been included in the Shelburne Ministry, had he lived three years longer; and it is probable that such a combination as that which he glanced at in his speech, with William Pitt and himself as secretaries, had been revolved in his mind, and perhaps in that of the Earl of

Shelburne. That it had either been talked of, or was supposed to be indicated by his speech and his change of attitude towards the Government, may be gathered from the remark of Horace Walpole, in a letter addressed to Sir Horace Mann on the day after the debate on the Earl of Bristol's motion, that Lord Lyttelton thought he had talent enough for a Secretaryship of State.[*]

Parliament rose without any change of Ministry, or the slightest brightening of the political prospect, however, and Lord Lyttelton retired to the seclusion of the Surrey dell which was his favourite place of residence during the latter part of his life, and the many beauties and advantages of which he extols in his letters. Hagley had never won much of his regard. It was far from the metropolis, and yet surrounded by towns, so that, as he complained to a friend, it afforded neither society nor seclusion. The extensive park was as public as a common, and the parish church stood within its bounds. To Lord Lyttelton, who enjoyed a congenial seclusion as much as he enjoyed congenial society, this was a great objection; and, besides this, its architectural excrescences displeased his eye, which regarded the

---

[*] "Letters of Horace Walpole."

natural with more favour than the so-called classical.

"The system of modern gardening," he says, in a letter to a friend, "in spite of fashion and Mr. Brown, is a very foolish one. The huddling together every species of building in a park or garden is ridiculous. The environs of a magnificent house should partake in some degree of the necessary formality of the building they surround. This was Kent's opinion, and where his designs have escaped the destruction of modern refinement there is an easy grandeur which is at once striking and delightful. Fine woods are beautiful objects, and their beauty approaches nearer to magnificence as the mass of foliage becomes more visible; but to dot them with little white edifices infringes upon their greatness, and, by such divisions and sub-divisions, destroys their due effect. The verdure of British swells was not made for Grecian temples; a flock of sheep and a shepherd's hut are better adapted to it. Our climate is not suited to the deities of Italy and Greece, and in an hard winter I feel for the shuddering divinities. At Hagley there is a temple of Theseus, commonly called by the gardener the temple of Perseus, which stares you in the face wherever you go, while the temple of God, commonly called by the gardener the parish church, is so industriously hid by trees from without that the pious matron can hardly read her prayer-book within. This was an evident preference of strange gods, and, in my opinion, a very blasphemous improvement. Where nature is grand, improve her grandeur, not by adding extraneous decorations, but by removing obstructions. Where a scene is in itself lovely, very little is necessary to give it all due advantage, especially if it be laid into park, which undergoes no variety of cultivation.

"Stowe is, in my opinion, a most detestable place, and has in every part of it the air of a Golgotha—a princely one I must acknowledge; but in no part of it could I ever lose that gloomy idea. My own park possesses many and very rare beauties, but, from the design of making it classical, it has been charged with many false and unsuitable ornaments. A classical park or a classical garden is as ridiculous an expression as a classical plumb-pudding or a classical sirloin of beef. It is an unworthy action to strip the classics of their heroes, gods, and goddesses, to grow green amid the fogs of our unclassical climate. But the affectation and nonsense of little minds is beyond description. How many are there who, fearful that mankind will not discover their knowledge, are continually hanging out the sign of hard words and pedantic expressions, like the late Lord Orrery, who, for some classical reason, had given his dog a classical name—it was no less than Cæsar! However, Cæsar one day giving his lordship a most unclassical bite, he seized a cane, and pursued him round the room with great solemnity and this truly classical menace, 'Cæsar! Cæsar! if I could catch thee, Cæsar! I would give thee as many wounds as Brutus gave thy namesake in the Capitol.' This is the very froth of folly and affectation."

The rural retreat for which Hagley was abandoned stood in a sequestered situation, near the church, at Epsom. It is called by some writers who have mentioned it Pit Place, which name is said to have been given to it on account of its site having been a chalk-pit; but in the newspaper accounts of Lord Lyttelton's death it is called Pitt Place, a name which, if it had not one before, may reasonably be supposed to have been given to it in respectful memory of the statesman whom he omitted no opportunity of eulogising and holding up to the reverential contemplation of posterity. Lord Lyttelton's reasons for its selection as a country residence, and for preferring it to Hagley, are pleasantly set forth in the following letter, which he wrote from Pit (or Pitt) Place to a friend :—

"You are not the only one of my many criticising friends who have expressed surprise at my taking so kindly to the Surrey dell, and becoming so dead to rural magnificence as to neglect Hagley's gaudy scene and proud domain. [Clara Haywood], in one of her visits to this place, told me that I looked like a toad in a hole. Be that as it may, it is shady, elegant, convenient, and snug—a term peculiar to English comfort, and not translated into any other language. Besides, a villa is a necessary appendage to that rank whose dignity you so often recommend me to maintain; and in what spot could a British peer find a more delightful retreat than mine, to solace himself in the interval of public duty? Or where is the Ægerian grot, in whose auspicious solitude he could better hold his secret counsels with the guardian genius of his country? But, *badinage* apart, its vicinity to the metropolis is one of its principal recommendations; and, to a man of my tendencies, a cottage at Pimlico is preferable to a palace in the distant counties. Here I find no inconvenience in a rainy day; the means of dissipating a gloomy temper are within my beckon. If I wish to be alone, I can shut my gates, and exclude the world; if I want society, my post-chaise will quickly bear me hence, or fetch it here.

"On the contrary, Hagley, which is certainly an Elysian scene, uniting beauty, grandeur, and convenience, does not possess any of these advantages; and I might die there of *ennui*, before anything like the necessary remedy could be found. In that spot, all delightful as it is, I cannot enjoy the society which I prefer; nor, when I am tired of company, is it possible for me to be alone. Manufacturing towns surround me on all sides, turnpike roads environ me, and the prospect from every window glares with such a variety of intruding objects that I have been often thankful to the shades of night for giving me to tranquillity and myself.

"Besides, the parish church is in my park; and I have more than once awoke from brilliant dreams by the cackling of gossips in full trot to a christening; nay, I have sometimes shuddered to see on my splendid lawns the dirges due and sad array of the rustic funeral. But this is not all. Coaches full of travellers of all denominations, and troops of holiday neighbours, are hourly chasing me from my apartments, or, by strolling about the environs, keep me a prisoner in it. The lord of the place can never call it his for a day during the finer part of the year. Nor am I proud, as others have been, of holding myself forth to the complimentary envy of those who come to visit it. My pride is not of that complexion; and the consciousness of possessing the first place of its kind in Europe is a sufficient satisfaction to me, without showing any preference to it as a rural residence.

"The little spot from whence I have the pleasure to address you has won my fondest attachment. H—— left me this morning. We passed the whole of yesterday evening in searching into the nature of the soul, and contriving ways and means for the final dissolution of the world. We are neither of us qualified to make any great figure in astronomy or metaphysics; nevertheless, we became very familiar with the heavenly bodies, and discoursed, with a most imposing gravity, on matter and spirit. We exercised all our ingenuity to find out in what part of the human frame the soul had fixed her abode, but were totally unable to make the discovery, till our friend, with his usual singularity of thought, determined it to be in every part where there is sensation, and particularly in those parts where sensation is most exquisite.

"But, as it is much easier to pull down

systems than to establish them, we destroyed the globe, and all that it inherits, with surprising expedition. A comet was seized upon by both of us, at the same moment, as the engine to be employed in the tremendous conflagration. The contest for the originality of this idea was carried on, with equal zeal, between us for some time, which my antagonist concluded by introducing another very interesting subject for inquiry—whether the great day of judgment was to precede, accompany, or follow this great event of the world's dissolution? In the course of his harangue, he rose to such a fervour of thought, delivered such forcible language, and intermingled such striking expressions from the Scriptures, that he grew pale beneath his own conceptions. The alarm was contagious, and made my blood curdle in its veins. I verily believe, if a rattling thunderstorm had immediately followed his oration, that our confusion would have been too serious to have admitted of an acknowledgment. The two ladies who composed our audience were thrown into such a terror of mind that I began to apprehend the evening's amusement would have concluded in sending two handsome and useful women to the Magdalen. My house, with all its advantages, is not calculated for the actual work of contrition, though it may prepare the way for it: and if such a scene of repentance had really happened, it would have constituted an era in my life sufficient to seduce the attention of mankind from all the past singularities of it."

The house from which this letter was written lies in a hollow, and cannot be seen from any of the roads which skirt three sides of the grounds, or from the footpaths through the old churchyard which adjoins the fourth. The entrance is through a gateway flanked by stone effigies of lions sitting on their haunches, and looking very steadfastly at the ancient hostelry over the way. A score of yards of a carriage drive, bordered with flowers and backed by old trees, are seen through the gate, and the roofs of the coach-house and stables rise above the high brick wall which surrounds the grounds; but from any other point only the venerable chestnuts and Scotch firs which screen the house can be seen. The place is now occupied by Mr. Rowland, the trainer, and the curious in family history and legend may be disappointed on learning that it underwent such extensive alterations about sixteen years ago as to be now almost a new house.

About the middle of October Lord Lyttelton was called upon, by the customs of society, to wear the outward sign of mourning for his cousin, George Edward Ayscough. Two years previously this contemptible individual had left England to recruit his health, which had been undermined by vicious excesses, by a Continental tour. He derived, however, but partial and temporary relief from the air of France and Italy, and, returning to England in the summer of 1779, he lingered for a short time, and died on the 14th of October. Nichol says that he "left behind a monument of unexampled disregard of every principle of virtue and decency in a journal of the most secret transactions of his life, in which, from most authentic information, I am assured that he, in the grossest terms, has recorded facts which Aretin himself would be ashamed to paint, and the most abandoned haunter of the stews would blush to read."*

The following letter, which seems to have been the latest which has been preserved,† was probably

---

* "Literary Anecdotes of the Eighteenth Century."

† It is stated in the preface to the second edition of the letters, published in 1806, that the thirtieth letter, which bore, in the manuscript copy, the conjectural date of the summer of 1775, appears to have been written the last of the collection; but this statement is contradicted by the internal evidence of the letters themselves. The letter referred to above could not have been written earlier than the time there assigned to it; and the forty-seventh, in which the suicide of John Damer is mentioned, and the fifty-seventh, written after the death of the Earl of Chatham, must have been written respectively in 1776 and 1778.

Y

written about this time, as it refers, in the last paragraph, to the gathering storm in Ireland, a subject which was then engaging much of Lord Lyttelton's attention :—

"I acknowledge, with a very serious concern, the indecisive and sluggish spirit of the present Administration. This political temper of our leading statesmen was amiable in its origin, perhaps pardonable in its progress, but is equally unaccountable and disgraceful, to say no worse, at this very important period. The humanity of the royal breast, co-operating with the moderate spirit of his immediate councils, and the general disposition of the nation, produced those lingering measures in the beginning of the present troubles which encouraged the insolence of democratic ambition. If half the regiments which have hitherto been employed in vain, with a proportionable fleet, had crossed the Atlantic at the early period of American revolt, the mis-shapen legions of rebellion would have been awed into submission, and the numerous loyal inhabitants would have had a strong hold to which they might have resorted for protection, instead of being urged, by the hopes of preserving their menaced property, to join the standard of rebellion, to which, by seduction, by habit, or by necessity, many of them vowed, and some of them have proved, their fidelity.

"This humane disposition of Government towards the colonies, which has proved a fatal error in the politics of our day, naturally led to another, which arose from the placing a confidence in, and drawing their intelligence from men, some of whom, I imagine, were as deficient in judgment as the rest were in honesty—I mean the American refugees. By their suggestions ministers were influenced to continue the inactive line of conduct, till independence was thundered in their ears, and circumstances seemed to announce that alliance which has since taken place between the natural enemies of this country and its revolted subjects. Permit me to observe that, in the early period of this unhappy business, the nation at large seemed indisposed to adopt the measures of fire and sword. The people, very generally, hoped and believed that the alternate anathemas and conciliatory propositions of our Acts of Parliament would have answered their beneficial intentions of quieting the disorders of the colonies; and I verily believe, if, at the period to which I allude, a Parliamentary motion had been made to provide for the sending a large fleet and army, with an active design, to America, that ministerial power would have met with a very numerous and respectable opposition; nor would the humanity of the nation at large have been satisfied with a design which portended the slaughter of British subjects; while faction would have lifted up its voice against it, as being framed upon the principle of extending, with drawn swords and bayonets fixed, the powers of corruption and the influence of the Crown.

"I again repeat that, at this time, there was a very general aversion in the British nation from entering seriously into the contest; for, even after the Americans had published their separation from Great Britain, and hostilities were actually commenced, the exertions of British valour were languid, and the rebels, at least on the sea, gained more advantages than they have since done with the open alliance of France and the secret aid of Spain. When that unnatural union took place, the British nation underwent a pretty general and very sudden change in sentiments; and many of the most rational friends of America could no longer consider its inhabitants as fellow-subjects when they humbly implored the ready ambition of France to support them in their disobedience to their lawful sovereign.

"At this period, I must acknowledge that my expectations were broad awake to the most vigorous exertions of the British Government. I did not doubt but the genius of my country would arise and shake his spear. Alas! one general was appointed upon a principle of reconciliation, and he does not reconcile; a second is named, and accoutred beyond example, for execution, and he executes nothing. A third succeeds, and new expectations are on the wing. Immense expenses are incurred, the national debt enormously increased, and no substantial advantages are obtained. At length my patience is almost exhausted; I begin to view the indecisive spirit of Ministry in a criminal light; and, if some promising symptom of a change in their measures do not appear at the meeting of Parliament, I will repeat what I have now written, and much more, in their very teeth. The place I hold shall not bribe me from letting loose the angry spirit of my reproach against them.

"But another scene is opening that is pregnant with more alarm, and may bring on a contest more trying to this nation than the Transatlantic commotions and the ambition of France. I allude to the growing discontents of Ireland. You must too well know that there are, at this moment, thirty thousand independent men in arms in that kingdom, who have erected their own standards, and are prepared either to repel a foreign invasion or to resist domestic tyranny. The Irish have long been an oppressed people; but oppression has not quenched their spirit, and they have seized on the present favourable moment to demand justice; nay, if they were to demand more than justice, England is not in a situation to refuse it. But of these matters I shall soon be better informed; and you may be assured of being the first repository of my future and more mature opinions. This is rather a disheartening subject. It demands my utmost resolution to look towards the storm which is gathering in the sister kingdom. If, however, that can be dissipated, and the bond of peace, which is already cracked, be restored, my fears will vanish, and I shall no longer doubt but that Great Britain and Ireland, in spite of American rebellion, of foreign foes, of an indecisive, timid, procrastinating Ministry, and of a noisy, malicious, hungry faction, will work out their own salvation, and close the present contest with added glory."

It is a circumstance which testifies strongly to the pains taken by Lord Lyttelton to obtain the fullest and most accurate information concerning the questions which came before the House of Lords, and confirms the assertion made in one of his letters, that his course in Parliament was the result of "curious research, ardent reflection, and deliberate preparation," that, before the meeting of Parliament in November, 1779, he went to Ireland, in order to acquaint himself fully with the state of affairs in that country, which could scarcely fail to become a subject of keen debate in the ensuing session. He was intimate with the Fortescues, who had estates in Ireland; but he determined to see the state of the country for himself, and to obtain the information which he considered essential on the spot, in preference to gathering the views and opinions of others, however deserving they might be of his confidence.

The duration of his stay in Ireland cannot now be ascertained; but he was there in the beginning of November, and it is improbable that he contented himself with a week's sojourn in Dublin. The origin and organisation of the Irish volunteers, the opinions of the commercial classes on the important question of free trade, and the feelings with which the connection with Great Britain was regarded by all ranks of the people, were the matters which chiefly engaged his attention; and he returned to England thoroughly informed on the Irish question, and determined to exert himself to the utmost to obtain an amelioration of the condition of Ireland, on the broad basis of justice.

CHAPTER XIII.

Lord Lyttelton's Secession from the Ministerial Ranks—Great Speech on the Irish Question—Opinions of the Whig and Tory Journals—Lord Sandwich and Miss Ray—Understanding between Lord Lyttelton and the Earl of Shelburne—More Calumnies of Horace Walpole—Lord Lyttelton's Famous Dream—Various Versions of the Story—New Light on it from the Family Archives at Hagley Hall—The Dowager Lady Lyttelton's Picture—True Circumstances of Lord Lyttelton's Sudden Death—His Will—Conclusion.

PARLIAMENT met on the 25th of November, 1779. Lord Lyttelton took a seat next to the Earl of Shelburne, and rose at an early period of the debate on the address to deliver his views on the Irish question, which was fast becoming one of the greatest importance. After a few words in condemnation of the general policy of the Government, he addressed himself to the subject upon which he had so carefully collected information, and at once fixed the attention of the House.

"No man," he said, "is more loyal than myself, or more ready to support every measure calculated to maintain the honour and dignity of the Crown and empire; but the times are critical, and require the unanimity which is so much talked of, but so little understood. Ministers talk of the necessity of union, while their own conduct is an example of the most jarring counsels and the most divided opinions. The foundation of unanimity is decision; can ministers say that their Government is decisive? What is their system of government? Who will be hardy enough to say that they have any settled plan? Fatal experience has shown the futility of their late policy; America shows the folly of ministers in a rash, ridiculous, extravagant war, which, instead of being governed by a wise, regular, and well-digested plan, is merely a chain of expedients— a repetition of instances of governing and dividing —an example of that wretched policy, *divide et impera!*

"What is their policy respecting Ireland? I hoped to have heard a plain and explicit declaration from ministers of some settled mode of meeting the complaints of the sister-kingdom, and applying an efficient remedy. The affairs of Ireland have come to a crisis; this is perhaps the last day we shall have to debate upon the subject—the last we shall have to consider a remedy. The eyes of the Irish Parliament, of the Irish associations, of the whole Irish people, are upon us: they have looked to this day with the most anxious expectation, and they will be governed by this debate. What is said by the British Parliament concerning Ireland will determine the fate of the country. We shall not again hear the language of complaint from Ireland; even now the Irish ask for relief in a different tone to that formerly used. They do not now beg it as a favour; they claim it as a right. Turn to the present state of Ireland; reflect on the crying necessities of the people, and on the number of armed men in the kingdom—men armed under associations, and not in the pay of the Government, nor even recognised by the Government.

"I have lately been in that country, and have endeavoured to fully inform myself respecting these associations; and I have found that, at the beginning of the present month, there were 42,000 men in arms, of whom 25,000 were as well trained and disciplined as our militia after a year's embodiment. I have conversed with several of the officers, and have inquired into the motive for arming; and I found that the first object was protection against foreign enemies, they having applied to Government for troops for the defence of the country, and been told that none could be spared, and that they must protect themselves. They endeavoured to obtain the sanction of the Government, but the Chancellor of Ireland [Lord Lifford] and the Chief Justice of the King's Bench [Lord Annally], opposed it on the ground that the levying of war without the knowledge and authority of Parliament was contrary to the meaning and spirit of the Constitution, and that, therefore, however worthy the motive for taking arms, and commendable their conduct and discipline, and however they might approve both as individuals, they could not, as lawyers, give their approbation to the movement, or cause it to be recognised by the Government, without warranting a breach of the Constitution."

Lord Lyttelton enlarged on this point, and called upon the Ministry to avow their principles, observing that, if what had taken place in Ireland had occurred in Worcestershire, he should certainly have told the promoters of the movement that they were acting contrary to the Constitution. He commented upon what had been said in the speech from the throne, and by the Earl of Chesterfield in moving the address, relative to the zeal of the nobility and gentry, who had raised new regiments and subscribed funds to aid the Government; and observed that the example would have been less particular and less confined, if England, like Ireland, had not been in such a wretched condition that people had little to give.

"The country," he continued, "has been ruined and disgraced by an irresolute, weak, and pusillanimous Administration. The people now expect a decisive Administration, not a Government of jobbers and jugglers. Why has one noble lord* resigned his seat in the Cabinet? Is it not because ministers cannot arrive at any fixed rule of conduct? The Government is to the world the best instance of its own want of firmness. It is a rope of sand, crumbling away day by day, until it comes to nothing. I beg noble lords to remember that the state of affairs is such that it demands fair, open, and avowed counsel—no whispering, no skulking, no delivering of opinions in private, and disavowing them in public. Parliament is the great council of the nation; and it is the duty of every one of your lordships to speak openly and ingenuously. It is not a time when dissimulation can be practised without entailing that disgrace on those that attempt it which ought ever to be their punish-

---

* Lord Gower, who had been President of the Council. There had been several changes immediately before the meeting of Parliament. The Earl of Hillsborough had taken the oaths that day.

ment, and which they very rarely escape; it is a time for speaking out plainly and honestly.

"For my own part, I speak from my heart; I wish to preserve my country, and I trust your lordships will give me credit for sincerity, and believe that I am not influenced by any pecuniary motives. It is true I have a place, which perhaps I shall not hold very long. I see noble lords smile; let them turn their eyes on their own pusillanimity, their own weak, ill-judged, and wretched measures, and then let them declare, on their consciences, who is most fitly the object of contempt—myself, openly and unreservedly speaking my real sentiments in Parliament, without regard to any personal considerations whatever, excepting only my position as an Englishman, my duty as a lord of Parliament, my duty to my king, and my duty to my country, which are with me, and ought to be with your lordships, above all considerations; or them, consenting, in a moment of public difficulty and danger like the present, to pocket the wages of prostitution, and to sit either in sullen silence, or, what in my idea is still more criminal, to rise and palliate the calamitous and disgraceful situation of the British empire, endeavouring to avert the eyes of the nation from the threatening cloud now hanging over our heads, and so near bursting that it behoves us to consider how to meet the coming storm.

"My lords, it is our interest to come directly to a satisfactory compromise with Ireland. Cast your eyes for a moment on the state of the empire: America, that vast continent, with all its advantages to us as a commercial and maritime people, lost—for ever lost to us; the West Indies abandoned; Ireland ready to part from us. Ireland, my lords, is armed; and what is her language? 'Give us free trade and the free Constitution of England, as it was originally, such as we hope it will remain, the best calculated of any in the world for the preservation of freedom.' This language, my lords, is not the language of an idle mob; it is the loud voice of the whole Irish people, who thunder it in your ears, and will be heard. The Irish Parliament itself says —Government there, my lords, as well as here, has a majority at command; but that majority dares not dissent from popular opinion in this particular; it is, therefore, the unanimous voice of Parliament, and through them of all Ireland —that nothing less than free trade will content them, and that they will have it. The associations, though originally armed for the defence of the country against foreign foes, within these two months have declared that they are ready to turn their arms against domestic enemies. They have not only received the thanks of their counties, but of both Houses of Parliament, and of the Lord-Lieutenant.

"Lay these matters, my lords, to your hearts; consider that these Irish associations are the Whigs of Ireland—men who detest tyranny, and consider passive obedience as a slavish doctrine preached only by tyrants, and which none but those who are lost to every sense of manly feeling, and unworthy to enjoy the blessings of freedom, would submit to. They complain, my lords, of oppression—that they are plunged into despair by the penury which it has entailed on them; they can bear it no longer, and they are ready to change their masters. Let me, my lords, repeat to you an expression which I heard from a gentleman in the Irish House of Commons, and which struck me very forcibly. Speaking of the situation of Ireland, her necessities, and her just rights, 'We have, sir,' said he, addressing the Speaker, 'our back towards England, and our face towards America.' My lords, this expression conveys a strong impression, not only of the present temper of Ireland, but of what may be her future views. It is worth while, surely, to put the matter out of doubt, to meet the difficulty like men, declare what relief you will give the sister kingdom, and endeavour to regain her confidence and esteem. Give her free trade, unload her pension list, lighten her burdens, and enable her to assist you, not in ministerial jobs, not in granting convenient sinecures to men who have done the country no public service, but in the essential points and considerations of a Government wisely conducted and founded on true Constitutional principles.

"Remember, my lords, that every advantage you give Ireland will be a double advantage to England: open her ports, let them be filled with shipping, and your marine will derive benefit from it. Ireland regards the Government of this country as fond of oppressing her, and unwilling to give her freedom. She wishes for a Whig administration, and expects relief only from the establishment of measures founded in Whigism. Do not, my lords, in times like the present, rely on the doctrine of prerogative. The press may teach you how much that idea is despised and exploded; every newspaper teems with libels on the king's ministers, which now pass as matters of course, and are multiplied in number and aggravated in quality beyond all example. In a word, my lords, Government must renovate the system before there will be grounds for hope of better prospects; the general relaxation of manners must be corrected, authority must show her face again, and due subordination must be restored."

The Earl of Hillsborough complimented Lord Lyttelton on his speech, observing that he had spoken with great warmth, and "with those commanding abilities which he so eminently possesses," and replied at considerable length to his arguments, assuring the House that nothing was to be feared from the armed associations of Ireland, and that ministers were prepared to give the sister kingdom "equal trade." This expression called up Lord Lyttelton again, to ask the new minister what he meant by it. Without an explanation, the speech of Lord Hillsborough amounted, he said, to nothing, and the people of Ireland would have nothing to depend upon but general promises conveyed in ambiguous terms. What he meant by free trade was unrestricted trade with any nation that was willing to trade with Ireland. Was this, he asked, what Lord Hillsborough meant by "equal trade?" The Earl of Hillsborough offered an explanation of the ministerial views, but all that he made clear was, that what they intended by "equal trade" was not what Lord Lyttelton and the people of Ireland meant by "free trade."

Lord Lyttelton rose again, and complained that the earl had left the question where it was before he spoke. He then recurred to the Irish volunteers, and said that if Ireland was left to protect herself, the inference was, that the military force appropriated and paid for her defence had been draughted to fight the Quixotic battles of Great Britain on the other side of the Atlantic. Ministers had stripped Ireland of her internal defence, and left her at the mercy of French and American freebooters. In reply to the assertion of the Earl of Hillsborough that many advantages had been derived from the Irish associations, he admitted the fact, but contended that the associations were illegal and unconstitutional. Yet the Government had assisted to arm them; ministers might express doubt, but the fact was notorious. The Lord-Lieutenant himself had admitted to him that seven thousand muskets had been distributed among them. The people of Ireland were resolute and determined; they had taken the Government into their own hands; the associations had chosen their officers, and, in some instances, dismissed them, when they found that they were not zealous in the cause of their country, or inimical to its supposed interests. The associations were composed of men of property, from the first noble downward, and the rank and file consisted of merchants, manufacturers, traders, and farmers. Indeed, the conditions of service excluded the indigent, as they provided their uniforms themselves and received no pay. He repeated some of his former arguments, and concluded by calling upon the Earl of Hillsborough to make a more explicit statement of the ministerial views and intentions, or look forward to the dire alternative of the total separation of Ireland from Great Britain.

Lord Lyttelton's speech won him encomiums from both sides of the House. The Earl of Shelburne said that he had spoken with great candour and distinguished abilities, and the industry he had displayed in making himself fully acquainted with the Irish question, all his statements on which were confirmed by addresses from both Houses of the Irish Parliament, and by private communications received by himself, had done him great honour. The Marquis of Rockingham's amendment was rejected, however, by eighty-two votes against forty-one, Lord Lyttelton voting with the minority, and the address was then agreed to without a division.

All the circumstances of Lord Lyttelton's

political status at this time show that he was regarded as a rising man, whose adhesion all parties were desirous of securing, and whose abilities and, more than these, uprightness and independence—rare qualities in those times—were hopefully regarded by the nation at large. His speech was described in the *Morning Chronicle* as "one of the most animated censures on the conduct of the Administration, for their want of decision, pusillanimity, and want of system, that ever was uttered in Parliament." Even the *Morning Post* acknowledged it to have been an "eloquent harangue,"—the Tory print, which Lord Lyttelton had stigmatised a few years previously as "a scandalous chronicle," which had been "not only saved from oblivion, but raised into universal notice and reception, from its abusive histories" of him, and which he had, in a letter to a friend, wished "in the bottomless pit, with its writers, printers, editors, publishers, collectors, and purchasers," for its "malignant, false, and detestable histories."*

Sir Nathaniel Wraxall, writing long after the event, says that "the Ministry sustained about this time a diminution of strength and loss of talents in the House of Peers, which an Adminis-

---

* "Letters of the late Lord Lyttelton." 1806.

tration so unpopular could ill afford, by the defection of Lord Lyttelton, who suddenly went over to the side of the Opposition. He was a man of very considerable Parliamentary abilities, who, notwithstanding many glaring vices of private character, might have made a conspicuous political figure, if he had not been carried off in the prime of life."*

À *propos* of Sir Nathaniel Wraxall's reflection on the private life of Lord Lyttelton, it may be remarked that a recent ministerial attack on the character of Charles Fox had, about this time, caused it to be asked in Whig circles and in the columns of Whig newspapers, how would the Government defend the morals of Lord Lyttelton? Lord Lyttelton was well able to defend himself; he was not a greater gambler than Fox, or a greater libertine than Lord Sandwich, though, if he had been less honest and independent, he might have exceeded both in their peculiar vices, and yet been visited at Pitt Place by the peers, temporal and spiritual, who attended the dinners and evening parties of the First Lord of the Admiralty, and listened enraptured to the vocalism of the unfortunate Miss Ray.†

---

* "Memoirs of my Own Time."
† Jesse's "Life and Times of George III." Miss Ray, the mistress of the Earl of Sandwich, was murdered by a jealous admirer, named Hackman.

The great speech which Lord Lyttelton made on the first day of the session seems to have been intended to be followed by another attack on the Ministry on the occasion of the Earl of Shelburne's motion, that the House should censure them for their neglect of Ireland. The resolution was moved on the 1st of December, when the Earl of Abingdon referred to Lord Lyttelton's speech of the week before, and stated that he had been informed by a person in the confidence of that "amiable nobleman," that Lord Lyttelton had declared that "the paltry consideration of place should not keep him from freely expressing his opinion of the criminal negligence of the Ministry;" and that, if he had lived to that day, he intended to have gone deeper into their conduct.*

But before the debate on the Earl of Shelburne's resolution came on, Lord Lyttelton had departed this life. He appeared to be in good health when he went to the House of Lords on the 25th, and he spoke with his usual animation, rising occasionally to an impassioned fervour. It was one o'clock on the morning of the 26th when the division was taken on the Marquis of Rockingham's amendment to the Address, and he was

---

* Hansard's "Parliamentary History," vol. xx.

then observed to look ill. He did not go to bed until some time afterwards, however, and it does not appear that he then complained of any indisposition. On rising he complained of headache, but this symptom passed off, and, in the course of the day, he went down to Pitt Place, where he was joined by a party of friends.

The incidents of the last two days of Lord Lyttelton's life have been related by the diarists and memoir-writers of the period in every variety of detail. Horace Walpole, who seems to have treated his friends at second-hand to every morsel of gossip that reached him, without taking the trouble to ascertain whether it had the smallest foundation in fact, wrote to Sir Horace Mann that Lord Lyttelton, after making a violent speech against the Government, looked ill, but went to Epsom on the following day with "a caravan of nymphs," and on the next night retired before supper to take a dose of rhubarb, returned to the supper-room, supped heartily, went to his chamber, and died in an instant. To the Rev. William Mason the same veracious gossip wrote that the noble subject of his scandalising pen supped on fish and venison with "four girls picked up in the Strand;" that, after supper, he complained of feeling ill, and retired to rest; that his bell rang ten minutes afterwards, and that his servant, entering his chamber immediately, found him at the point of death.

Disentangled from the web of fiction which calumny has woven around the facts, the story of Lord Lyttelton's last hours of life is much less sensational than it appears in the pages of Walpole and Wraxall, but still remarkable enough. The newspapers of the period are less amusing than the gossip of the Strawberry Hill letter-writer; but they give us facts, and facts are the materials of which a biography should be composed. From these it may be gleaned that the party assembled at Pitt Place on the 26th of November comprised Lord Lyttelton, Mr. Fortescue (eldest son of Lord Fortescue), Captain (afterwards Admiral) Wolseley, Mrs. Flood, and the Misses Amphlett,* who are described in Lord Lyttelton's will as the daughters of his "dear friend and relative, Mrs. Mary Amphlett, of Clent." In this society all traces of fatigue and symptoms of indisposition vanished, and Lord Lyttelton retired to rest, apparently in his usual health and spirits.

It was then, according to reports subsequently

---

* Peter Cunningham, though he appends a note to Horace Walpole's calumnious statement respecting the party at Pitt Place, says that "two of them were Margaret and Christina Amphlett, who were provided for in his will," leaving it to be inferred that these young ladies, members of a respectable Worcestershire family, were two of the "four girls picked up in the Strand."

circulated, that he dreamed that he saw a lady who had been dead several years, and that she warned him that he would die on the following night at twelve o'clock. The various accounts of this nocturnal visitation differ both as to its nature and the person from whom the warning proceeded. Sir Nathaniel Wraxall calls it an apparition, and blunders so far as to say that it was the ghost of Mrs. Dawson, who continued to inhabit this sublunary sphere long after Lord Lyttelton's decease! Pennington, repeating the gossip of the day, says, "the vision is said to have appeared in the form of Miss ——, a young lady whom he had seduced with circumstances of great profligacy, and who was then dead."* There is as little truth in one story as in the other. Lord Lyttelton is said to have related his dream to his guests on the following morning, while they were assembled round the breakfast-table; and it is not at all probable that he told the story as rumour told it afterwards, or that he gave one version of the story to his friends, and another to his valet, who is said to have received it from him, and to have repeated it to the Dowager Lady Lyttelton with every supernatural accessory with which it has been told in later times.†

---

* "Memoirs of Elizabeth Carter."
† Wraxall's "Memoirs of my Own Time."

It is worthy of remark that, in the announcement of the event in the newspapers, the magazines, and the "Annual Register," no mention is made of any remarkable circumstance in connection with it. The first report of the dream which I have been able to discover, occurs in a letter from Mrs. Delany to her niece, Mrs. Port, written from St. James's Place, on the 9th of December, and in which she mentions Lord Lyttelton "seeing a bird turned into a woman, who gave him warning of his approaching end." Mrs. Delany adds a "hearty dinner" to the supper of fish and venison mentioned by Walpole, and refers to the unfortunate nobleman's "flow of spirits," after which, she says, he "complained of a pain in his stomach, which lasted but a little before he expired at once."

About six months afterwards, when Johnson, Boswell, Croft, and Henderson were taking tea one afternoon with Dr. Adams, in the latter's rooms at Oxford, Boswell mentioned Lord Lyttelton's "vision," and "the prediction of the time of his death, with its exact fulfilment."

"It is the most extraordinary thing which has happened in my day," observed Johnson. "I heard it with my own ears from his uncle, Lord Westcote. I am so glad to hear every evidence to the spiritual world, that I am willing to believe it."

"You have evidence enough," said Dr. Adams. "Good evidence, which needs not such support."

"I like to have more," rejoined Johnson, as if he had a lingering doubt on the subject, which could only be kept at rest by a constant succession of evidences.

Lord Westcote was a brother of the first Lord Lyttelton, and an Irish peer, afterwards created Lord Lyttelton of Frankley. The version of the story of Lord Lyttelton's dream and death which Johnson received from him remained unknown until November, 1874, when the present Lord Lyttelton communicated to *Notes and Queries* the following narrative, which was drawn up by Lord Westcote, and was, no doubt, that which had been verbally communicated to Johnson :—

"On Thursday, the 25th of November, 1779, Thomas Lord Lyttelton, when he came to breakfast, declared to Mrs. Flood, wife of Frederick Flood, Esq., of the kingdom of Ireland, and to the three Miss Amphletts, who were lodged in his house in Hill Street, London (where he then also was), that he had had an extraordinary dream the Night before; he said he thought he was in a room which a Bird flew into, which appearance was suddenly changed into that of a Woman dress'd in white, who bade him prepare to Die;

to which he answered, 'I hope not soon, not in two Months;' she replied, 'Yes, in three Days.' He said he did not much regard it, because he could in some measure account for it, for that a few days before he had been with Mrs. Dawson, when a Robin Redbreast flew into her room.

"When he had dressed himself that day to go to the House of Lords, he said he thought he did not look as if he was likely to Die : In the Evening of the following Day, being Friday, he told the eldest Miss Amphlett that she look'd melancholy; but, said he, 'You are foolish and fearfull, I have lived two Days, and, God willing, I will live out the third.' On the morning of Saturday he told the same ladies that he was very well, and believed *he shou'd bilk the ghost*. Some hours afterwards he went with them, Mr Fortescue & Captain Wolseley, to Pitt Place, at Epsom; withdrew to his bed-chamber soon after eleven o'Clock at night, talked cheerfully to his Servant, and particularly inquired of him what care had been taken to provide good Roles for his breakfast the next morning; Stepd into Bed with his Waistcoat on, and as his Servant was pulling it off, put his hand to his side, sunk back, and immediately expired without a Groan. he ate a good Dinner after his arrival at Pitt Place that day, took an egg for his supper, and did not seem to be at all out of Order, except that while he was eating his Soup at Dinner he had a rising in his Throat, a Thing which had often happened to him before, & which obliged him to spit some of it out. his Physician, Dr Fothergill, told me Lord Lyttelton had, in the summer preceding, a bad pain in his side; & he judged that some great Vessel in the part where he had felt the Pain gave way, & to that, he conjectured, his Death was oweing. His Declaration of his Dream, and his Expressions above mention'd, consequential thereunto, were, upon a close inquiry, asserted to me to have been so, by Mrs Flood, the eldest Miss Amphlett, Captain Wolseley, and his Valet de Chambre Faulkner, who dress'd him on the Thursday, and the manner of his Death was related to me by William Stuckey, in the presence of Mr Fortescue and Captain Wolseley, Stuckey being the Servant who attended him in his Bed Chamber, and in whose Arms he died.

"WESTCOTE.

"February the 13th, 1780."

This statement, while it confirms the story of the dream in its simplest form, explains it in a natural manner. Dr. Fothergill's evidence accounts for Lord Lyttelton's death, conformably with the newspaper announcements which mentioned its cause; while the fish and venison supper of Walpole's story diminishes to an egg. Lord Westcote's mistake as to the number of the Misses Amphlett may have originated in inadvertence.

It is remarkable, however, that, though Lord Westcote refers to Mrs. Flood, the eldest Miss Amphlett, and Captain Wolseley as his authorities for the account committed by him to writing, a different version of the story was given to the late Dowager Lady Lyttelton (a daughter of the second Earl Spencer) by a son of the Mr. Fortescue who was one of Lord Lyttelton's guests at the time of his death. This lady says:—

"Mr George Fortescue called upon me one day in town, & in a conversation on the subject of an article in the *Quarterly Review*, which ascribes the authorship of Junius to Thos Ld Lyttelton, he told me, that he had often heard from his father Ld Fortescue, some details of the death of Thomas Ld Lyttelton, which must be true, & are rather curious. He said that L^d, then M^r, Fortescue was in London on the morning of ... 17 and went to see Ld L. his first cousin, who was then also in town, & had on the day before made a fine speech in the H. of L^ds. He found him in bed, tho' not ill; and on his rallying him for it, Ld L. said: 'Well, if you will wait a little in the next room, I will get up & go out with you.' He did so, & the two young men walked out into the streets. In the course of the walk, they crossed the church yard of St James's Church; and Ld L. pointing to the gravestones, said: 'Now look at all the vulgar fellows, they die in their youth; at five & thirty. But you & I, who are gentlemen, shall live to a good old age.' The walk ended by their getting into a carriage and driving together to Ld L.'s house at Epsom, where was a party of his friends. They dined cheerfully, & no allusion was made to any remarkable occurrence. In the evening, Ld Lyttelton withdrew to his room earlier than Mr Fortescue, who so far from having any anxiety or curiosity on his mind respecting his cousin, sat before the fire in the drawing-room with his feet on the fender, and dropped asleep. He was aroused by Ld L.'s servant rushing into the room and saying, 'My Lord is dying.' He 'ran upstairs and found that all was over. His servant said that he had got into bed, and asked for his usual medicine, a dose of rhubarb. Finding it ill mixed, he desired the servt. to mix it again. No spoon being at hand, the man began to mix it with a tooth pick that lay on the table. 'Dirty fellow!' said Ld L., 'go down & fetch a spoon.' He obeyed, and on returning to the room found his master speechless, fallen back on the pillow, & in the last agonies. Mr Fortescue heard nothing then, nor for some days after, of the dream or the prediction of his death, which Mr Fortescue seemed inclined therefore wholly to disbelieve. S. L." *

How are we to reconcile this statement with the account which Lord Westcote received from his nephew's other guests? The question becomes more perplexing as we push the investigation farther, every teller of the story varying the circumstances, and omitting some of the details or adding others.

Sir Nathaniel Wraxall says that, dining at Pitt Place about four years after the death of Lord Lyttelton, he "had the curiosity to visit the bed-chamber where the casement window,

---

* This document, the narratives of Sir Digby Neave and Russel, the Guildford organist, and the letter of Mr. G. M. Fortescue to the Hon. Miss Lyttelton, given in succeeding pages, were communicated to *Notes and Queries* by the present Lord Lyttelton, and are reproduced in the present volume by the kindness and courtesy of D^r. Doran.

at which Lord Lyttelton asserted the dove appeared to flutter was pointed out to me; and at his stepmother's—the Dowager Lady Lyttelton's, in Portugal Street, Grosvenor Square, who, being a woman of very lively imagination, lent an implicit faith to all the supernatural facts which were supposed to accompany or precede Lord Lyttelton's end—I have frequently seen a painting which she herself executed in 1780, expressly to commemorate the event. It hung in a conspicuous part of her drawing-room. The dove appears at the window, while a female figure, habited in white, stands at the foot of the bed announcing to his lordship his dissolution. Every part of the picture was faithfully designed after the description given to her by the *valet de chambre* who attended him, to whom his master related all the circumstances."

The Rev. Bouchier Wray Savile, in his work on apparitions, reports the conversation as it is given in Lord Westcote's document, but says that the lady of the dream was Mrs. Amphlett. Both accounts are contradicted by the statement in Nash's "Worcestershire," that Lord Lyttelton made a vain attempt to address the figure. Mr. Savile refers to an account of what passed at Pitt Place, written by Mr. Russel, a music-master, at Guildford; and says, quoting this narrative, that Lord Lyttelton's valet "came down to fetch some mint water, leaving his lordship alone. At that moment the clock of the parish church, which of course had not been tampered with, began slowly to strike the true midnight hour. The valet returned to his master, and called out loudly; the company ran upstairs, and found his lordship quite dead."

Unfortunately for the credibility of this story, Mr. Russel is said to have given a different version of the affair to Mrs. Lefroy, who committed it to paper, as follows:—

"Lord Lyttelton occasionally resided at a house in or near Epsom, where Mr. Russel was in the habit of attending him, and performing for his amusement. Having received a summons for one particular evening, Mr. Russel rode to Epsom, and, putting up his horse at an inn there, walked to Lord Lyttelton's house. On entering the courtyard, he was struck with the number of carriages which filled it. On reaching the house, he was conducted to an apartment in which was a pianoforte,—the room served as an ante-room to the dressing-room. The folding-doors between the two apartments were thrown open, and as he sat at the pianoforte, Mr. Russel could perceive that the drawing-room contained a large party, almost entirely consisting of gentlemen. Mr. Russel had not played long, when he was astonished at hearing a loud noise of shouting and laughter from the company in the drawing-room, the gentlemen pulling out their watches and exclaiming, 'We shall jockey the ghost after all; there will be no ghost to-night, I fancy,' and other words to that effect. A lady, related to Lord Lyttelton, came from the drawing-room, apologising to Mr. Russel for the interruption to his music caused by all this noise, adding that Lord Lyttelton had been suffering from great depression of spirits, and that the present party had been assembled for the purpose of amusing him and dissipating his melancholy. Many times during the course of the evening these shouts and exclamations were heard.

"Mr. Russel was at last given to understand that he might finish. Lord Lyttelton came to him, and, having paid him handsomely for his performance, desired him to take his supper in the house. This Mr. Russel declined, but said that, with his lordship's leave, he would take a glass of wine, and for this purpose he would step into the butler's pantry as he went out. He did so, and while drinking the wine, Lord Lyttelton came into the pantry, and seating himself on the plate-chest, complained to the butler of feeling very unwell, and in great pain. The butler proposed mixing him a glass of brandy and rhubarb, and Lord Lyttelton agreeing to it, Mr. Russel wished his lordship a good night, and took leave of him. On his way through the offices, one of the gardeners whom he happened to meet lighted him out, and was making some observation to him on the uproar which had been so often heard during the evening, when, just as they reached the outer door, a most dreadful scream was heard from the interior of the house. 'And this,' said the gardener, 'is worse than all the rest.'

"Mr. Russel wished him good night, and stopping only a few minutes at a lady's house in Epsom to deliver a message, proceeded to the inn where he had left his horse. Just as he reached the inn door, he heard some one exclaiming, 'I must have a horse to ride to London immediately, for my lord is dead.' On looking at the person who spoke, Mr. Russel perceived it to be the gardener who had lighted him out of the house. He now informed him that Lord Lyttelton had fallen off the plate-chest speechless, and died as he was being carried upstairs."

It is impossible to reconcile this narrative

with the statement of Mr. Fortescue, which must be regarded as the more worthy of credence. But there is yet another account, namely, that given to the present Lord Lyttelton by Sir Digby Neave, in September, 1860, and which is as follows :—

"In 1828, Mr. Taylor, of Worcester Park, near Ewell, who was then above eighty years of age, told me, then residing at Pit Place, that he was in the neighbourhood during the year 1779, and heard particulars of the illness and death of Lord Lyttelton from an Italian painter visiting at Pit Place at the time of Lord Lyttelton's death.

"Lord Lyttelton had come to Pit Place in a very precarious state, and was ordered not to take any but the gentlest exercise. Walking in the conservatory with Lady Afflick and two Misses Afflicks, a robin perched on an orange-tree close to them. Lord L. attempted to catch it; but failing, and being laughed at by the ladies, said he would catch it if it was the death of him, and succeeded, putting himself in a great heat by the exertion. He gave the bird to Lady Afflick, who walked about with it in her hand.

"Lord Lyttelton became so ill and feverish

that he went off to London for advice to a house in Bruton Street. In his delirium he imagined that a lady with a bird in her hand, drawing his curtain, told him he would die.

"Dreams being the *Galamatia* of waking thoughts, it needed no ghost to fix such an impression on the mind of a sick man, and this may be said to clear away supernatural agency thus far. As to death occurring at the moment indicated by an apparition, and the putting on of the clock by his friends—from the habits of his boon companions in the house at the time, and the report of the Italian painter, his informant, Mr. Taylor was satisfied as to its being a fable invented to mystify the public, as the actual circumstances attending his death were as follows :—

"Being in bed opposite a chimney-piece with a mirror over it, he desired a valet to give him some medicine, which was on the chimney-piece. Seeing him mixing it with a tooth-brush, Lord Lyttelton raised himself up and rated him, but he was so weak that his head sunk below the pillow on to his chest, and he gasped for breath. His valet, instead of relieving him, in his fright left the room, and death ensued before assistance could be given.

"DIGBY NEAVE.

"Mr. Taylor, of Worcester Park, told me the names of the party in the house. I only recollect that Mr. Michael Angelo Taylor was one of them. He named that Lord L. had become possessed of Pit Place in payment of a debt of honour."

It is obvious that the most credible member of this "cloud of witnesses" is Mr. Fortescue, whose only surviving son addressed the following letter to the Hon. Miss Lyttelton, no longer ago than September, 1874:—

"Dropmore, Maidenhead, *Sept.* 4, 1874.

"DEAR MISS LYTTELTON,—My father attached no credit to the Lyttelton Ghost Story.

"He told me once that he was at Pitt Place at the time that Lord Lyttelton died there; that though in weak health, Lord L. was in good spirits, giving certainly no evidence of his having received any premonition of an early demise; and that, on the night of his death, there was, as far as he knew or heard, no unwillingness on Lord L.'s part to retire to bed, and no putting forward of the clock; and that it was not till some time after the event that he heard of the female apparition having announced to him

(Lord L.) the day and hour of his death, &c. My father, I think, told me, that Miles Peter Andrews and another gentleman, whose name I have forgotten, were guests with him at Pitt Place at the time.

"G. M. FORTESCUE."

Andrews was the gentleman to whom, according to a ridiculous story which has been told by Plumer Ward and others, the ghost of Lord Lyttelton appeared at Dartford on the night of the unfortunate peer's decease. According to this story, Andrews was at Pitt Place in the course of the day, but left, before night, for Dartford, thirty miles off. Mr. Savile relates that "the party at Pitt Place were additionally horrified by receiving intelligence on the following morning that the mother of the Miss Amphletts had expired in Warwickshire, unknown to them, at the very time when she appeared to Lord Lyttelton, on the Thursday night, and warned him of his coming doom." But, a little farther on, Mr. Savile says that Mrs. Cameron (a married sister of the Misses Amphlett) stated that she heard Mrs. Flood tell Mrs. Amphlett the story of the ghost of Lord Lyttelton appearing to Andrews!

After all this contradictory evidence, which is

adduced only for the purpose of sifting to the bottom the rubbish which has been heaped over the facts, we may ask ourselves whether there was even a dream? Thus much may be admitted; but the most remarkable matter connected with Lord Lyttelton's death seems to me to be the observation which the unfortunate nobleman made to Mr. Fortescue in the churchyard, as to "vulgar fellows" dying at thirty-five—the age at which he died himself so soon afterwards.

Whatever may have been present to Lord Lyttelton's mind in the vivid and remarkable dream concerning which so much has been written, his character disposes us to believe that the impression that remained on waking must have been deep and grave. Elizabeth Carter, who knew him well, wrote to her friend Mrs. Vesey: "We have received a very circumstantial and authentic account of Lord Lyttelton's dream, which you mention. Through all the affectation of disregarding it, it appeared plainly, I think, that it made a strong impression on his mind, though not in such a way as seemed to be much for his benefit, or he would have made a different kind of preparation for the event."

The lady's biographer, Pennington, with more of the spirit of Christian charity than most of those who have written about Lord Lyttelton, observes upon this passage of the pious and learned Elizabeth's letter, that her reasoning "seems by no means conclusive. In all cases of supposed warnings, whether occasioned by a troubled conscience within, or by any natural, though perhaps not easily accounted for, circumstance without, God only can judge of the effect which may be produced by it on the heart. Lord Lyttelton never appears to have braved the prediction, though he often alluded to it in conversation; and God only knows what resolutions of amendment he may have made, how sincerely determined on repentance, and how fervent have been in private prayer to Him during those three days."

It is a curious illustration of the pertinacity with which errors are clung to by persons who may readily inform themselves of the truth, that most narrators of the story of Lord Lyttelton's dream and death repeat the mistake as to the interval between the prophecy and its fulfilment. Lord Lyttelton spoke for the last time in the House of Lords on Thursday night, went down to Epsom on Friday morning, dreamed his remarkable dream on Friday night, and died at midnight on Saturday. The mistake seems to have originated in a statement made to the Rev.

William Mason by Horace Walpole, that Lord Lyttelton had on Thursday expressed to a friend a presentiment that he should live only till Saturday, and that on Saturday he had said, "If I survive to-day I shall go on." The remark which he made on the day of his death is said, upon other authority, to have been, "I believe I shall jockey the ghost after all;" and this he is said to have made to Mrs. Flood, when night was approaching, and he found himself still as well as usual.

The account of his last moments given by the newspapers of the period agrees substantially with the details communicated by Horace Walpole to Sir Horace Mann and the Rev. William Mason. The cause of death is said to have been "a concretion of blood about the heart and arteries, to which surgeons give the name of polypus," and which is said to have burst. The record of his death in the *Annual Register* is unaccompanied by a single line of comment, and appears to have been copied *verbatim* from the journals of November 29th. On the 30th the *Gazetteer* contained the following paragraph, which, on the following day, was adopted, without acknowledgment, by the *Morning Chronicle*:—"The death of Lord Lyttelton is sincerely to be lamented. His lordship, as is too frequently the case with men of high birth, great fortune, and superior abilities, gave too much way to the levities of youth; but, from the greater regularity of his late conduct, there was reason to believe that his character would have merited the esteem, as much as his talents deserved the respect, of the world. His Parliamentary character was most deservedly high, as an able, manly, and most eloquent speaker, possessing all that independence of spirit and noble disdain of Court influence, from any pecuniary consideration, which so well becomes the character of a real nobleman, and which is so necessary for the preservation of our excellent Constitution. His speech in the House of Lords on Thursday was replete with political knowledge and the most clear and forcible reasoning."

He had made his will a few weeks before his death, appointing as executors his uncle, Lord Westcote, who was the sixth son of Sir Thomas Lyttelton, and succeeded to the title and the estate of Hagley; his brother-in-law, Lord Valentia; and his friend Roberts. The Arley estate was bequeathed to his nephew, the Honourable George Annesley, subject to the payment of the following annuities: two hundred pounds to Lady Valentia, three hundred pounds to Mrs. Dawson, and one hundred pounds to Clara Haywood. To each of these ladies, and to others of his friends, munificent bequests were made out of the personalty: to Lady Valentia, one thousand pounds; to Mrs. Dawson, one thousand pounds; to Clara Haywood, two thousand pounds; to his niece and godchild, to whom he had given the fanciful name of Honeysuckle, two thousand pounds; to Margaret Amphlett, five thousand pounds; to Christina Amphlett, two thousand five hundred pounds; to the Hon. Mr. Fortescue, three thousand pounds; Miles Peter Andrews, seventeen hundred pounds and his gold watch; to George Bodens, five hundred pounds; and to another gentleman, named O'Byrne, five hundred pounds A diamond bow, which had cost fourteen hundred and thirty-eight pounds, was directed to be sold, and the proceeds to be divided equally between Margaret and Christina Amphlett.

The residue of his personal property was bequeathed to the executors, with the exception of his manuscripts, which were confided to Roberts, who selected from them the contents of the small volume of short poems published in the following year. These effusions do not entitle Lord Lyttelton to an exalted place among the British poets, but most of them will bear comparison with the best of the fugitive poetry of the period, without discredit to the author. One piece is remarkable for its striking resemblance to the lines of Byron, commencing—" Born in a garret, in a kitchen bred," for which it may have served as a model. The amatory poems are conceived with exuberant warmth and too vivid suggestiveness; but the best of them are marked by the lightness, grace, and fancy of the similar compositions of Moore.

The readers of this biography may form their opinions of Lord Lyttelton's character for themselves. They have been shown the man as he was, with all his faults and with all the sterling qualities which endeared him even to those who frowned upon his early frailties; and have seen how his traditional repute as "the wicked Lord Lyttelton" grew out of the calumnies of political opponents, who disliked and feared him for his honesty and his independence, and the condemnatory generalisations of the Pharisees, who would have had it believed that a man who could not pronounce their Shibboleths after their own manner must necessarily be a monster of vice. The character of a strictly virtuous man is not claimed for him: judged by the standard of the present day, how many of those who mingled in the public life of the last century can justly receive that character? But his failings were more than counterbalanced by the noble qualities which are sufficiently attested by the sneers of his political opponents, and by the amiability which won for him the regard of men like the Earl of Chatham and Earl Temple, of women like Mrs. Montagu and Miss Carter.

If we turn from his private life to his public career, where shall we find, among the men of his generation, another who, in his thirty-sixth year, displayed equal talents; or, at any period of life, as much of the honesty and independence which made him so conspicuous by their uniqueness on the political arena of the eighteenth century? It is not much, perhaps, that he had few rivals as an orator; there was eloquence enough and to spare, in that day, in both Houses of Parliament. The public men who were more rare in the Georgian era than orators were those who, as has been said of Andrew Marvel, were "bold enough to be honest, and honest enough to be bold;" and among the few to whom that character can be applied THOMAS LORD LYTTELTON shines conspicuously to the mental vision of all who do not shun the light.

THE END.

CHARLES DICKENS AND EVANS, CRYSTAL PALACE PRESS.

www.ingramcontent.com/pod-product-compliance
Lightning Source LLC
Chambersburg PA
CBHW032045220426
43664CB00008B/872